Seriously
Funny

Disability in Society

Ronald J. Berger, series editor

Seriously *Funny*

Disability and the Paradoxical Power of Humor

Shawn Chandler Bingham
Sara E. Green

LYNNE
RIENNER
PUBLISHERS

BOULDER
LONDON

Published in the United States of America in 2016 by
Lynne Rienner Publishers, Inc.
1800 30th Street, Boulder, Colorado 80301
www.rienner.com

and in the United Kingdom by
Lynne Rienner Publishers, Inc.
3 Henrietta Street, Covent Garden, London WC2E 8LU

Library of Congress Cataloging-in-Publication Data
Names: Bingham, Shawn Chandler, 1976– author. | Green, Sara E., author.
Title: Seriously funny : disability and the paradoxical power of humor /
  by Shawn Chandler Bingham and Sara E. Green.
Description: Boulder, Colorado : Lynne Rienner Publishers, Inc., [2016] |
  Includes bibliographical references and index.
Identifiers: LCCN 2016016378 | ISBN 9781626375208 (hardcover : alk. paper)
Subjects: LCSH: Sociology of disability. | Disabilities—Humor. | Wit and
  humor—Social aspects.
Classification: LCC HV1568 .B56 2016 | DDC 305.9/080207—dc23
LC record available at https://lccn.loc.gov/2016016378.

British Cataloguing in Publication Data
A Cataloguing in Publication record for this book
is available from the British Library.

Printed and bound in the United States of America

The paper used in this publication meets the requirements
of the American National Standard for Permanence of
Paper for Printed Library Materials Z39.48-1992.

5 4 3 2 1

Contents

Acknowledgments

Stand-up comedy typically comes to life through the perspective of one person onstage holding a microphone and a point of view. Academic books have a very different kind of birth. There are no "open mic" nights for such projects, and they are rarely the result of the labor of one or two authors, or even a small group of people. We have many people to thank for their support, thoughts, critiques, stories, and patience. Andrew Berzanskis and Lesli Brooks Athanasoulis at Lynne Rienner Publishers worked closely with us over several years as this project evolved, and Lynne Rienner was willing to take on an unconventional topic that merges two seemingly unrelated areas. We extend our sincere gratitude to the comedians who took time out of their busy professional lives to participate in the project and trusted us with their stories. We have much to learn from them about social observation and successfully reaching a broad public audience. We are also grateful to our students, Amy McDonough, Justine Egner, Shahira Saad, Melissa Welch, Meghan Bowman, Blake Martin, Cortney Mihulka, Amanda Plazarin, Linda Rogers, Jessica Schoenfeld, and Toney Matthew, who assisted with various aspects of the project. A number of colleagues provided insightful critiques and suggestions, including Allison Carey, Beth Haller, Anthony Ladd, Ben Shepard, and James Thomas. Financial support provided by the University of South Florida Humanities Institute allowed us to gather historical data for the project, which was done through access to the Emerson College Library's American Comedy Archives. Finally, we would like to thank our families for humoring us throughout this project and for taking our interest in it seriously. Their own use of humor served to ground us and provided a testing ground throughout our work on the book.

—*Shawn Chandler Bingham*
—*Sara E. Green*

1

The Social Significance of Disability Humor

Someday, I'm afraid, the eggheads will take [Red Skelton] up and start reading social significance into his antics. Let's hope they don't, because this has
ruined many a good performer.
— *Groucho Marx (1959, p. 105)*

McCurdy's Comedy Theatre (and Humor Institute) is tucked in the back of
a 1970s strip mall in the center of Sarasota, Florida. On a March night,
members of a mostly gray-, white-, and blue-haired audience park their
Buicks and Cadillacs and line up at the entrance. They are flanked by thirty
years of photographs depicting well-known comedians who have played the
club. Most who wait in line grew up in an era when institutionalization was
the norm for people with lifelong impairments.[1] Yet they wait in line for a
performer with cerebral palsy to dole out a heavy dose of cerebral humor.

The weekend headliner is Josh Blue, the 2006 winner of the NBC television show *Last Comic Standing*. His long scraggly beard and disheveled
hair give him the look of a Colorado snowboarder or 1970s-era soccer
player. He thanks the crowd for staying up past their bedtime, and for the
next hour lays out a one-man drive-by examination of parenting with a disability, traveling with the Paralympic soccer team, and the strange reactions
he gets doing something as simple as grocery shopping. If Blue tap-dances
on the acceptable line of self-deprecation, the jokes often mask a more interesting social critique: "People ask me if I get nervous before coming up
onstage. I say, 'Heck no! I've got this many people staring at me all day!'"
(Blue 2006b). And just when the audience is fully comfortable laughing at
jokes about disability, he yanks the carpet out from under them, reminding
them that humor lives in ambiguities, not in a world of black and white: "I
would like to inform you that you all are going to hell tonight for laughing

1

at me. But, it's okay. We'll be hanging out. I hear the Devil's got good weed!" (Blue 2006b).

A (Groucho) Marxist take on this showground might suggest that Blue is simply a comedian doing what comedians do best: amusing people by using personal experiences to make them laugh. However, while entertainment may well be Blue's main goal, the fact that the personal experience on which his performance draws includes cerebral palsy forces his audience to move beyond the comfortable modern practice of politely ignoring impairment. His set is a mirror and a measuring stick, provoking not only laughter but also thought and discomfort. Through his humor, he forces the audience to engage with their own preconceived notions of what disability is and is not. He brings the elephant in the living room that is disability to center stage and makes it impossible for audiences to politely turn away. Far from echoing Groucho Marx's (1959, p. 105) fear that "eggheads will . . . start reading social significance" into the antics of comedians, Blue and other disabled comedians themselves consciously use humor in a socially significant manner (Bartholomy 2012, p. 1). They maneuver in an arena where social critique, education, activism, entertainment, and perhaps exploitation are fused in the act of performance. Where else is disability brought so fearlessly, and aggressively, to the attention of a nondisabled crowd? And where else does the crowd pay $20 and the price of a two-drink minimum to hear it?

Of course, the social significance of humor is neither new nor unique to disability content. Contrary to the apparent wishes of Groucho Marx, comedy and humor have long provided a lens into social life. In other words, humor has been used as a way to encourage, even force, others to view an aspect of the human experience from a perspective with which they may not be personally familiar or to consider sides of an issue to which they usually stand in opposition. From the searing critiques of William Shakespeare and the political maneuverings of the medieval court jester to the more modern racial comedy of Richard Pryor and political comedy of Jon Stewart, humor has been used as a tool with which to both challenge and redirect power.

A stage like McCurdy's Comedy Theatre serves as a complex social space for modern comedians and audiences. Neither a one-dimensional ring for amusement, nor a simplistic soapbox veiled as comedy, it is an arena in which comedians such as Blue mediate (Mintz 1985) routine and authentic experiences to others in an active, and sometimes activist, manner. Just as stand-up comedian Lenny Bruce used humor to question and problematize US norms of censorship, Blue and other performers with disabilities begin with an understanding of the assumptions about disability with which audience members enter the arena. Then, they actively engage with those assumptions, twisting and challenging them. If they are successful, audience members leave the performance with understandings of the disability experience that are at least slightly, and perhaps profoundly, altered. In other words, the performance is a mediator through which old assumptions are converted into new understandings. In mediating the disability experience for audiences in this way, the humor of these comedians serves as a deft social indicator by creatively unlocking social norms about disability that might not be adequately unveiled through traditional methods of studying social phenomena. They make the personal very public and in so doing disorder, deconstruct, and reorder conventional views of disability and other broadly held norms about the body. In this way, disabled comedians engage in a kind of "carnival consciousness" in which humor is used to resist and challenge oppressive social arrangements (Bakhtin 1981, p. 49). This kind of humor provides an empowering and accessible opportunity for comedians with disabilities to help create new narratives about the disability experience.

A wide range of comedians with disabilities such as Blue have recently been reclaiming the comedy stage as a political space in which to contest inequality. Disability humor has been called an "emerging, liberatory art form" (Reid, Stoughton, and Smith 2006, p. 640), and the past decade in particular has been its advent season. Media outlets such as NBC, HBO, and BBC have prominently featured comedians with disabilities, as have major venues such as London's Soho Theatre. As Beth Haller puts it in the introduction to a special issue on disability and humor in *Disability Studies Quarterly:* "Disability humor is out of the closet" (2003, p. 2). Comedic tour groups, including Abnormally Funny People, the Comedians with Disabilities Act, and the Preferred Parking Comedy Tour, have moved beyond college campuses to national tours and comedy clubs. Many of the comedians within those groups also have solo careers. This renaissance is bringing alternative narratives of the disability experience to a wider audience than might have been possible just a decade ago (Bartholomy 2012; Haller 2010; Haller and Becker 2014; Kuppers 2011).

The work of disabled comedians highlights the utility of humor as an alternative lens into social life, especially the complexity of disability. Carrie Sandahl and Philip Auslander (2005) argue that disabled performers disturb traditional performance aesthetics as well as traditional understandings of disability. The work of disabled comedians also provides a fascinating chance to use disability to explore the paradoxical functions of humor. Humor can heal, yet it can also cut us deeply. It can bring us together and ease tension but, just as quickly, it can highlight difference and reinforce hierarchy. We, the authors of this book, have experienced these various functions in our everyday lives as family members of individuals with disabilities. Shawn Bingham grew up watching his adopted brother with fetal alcohol syndrome (FAS) deftly maneuver social situations using a lightening quick wit. He remembers studying the textbook definitions of FAS as a graduate student in the University of Maryland library and wondering how, despite all of the cognitive and emotional limitations that can create obstacles for young people with FAS, his brother had a mastery of humor that was used so strategically: as a form of tension relief, likeability, and networking—ultimately, a unique survival mechanism. Over the course of his lifetime, his brother has drawn on humor as a form of capital that has endeared him to people, creating a kind of safety net that softens some of the negative experiences that come along with FAS.

Nearly thirty years after her daughter Amanda was diagnosed with spastic cerebral palsy, Sara Green can still see two images that flashed through her mind just after receiving the news. One image was based on a painful memory of schoolchildren jokingly calling each other "spastic" to tease, taunt, and bully. This image triggered a sickening anticipation that her daughter would suffer the dual indignity not only of being the direct target of demeaning jokes, but also of having an aspect of her bodily experience used as a generalized derogatory term when nondisabled people tease and taunt each other. Can there be a more powerful insult? How on Earth would her daughter deal with this? How could she possibly protect her daughter from the painful tragedy of this kind of humor? The second image, though, followed rapidly and was much more encouraging. It was the memory of a stand-up routine in which popular comedian and television star Geri Jewell, who shares Amanda's diagnosis, asks the audience if they know what the worst thing about being a woman with cerebral palsy is? As the audience sits in stunned and embarrassed silence, she tells them that it's trying to put on mascara—miming the impossible task of attempting to do this with hands that don't obey the brain's commands. Every woman in the crowd can empathize with the futile impossibility of this situation, and the room explodes with laughter. Sara remembers with absolute clarity thinking: "Well if that's really the worst thing, we'll be able to deal with this. Maybe it isn't such a tragedy after all."

In disability studies, a distinction has been made between *disabling humor* that (like the taunts of school children) denigrates people with disabilities by making them targets of derisive jokes, and *disability humor* that (like Jewell's performance) enlightens others about the disability experience, affirms the humanity of individuals with impairments, counters the widespread view that disability is a tragedy, and challenges stereotypes (R. J. Berger 2013; Reid, Stoughton, and Smith 2006). Disabling humor remains common in popular culture and is reflected in comedy films such as *There's Something About Mary* (Lebesco 2004; Wolfe 1998) and the stand-up of the Blue Collar Comedy Tour. Like other stereotypical media portrayals of disability, these performances reinforce traditional notions of disability (Norden 1994; Haller 2010). Yet we have also seen an increase in the popularity of humor (whether onstage or in everyday interaction) used as a weapon to contest traditional norms of disability (Davies 2005). Beth Haller and Sue Ralph (2003) suggest, for example, that John Callahan's popular children's cartoon character Pelswick is empowering because he comes across as a smart, cool, funny eighth-grade wheelchair user who gets into hilarious situations with his peers. "The show focuses on Pelswick's interactions with others and the world around him, not his disability" and "normalizes and demystifies the disability experience for his audience" (Haller and Ralph 2003, p. 2). Some comedy seems to function in disabling and empowering ways at the same time—*South Park,* for example (Haller 2003; Reid-Hresko and Reid 2005; J. White 2005).

Kim Reid, Edy Stoughton, and Robin Smith (2006) argue that comedians with impairments may be uniquely positioned to engage audiences in affirming disability humor, which has the potential to change the narrative of the disability experience. Specifically, comedians and other artists with disabilities can use their insider perspective to set the audience at ease while simultaneously unveiling, challenging, and critiquing the widespread belief that having an impairment is inherently tragic (Albrecht 1999; Baum 1998; Haller and Ralph 2003; A. Lewis 1995). Haller suggests that "disability humor appears to be a way in which the disability community is gradually sliding its issues into the mainstream culture" (2003, p. 3). Jewell is often cited as an early example of a comedic performer who helped mainstream audiences relate to the disability experience. As a person with cerebral palsy, she successfully used self-deprecating humor to poke fun at her own experience in ways that were both palatable to audiences and powerful in reframing the disability experience for millions of television viewers (R. J. Berger 2016). Jewell's work is often starkly contrasted with that of Jerry Lewis, who, though not disabled, took on the persona of a person with an impairment in his comedic performance. Though certainly not the only difference between Jerry and Geri, Jewell's position as an insider to the disability experience may play an important role in the acceptance of her work as disability humor rather than disabling humor. Recent research on the acceptability of cartoons with disability content conducted by Morgan Ellithorpe, Sarah Esralew, and R. Lance Holbert (2014) suggests that humor with disability content is more acceptable to audiences when the humorist is known to be a disability insider. The insider status of the humorist is especially important to audience members who have personal or family experience with disability.

Even for humorists with insider disability status, however, the line between disability humor and humor that is disabling is not always easy to draw (Rosenbaum 2003). Disabled comedians who take their humor to the stage can create ironic quandaries for audiences (Shultz and Germeroth 1998). In the era of political correctness, how might they be judged by other audience members if they laugh at self-deprecating jokes told by disabled comedians? Should disabled people be the only ones allowed to laugh at disability humor? Should audiences laugh if a comedian with one kind of impairment tells jokes about someone with another? Are they laughing because they are embarrassed, or because they see something truly humorous in what is going on?

For many people, the idea of coupling disability with humor is troubling. In a world that equates disability with personal tragedy, the two can seem odd and disturbing bedfellows (Albrecht 1999; Haller 2003). How can there be anything funny about personal tragedy? In describing this book project to others, we have frequently gotten blank stares and awkward reactions. One friend suggested that the project itself might offend other colleagues and asked Shawn: "Shouldn't you be writing that *after* you get tenure?" But if we heed the anthropologist Mary Douglas's (1968) poignant argument that there is a connection between joking and social structure and values, it seems important to examine how disability and humor are intertwined. As family members of people with impairments, we know that humor and disability coexist in complex, sometimes painful but also often empowering, ways. It is our goal in this book to explore these complexities—focusing specifically on the perspectives of comedians with disabilities who take the enormous risk of using disability to get a laugh in the context of public stage performance. The role of humor in reinforcing and resisting existing narratives of disability, mediating the disability experience for others, and creating new narratives of disability is the major theme of this book.

Mapping Disability Through Humor

In the project on which this book is based,[2] we aimed to do what Tanya Titchkovsky (2003) calls "mapping disability" by using humor as a lens into the disability experience. That is, we employ humor as an index and epistemological tool to examine disability in social context. We also reverse the lens, using disability as a way to better understand humor. We began the project with two seminal questions. First, how does humor function as a tool to investigate and analyze the disability experience, and what can be learned from this? Second, how is disability humor used to mediate the disability experience to an audience? To examine the first question, we built on Linda Francis's (1994) argument that comedy draws on cultural expertise to get people to laugh. That is, we aimed to explore the ways that humor can link to cultural expertise, social analysis, and the disability experience. We take an interdisciplinary approach, drawing on humor, disability, and social science theories to analyze how humor can be used as a sociocritical tool to disorder, question, reorder, and reconstruct traditional narratives of disability. For our second major question, we draw on the work of humor theorists such as Lawrence Mintz (1985) to examine how disability humor is used to mediate the disability experience to an audience, which could be either a group in a comedy club or one individual in an everyday interaction.

We were particularly drawn to the comedic arena as a fascinating space of public sociology in which people of all backgrounds pay money to listen to comedians talk about taboo and controversial issues in an entertaining way. The comedian is uniquely licensed to discuss issues that are unmentionable in other contexts, including disability. If, as has been claimed, the comedian can serve the role of cultural mediator, amateur anthropologist, or public sociologist (Bingham and Hernandez 2009; Douglas 1975; Mintz 1985), we wanted to examine the ways that the performance of disability humor can illuminate or unveil for an audience an entire set of unknown and unexpected layers of the disability experience, including social structures, norms, and values. In addition, disability comedy is not simply about language. Since performers are onstage, they present their message in corporeal form (Kuppers 2003). They also mediate disability through reembodiment. That is, in mediating disability, the comedian goes beyond simply talking about bodily aspects of the disability experience to embodying the experience onstage in real time.

Recent research has examined the content of comedic performances that address disability (Reid, Stoughton, and Smith 2006). Yet despite the rise of disability humor as a form of activism, scholars continue to define disability humor as an undertheorized area (Coogan 2013; Haller 2003; Mallett 2010). If, as Gary Alan Fine and Christine Wood argue, jokes and joking are a "means of recognizing a group's relationship to civil society" as well as a way to be "cognitively—and potentially politically—relevant" (2010, p. 299), then disability, a category that crosses demographic boundaries, necessitates further inquiry. Following Albert Robillard's critique of previous analyses of disability humor, our work moves beyond "literary analysis" by drawing on the interviews of "actual lay and professional comedians" who are discussing and describing their own interactions (1999, pp. 61–62). We have added to this line of inquiry by conducting in-depth, semistructured interviews with ten professional comedians with disabilities about the role humor has played in their lives and their work (see the Appendix at the end of the book). In so doing, we hope to bring the voices of these comedians from the stage to the academic discourse on the use of humor as a means of reconstructing narratives of disability. Since much of the social science literature devoted to humor addresses its functions as a tool of coping, acceptance, and social navigation (Moran 2003), we turned our focus to humor as a means of dealing with uncomfortable interactions, including conflicts and microaggressions. We wanted to examine the ways in which humor might also be used to resist and reframe discomforting social situations, manage identity, and deal with the emotions of others in an active and empowered way. As you will see from the biographical sketches that are included in the Appendix, we interviewed a diverse group of male and female comedians from Canada, the United Kingdom, and the United States. These comedians represent a range of disability experiences. Their impairments include: blindness, cerebral palsy, deafness, dwarfism, learning disabilities, mobility impairments, and stuttering. Collectively, they represent a variety of social experiences including: marriage, partnership, and singleness; parenthood; sexual identities; athletic competition; undergraduate and graduate education; and careers on and off the stage. All are currently working as professional comedians who tour—some extensively and internationally.[3]

In the project and these interviews, we took an interpretive approach consistent with principals of one kind of emancipatory research that has gained considerable ground among scholars in disability studies. The strongest version of the emancipatory methodological perspective within disability studies argues that research and activism are two sides of the same coin and that research that does not directly support the cause of revealing and removing social and economic barriers is to be avoided. This version of the emancipatory research perspective is not without its critics, who, among other things, fear that the voices of individuals with impairments whose stories do not conform to the narrative that the disability movement feels it needs to tell to accomplish its goals might be silenced (Shakespeare 2014). Another approach to emancipatory research is grounded in the interpretive tradition and takes the stance that giving voice to the diverse views of marginalized people has emancipatory value in itself. Scholars who use this approach argue that bringing a variety of perspectives on disability and impairment to the attention of professional and academic communities has the potential to increase understanding and facilitate change (R. J. Berger, Feucht, and Flad 2013; Blaikie 1993). We share this view and approached our interviews with comedians from what we call an interpretive-emancipatory perspective.

Our goal in this project was to bring the perspectives of comedians with disabilities to the attention of academic audiences—in and outside of disability studies. We wanted to offer the comedians an opportunity to tell the stories they want us to hear about their disability experiences and the impact of both disabling and disability humor in their lives. We particularly wanted to explore the ways in which they negotiate the interesting and risky social space that lies at the intersection of disability and professional comedic performance. We were also interested in their views on how the performance of disability on the comedic stage might support or diverge from the goals of the disability movement. While these goals and our methods are consistent with those of an interpretative-emancipatory perspective, there is an interesting twist in this project. The goal of interpretative methodology is often to give voice to perspectives that are silenced because they come from people who occupy marginalized positions in society (Blaikie 1993). As people with impairments who are disabled by negative social attitudes, physical and economic barriers, and hegemonic cultural notions of what it means to live a normal life (ableism), these comedians clearly occupy marginalized positions. As public performers, however, they actively resist being silenced. It is likely, in fact, that collectively their work has more far-reaching impact on general populations than does academic scholarship on disability. They may have wider impact than more serious-minded disability activists. As a consequence, our goal was not to give voice to these comedians. They have voices (and microphones) and are unafraid to use them. Our goal was, rather, to bring to the attention of the academic community their perspectives on the experience of being public performers with disabilities and their views on the ways in which their work intersects with, challenges, or supports the work of disability activists and scholars. In this way, we seek to engage as researchers "with those seeking to emancipate themselves" (Oliver 1997, p. 25) by "breaking down stereotypes of people with disabilities one laugh at a time" (as quoted at joshblue.com 2014).

Organization of the Book

Since this book is part of the Lynne Rienner Disability Series, it is likely that readers will come to it with a far greater understanding of the complexities of disability than of humor. So, in the next chapter, we spend some time examining scholarship on the many interdisciplinary functions of humor. These functions and their related concepts provide important scaffolding for the analysis in subsequent chapters. While the experiences of the ten comedians we interviewed (Josh Blue, Liz Carr, Steve Danner, Tanyalee Davis, Nina G., Terry Galloway, Kim Kilpatrick, Simon Minty, Alan Shain, and Maysoon Zayid) form the core of this book, we also wanted to place their work in the context of the historical linkages between disability and humor. In Chapter 3, we explore the ways in which disability and humor have been linked across time, beginning with the Greco-Roman era and moving through the Middle Ages, Renaissance, Enlightenment, vaudeville, and the rise of stand-up comedy. We pay particular attention to how the relationship between humor and disability shifted as the dominant narrative of disability changed from one of moral weakness to one of illness and personal tragedy as well as how humor can be used as an index of larger attitudes about disability. In Chapter 4, we bring these historical linkages to the present by exploring the intersection of disability and humor in the everyday lives, work, and professional aims of the comedians we interviewed.

We had other objectives beyond the broader themes of humor as a means of analyzing and mediating the disability experience. We also wanted to create interdisciplinary links, bridging some of the work that has been done on parallel tracks in disability studies, humor studies, and the social sciences. Scholars in sociology, cultural studies, and philosophy have developed theories on humor, but few have included disability in their analyses. Even less frequently have scholars attempted to synthesize comedic theory with social science and disability studies approaches toward disability into an interdisciplinary approach to understanding the complex relationship between disability and humor. In Chapter 5, we examine ways in which models of disability and theories of humor can be linked and provide examples of these linkages from the work of the comedians we interviewed.

Finally, we wanted to use disability as a way to better understand humor—especially the tension that exists between humor and notions of political correctness. The disability rights movement has made progress in terms of how the public speaks and thinks about disability. While all of the comedians we interviewed classify themselves as part of that movement, they often walk a fine line between exploiting and challenging notions of disability for a laugh. In Chapter 6, we examine these paradoxes and the ways in which comedians negotiate this sticky territory in their everyday lives and in the context of their stage performances. In the final chapter, we pull together what we have learned about the complex relationship between disability and humor and make suggestions for future research. We have aimed for a type of emancipatory research that brings to the scholarly discourse comedic insight into such issues as living with disability, performing disability humor in an era of political correctness, and the responsibility of representation. The experiences of the professional performers who graciously shared their stories with us can help shed important light on the broader and evolving definitions of humor and disability.

Notes

1. We differentiate between the concepts *impairment* and *disability*. Following the social model of disability, we associate *impairment* with bodily differences currently conceived to be outside of the range of "normal" variation—recognizing that normal is also a social construct that varies with social, cultural, and historical context. *Disability,* however, is conceived as a more complex phenomenon that stands at the intersection of bodily difference and the social, cultural, and physical environ-

ments that impose layers of disadvantage on people whose bodies do not fit neatly within current concepts of normality. We find value in both the UK convention of speaking of *disabled people* to emphasize the degree to which environments act on people with impairments to disable them and the US convention of using *people with disabilities* to put the person first and emphasize the fact that disability is only one piece of an individual's identity. We therefore use these terms interchangeably in the text. In quotations from interviews and other sources, we use terms as they are included in the source verbatim.

2. Previous versions of portions of this book were published in *Humanity and Society*, OnlineFirst, December 17, 2015; and Green and Bingham, forthcoming.

3. Our interviews were between one and a half and three hours in length, and they were conducted in a format and location chosen by the participants. Interviews were semi-structured. We used an interview guide to make sure that all participants were given a chance to cover the same ground, but participants were given wide latitude to shape the course and content of the interview. These interviews were part of a larger project that was reviewed for compliance with ethical standards for research with human subjects and approved by the University of South Florida Institutional Review Board. During the consent process, participants were asked whether they would prefer to remain anonymous or to be identified in publications resulting from their interviews. All chose to be identified in our work by the names that they use onstage.

2

Humor as Aesthetic, Analysis, and Activism

San Francisco's Purple Onion, a famed cellar club in the North Beach area, has hosted Woody Allen, Richard Pryor, Robin Williams, and Zach Galifianakis. On a spring night in 2012, Nina G. is introduced to the audience there as America's only female comedian who stutters. She has played major comedy clubs before—Los Angeles's mainstay the Laugh Factory and San Francisco's Punchline—as well as college campuses up and down the West Coast. But this is new territory for almost every audience member. In less than five minutes, Nina G. breaks through what she calls the "fifth wall" of comedy—leading the audience away from laughter that seems to nervously coincide with her stutter to roaring applause that follows her jokes about the ridiculous responses she experiences in everyday life. Often, the jokes come from a place of frustration with living in an ableist world in which people with disabilities are devalued and discriminated against. In her interview, she says:

> Having a disability is a-a-a minority experience. . . . Things happen to you. . . . If you are able-bodied, you are not going to have those. . . . For a lot of us, we can get really angry or we can make fun of it. . . . The humor opens a door that otherwise may not be open in terms of communicating the message. . . . A lot of comedy comes out of [what] irritates you. . . . For Seinfeld, it was . . . not f-finding a sock in his dryer that irritates him. For others, it was their parents that irritated them. When you have a disability, there's this whole world of inaccessibility and discrimination which could irritate you.

Nina G. wields humor as both a mirror and a sword, as a way to educate people and directly challenge this mistreatment. And the beauty of being onstage with a mic is that she does not have "to educate every single person every single time. . . . It's kind of addressing [it] in bulk." Sometimes, this education can be blunt: "People tell me that that stuttering isn't a real d-dis-

13

ability, but the Americans with D-D-Disabilities Act . . . says that a disability is a physical or or mental impairment that substantially r-r-results in having to deal with assholes."

In her everyday life, though, Nina G. uses her humor in many different ways, sometimes to circumvent potential awkwardness and set people at ease: "I went to a job interview . . . and . . . I told them . . . 'I stutter. So, you're going to have to wait for all of my really insightful things that I'm going to say and all of my g-g-good ideas.'" In her role as a disability educator, humor is often deftly employed "as a way to make people c-comfortable." Nina G.'s roles as educator, activist, and comedian highlight the multiple functions of humor in everyday life as well as the varied ways that it can be used to know the world. Through humor she brings conflict and comfort, mirror and (metaphorical) machete. Breaking down the fifth wall, Nina G. takes audiences into a new realm—sometimes one letter at a time.

In this chapter, we explore these various roles of humor as forms of inquiry and epistemology—as ways of knowing the world. This may seem a somewhat peculiar notion. Humor is often viewed as folk knowledge or common sense, but rarely as a serious method of understanding social life. Clearly, though, humorists take up serious matters as their subjects: power, dominance, ethnicity, race, gender, sexuality, disability, aging, and so forth. Likewise, much has been learned about the social world through academic inquiry into the functions of humor in everyday life: social cohesion, promoting stability or change, status, healing, coping, teaching and learning, persuasion, or arguing (Nilsen 1993). We can also gain significant comparative insight into other cultures by using humor as an index of social values: as a map, marker, and method of inquiry. Humor is used in a wide range of fields to present and solicit information in a nonthreatening and accessible manner (Bonaiuto, Castellana, and Pierro 2003; du Pre 1997). It has benefits for obtaining and transmitting information to others, from pedagogy to persuasion (Bingham and Hernandez 2009; Hobbs 2007).

Art and literature have long been recognized as indices providing us with a measure of cultural sophistication and serving a conscientizing function (Bingham 2012; Dutton 2009). Other creative outlets, such as play, have been valued for helping individuals learn to navigate and solve problems. Likewise, the aesthetic of humor contains its own analytical elements and approaches. It offers the same avenues for inquiry, problem solving, and sensemaking that are found in these other forms of creative process. Humor can function as a tool with which to navigate complex interactions in a variety of contexts such as the workplace (Romero and Cruthirds 2006) and health care settings (Taber, Redden, and Hurley 2007). Humor is also used as a tool to process life experiences, make meaning, and interpret and deal with novelty (Decker 2004). As we show in Chapter 5, the humor aesthetic contains specific critical elements that allow analysis and evaluation

to take place. Creating humor, according to all of the comedians we interviewed, allows them to make sense of the world while also challenging
existing assumptions about that world.

Perhaps one of the best pop cultural examples of this is the work of
comedian Lenny Bruce, whose countercultural humor in the 1950s and
1960s challenged dominant cultural ideas of race, sex, prudence, and language. Considered by many to be the father of stand-up comedy in the
United States, his work influenced popular culture and a long line of professional comedians. This certainly is largely due to his use of comedy as a
form of social and cultural inquiry, as argued by Ronald Collins, who depicts
Bruce as: "A comic sage . . . a scholar of sleeze . . . who revealed the gap
between the real and the official . . . unmasked the mask man . . . delighted
in exploring why certain words were forbidden . . . and challenged 'community standards' by questioning whether the community *actually* held to these
standards" (2002, pp. 20–21; emphasis in original). Bruce's work illustrates
that some aesthetic tools of humor—inversion, skepticism, and comparative
thought process—align with more complex epistemologies that we often
associate with more formal modes of inquiry. Humor can deconstruct,
unmask, and debunk the status quo by reordering and reversing traditional
perspectives (M. Davis 1993). In their many forms, humor and comedy can
foster inquiry, analytical questioning, and evaluation, all functions that parallel tasks undertaken by sociologists, anthropologists, and other professional cultural critics.

Consider the example of satire, a form of humor that engages sense-
making strategies. Through satire, the author and the audience can deal
with issues that might otherwise go unaddressed and unexpressed (Brody
1999). In this context, the satirist is the ultimate participant observer who
can question assumptions without consequence, expressing what others
cannot (Brody 1999). He or she "constructs" sense for an audience by spec-
ifying, naming, and laying bare the boundaries of social life (Brody 1999).
Far from being hasty or reckless, the act of creating satire is intentional,
and often a calculated process: "The satirist writes in order to discover, to
explore, to survey, to attempt to clarify" (Griffin 1994, p. 39). As a form of
inquiry, satire tests patterns (Bakhtin 1984), encourages skepticism, and
even provokes (Griffin 1994). As opposed to false certainty or simply reinforcing orthodoxy and tradition, satire draws on irony and paradox to generate doubt, disorder, and disbelief. In this way, the audience can be awak-
ened. Mikhail Bakhtin posits that the world is "seen anew" (1984, p. 66)
through humor. Perhaps, as Peter Berger argues, there are things we can
only see (or hear) when we use the lens of humor:

> Indeed, an argument could be made that the social scientist who does not
> perceive this comic dimension of social reality is going to miss essential fea-

tures of it. . . . These remarks, needless to say, are not meant to denigrate the serious study of society but simply to suggest that such study itself will profit greatly from those insights that one can obtain only while laughing. (1963, p. 165)

As we demonstrate below, these arguments have implications for generating and transmitting newer narratives of disability as well as reconciling disability humor with the philosophies of political correctness.

Perhaps the most compelling quality of humor as a lens is its interdisciplinarity. Cognitively and culturally, it is ubiquitous in its scope and influence. It can be found embedded in our experience of mental health, emotion, identity, memory, learning, status, cultural and social norms, and social action. Humor is both lubricant and abrasive (Tavernier-Courbin 1985), form and function. As an aesthetic, analytic, and activist tool, it can serve individual and social goals. Beyond entertainment, it provides tension relief, ammunition for attack or acceptance into a group, and a way to challenge and unveil social norms. If it has kept social scientists frustrated and busy in their attempts to map its elusiveness, it may be because of its promise as an open window into the sociological, psychological, anthropological, and educational—simultaneously.

Humor and Social Interaction

Everyday interaction, of course, provides the most common arena for the use of humor. In this realm it can operate as an active tool for social navigation, particularly as a part of interactional strategies within a larger group. These functions are well studied in the social sciences, and even widely recognized in the popular media. In general, humor is an important tool for developing and sustaining social relationships (Derks and Berkowitz 1989). It is also routinely associated with likeability (D. Long and Graesser 1988), approachability, and flexibility by a range of groups: voters, potential employers, students, singles seeking dates, and television audiences (Zhang and Zinkhan 1991). But it is more than a popularity device. It operates as a method of identifying and building support with others and a way to differentiate through contrast (Meyer 2000). It provides group boundaries through clarification of norms and enforcement of those norms (Meyer 2000), especially through laughter directed at an individual.

Humor can profoundly impact situational structure. Indeed, our own interest in this project began with the role that humor plays in providing a unique context to engage in transformative dialogue (Romero and Cruthirds 2006) and as a safe arena for discussing taboo topics (Freud 1960; Rodrigues and Collinson 1995). From the office to the classroom and clinic, humor and comedy can be used to call attention to particular topics (Foot 1991), redirect conversation in situations of awkwardness (Norrick 1993), and facilitate more open communication and relaxation (Graham, Papa, and Brooks 1992). Its role in facilitating interaction between patients and health care providers has been widely recognized in areas such as nursing and psychotherapy (Hampes 1993). Humor can be used in the classroom as an innovative way to engage students and improve learning outcomes for a range of disciplines, from sociology and psychology to literature and nursing (Berk 2000; Bingham and Hernandez 2009).

Humor as a Way to Shape Perceptions

These functions probably do not surprise most people, especially those with a sense of humor. But a lot less is known about the specifics of the process—*how* and *why* humor functions as such a tool. For example, how is humor used to manage the emotions of others, navigate awkward situations, and shape perceptions of our identity? Linda Francis argues that humor can be a deft tool of "interpersonal emotional management" (1994, p. 154). Her work makes an important contribution by pointing out that this type of management involves a level of cultural sophistication not always attributed to those possessing a sense of humor: (1) expertise in cultural performance; (2) understanding definitions within a common culture or shared situation; and (3) the ability to take the role of others (Francis 1994). From this perspective, humor is not simply reactionary and impulsive. It draws on cultural expertise and is mediated through an expert cultural performance. Francis also suggests that the use of humor in social interaction is a kind of cultural performance requiring knowledge of cultural symbols and meanings. Being funny builds on an understanding of cultural norms, values, and practices as well as insight into how participants in the situation will be affected by humor. This, of course, requires the ability to engage in role taking, as Francis argues: "The creation of amusement in others most definitely requires the ability to look through their eyes" (1994, p. 157).

Many comedians, for example, can articulate differences in how specific audiences will react to particular jokes. All of the comedians we interviewed for this project spoke clearly about the subjectivity of group humor, particularly in terms of political correctness. They understand that their stage success depends on shared meaning through language or other symbols such as physical comedy. They learn to play to the crowd, or, to use Francis's words, to manipulate shared "symbols and subjects with specific meaning" to a particular group (1994, p. 161). Without first having a common cultural understanding of the disabled and the nondisabled worlds, these comedians could not unpack the incongruities or then reframe traditional norms in ways that provoke laughter. To put it another way, absent such insight and understanding into culture and social life, they could not engage in this type of "emotion work" (joke construction and telling) that can be used to alter the emotions of an audience (elicit laughter) (Francis 1994).

On a group level, we can see attempts at this type of emotion management—humor as persuasion—in advertising and in the legal system. In the construction of ads, the "mere association" of humor with a product can "enhance product evaluations and product choice" (Strick et al. 2011, p. 16). Within the US legal system, traditionally idealized for its objectivity, humor and wordplay serve as highly valued evidence of forensic skill (Hobbs 2007). From informal court-mandated mediation to oral arguments before the US Supreme Court, humor is used as a form of "persuasive advocacy" (Hobbs 2007, p. 124). Attorneys have been observed using humor aggressively to ridicule the plaintiffs' claims and to portray them as "laughable and unworthy of serious consideration" (Hobbs 2007, p. 150). In this context, the lawyer engages in a comic performance that allows him or her to display linguistic skills for the audience, contributing to overall credibility (Hobbs 2007).

Humor and Coping

Humor is perhaps most well known in popular culture as a mental health antidote for stress. Indeed, from corporate training sessions to advice columns, the notion of humor and laughter as therapy is widely accepted. But the social sciences have also given significant attention to the relationship between humor and mental health. Much of the psychological research on humor and laughter has centered on their stress-moderating effects on mental health "maladies" such as depression, anxiety, mood, anger, and low self-esteem (Abel 2002; Cann, Holt, and Calhoun 1999; Martin et al. 1993). Humor has also been proposed as a source of hope and hopefulness, particularly in times of stress (Herth 1993; Snyder 1994; Vaid 1999; Vilaythong et al. 2003).

While these functions are important, the use of a narrow tragedy/ comedy frame has limited study of the relationship between humor and coping. In fact, a significant portion of the coping literature frames humor in opposition to other value-laden terms with negative associations. Words such as "struggle," "suffer," and "endure" are routinely assumed to be necessary elements of the humor-coping relationship: humor helps one passively endure individual struggles and suffering. Sigmund Freud's work, for example, illustrates this idea: "Its fending off of the possibility of suffering places it among the great series of methods which the human mind has constructed in order to evade the compulsion to suffer" (1928, p. 3). A brief examination of the etymology of the word "cope" does provide some explanation for why its interpretations vary. It comes from the Old French *couper*, which translates as "to strike or to cut." But the meaning of the word has evolved from "to come to blows with" (fourteenth century) to "handle successfully" (seventeenth century), and even "to traffic" based on the Flemish version of the word used in North Sea trade. More modern interpretations suggest that it is to effectively handle some occurrence or situation.

This binary tragedy/comedy frame is all the more apparent in academic explorations linking humor with disability, which until recently have been dominated by extremely limited interpretations of coping. Such binary framing of the relationship between humor and disability has a number of ironies and incongruities: people with disabilities have traditionally been seen as chronically sorrowful, suffering, and grieving (Rieger and Ryndak 2004). At the same time, though, they have served as a population worthy of being laughed at. They are at higher risk for depression and other secondary mental health conditions due to stigma and external factors (Green 2007). Yet they are often expected to be "silent about the body" while being "cheery about impairment" (Stronbach and Allan 1999, p. 38). Much of the focus has been on the individual's use of humor for internal self-benefit: to change mood and self-esteem; to decrease the tensions and stressors that come with having a disability; in short, to laugh to keep from crying. Other research has reinforced the tragedy/comedy frame by assuming that humor is related to cognitive functioning. This has resulted in questions about whether or not some individuals with disabilities have the ability to create humor at all (Rosqvist 2012). The overrepresentation of research on how humor helps people cope with the emotional distress presumed to naturally accompany impairment is likely a result of the widely shared cultural notion that disability is a personal tragedy. Some research, however, has broken out of the pattern by exploring the ways in which people with impairments are called on to use humor to manage their own reactions to socially awkward situations and the emotional responses of others. Spencer Cahill and Robin Eggleston (1994), for example, examine the complex ways in which wheelchair users employ humor to disarm potentially difficult encounters with other people in public spaces.

In this project, we aimed to expand our understanding of coping through one of its synonyms—*encounter*. Using humor as a way to encounter an environment provides a different frame, one that takes into account the complexities of interpreting, analyzing, and navigating situations. For this, we drew on the work of Rollo May, who claimed that humor is "an expression of our own uniquely human capacity to experience ourselves as subjects who are not swallowed up in the objective situation. It is the healthy way of feeling a 'distance' between oneself and the problem, a way of standing off and looking at one's problems with perspective" (1953, p. 54). Paradoxically, humor allows us to distance ourselves from situations in order that we may encounter them in a more deliberate and strategic way. In our field, this is referred to as the *sociological imagination*—the ability to locate oneself in a larger social context. Such distancing has several effects, according to Herbert Lefcourt: it allows individuals to "actively engage" in stressful situations, but with a lesser "emotional reaction" to those situations (1996, p. 59). This ability to distance from embarrassments and defeats also prevents an overinflated sense of self-importance (Lefcourt 1996). The use of humor, then, is not one-dimensional coping in the sense of self-pity, or simply laughing to keep from crying. Coping in this sense is a more active process than its traditional interpretations might suggest.

We can see this more complex understanding of coping and humor in the recent studies that link the two concepts with disability in the family experience. These perspectives provide insight into a deeper conception of coping—as encounter, navigation, and traffic. Humor provides families with disabilities alternatives to traditional understandings and expectations of the patient response, especially tragedy and helplessness (Brooks, Guthrie, and Gaylord 1999). For the individual, humor can function as a self-evaluation tool. For example, among stroke survivors, conversational humor has been found to function as a way to reevaluate their sense of self-worth and their self-sufficiency, both of which are important in forming relationships with others (Heath and Blonder 2003). Likewise, humor allows individuals to reclaim their own subjectivity by "being part of the joke," rather than an object of the joke (Rosqvist 2012, p. 245). In this way, individuals can use humor to control and manage interpretations that others have of disability. As part of this stigma management, they can also use humor to deflect the attention that others pay to disability (Taub, McLorg, and Fanflik 2004). But humor additionally provides positive empowering functions to the larger family group as they interpret and navigate the disability experience in daily life. For example, humor can be an important vehicle for revealing feelings about illness to the larger family group and for communicating about other sensitive subjects (Brooks, Guthrie, and Gaylord 1999; Rieger 2004; Rieger and Ryndak 2004; Rieger 2005). In addition to structuring and guiding conversations around illness, it assists with creatively integrating illness into the family experience (Brooks, Guthrie, and Gaylord 1999). This can range from humor as a form of problem solving, to preventing conflicts and other situations where outsiders to the disability experience insult or laugh (Moran 2003; Rieger and Ryndak 2004).

In these examples, coping is occurring. However, it is a more active and engaged process that deals not simply with the biological or the psychological, but also with factors and situations external to the individual as well as the family. This notion of coping goes beyond positive adjustment as an aspect or indicator of individual mental health. In a much more interdisciplinary way, this kind of coping incorporates emotional response and self-perception with understandings of larger structures, social values, groups and group process. In short, it is an interdisciplinary form of problem solving. The net effect is a new form of control and freedom to express oneself, restore one's self-image, and establish a sense of normalcy (Jarzab 2004). This agency also frees people with impairments in important ways from "embodied social constraints" associated with the disability experience (Rieger and Ryndak 2004). By helping to foster a "playful spirit," humor helps disprove assumptions that the disability experience must or should be somber or solemn for families (Rieger 2004). These types of explorations have deepened our understandings of the complex relationships between humor, coping, and disability within the family context. Humor, though, is a form of agency and a navigational tool used in a range of arenas, including the political. In the remainder of this chapter, we examine ways in which humor operates on a broader level as a form of social and political action.

Carnival Consciousness: Humor as a Tool for Subversion, Activism, and Social Change

> Power, money, persuasion, supplication, persecution—these can lift a colossal humbug—push it a little—weaken it a little, century by century; but only laughter can blow it to rags and atoms at a blast. . . . Against the assault of laughter, nothing stands.
> —*Mark Twain (as quoted in Sanders 1995, p. 14)*

A common theme can be found throughout historical, political, psychological, philosophical, and sociological inquiry into humor: transformation. Through its many interdisciplinary functions—entertainment, mediation, analyses, investigation, protest—humor alters dynamics. It can transform perspective, outlook, and group dynamics. And it can provide a vehicle for new forms of agency. Our interest for this project centered on the more subversive aspects of humor's *transformation* capabilities. The Latin translation of the word means "to change the shape of," a fitting definition, considering the ways that humor is used to do just that—challenge and invert dominant values, cultural ideas, and common logic. Subversion has been a central element of humor, from Greek comedy and the Renaissance jester to the twenty-first-century humor of the disabled comedians in the Abnormally Funny People comedic tour group. It is a dominant objective of a number of genres of humor, including irony, satire, and parody. To the extent that these genres question common sense and push cultural boundaries, they aim to transform our perspective.

As we show in Chapter 3, folly and subversion have often been intertwined. A good starting point to explore this link is Russian philosopher and cultural critic Bakhtin (1984), who wrote about the social function of folly in the form of carnival exemplified in the Feast of Fools (a French medieval festival). *Carnival* was both a social institution and a form of consciousness. It was a place where folly profaned and subverted hierarchies of social life—etiquette, reverence, piety, accepted truths, and hierarchies of social life were all reversed. The result was a world turned upside down, where privilege was challenged and hypocrisies were revealed. More than simple revelry, the event was a "sustained protest against the monological misrule of officialdom" with the specific aims to "transform canonical orders of truth, [and] rupture established hegemonies" (Irving and Young 2002, p. 25). In other words, folly functioned as resistance and transformation.

Three specific Bakhtinian ideas on carnival and humor have important implications for our project: diversity, openness, and creativity. Carnival humor celebrates difference, pluralism, and the Other (Bell and Gardiner 1998; Irving and Young 2002). In this arena, new voices and perspectives were privileged through folly—the lower levels of society were empowered to question the higher levels. Because of his interest in discovery and freedom, Bakhtin wrote about "unfinalizability"—the idea that all of life is not fixed unless it is rendered so by authoritarian structures that suppress by monopolizing meaning and truth (Irving and Young 2002, p. 21). Carnival and its elements help to reveal truths about difference, especially the reality that these truths were both arbitrary and relative (Sobchack 1996). Indeed, for Bakhtin, humor and laughter revealed a lot:

> Laughter has a deep philosophical meaning, it is one of the essential forms of the truth concerning the world as a whole, concerning history and man; it is a peculiar point of view relative to the world; the world is seen anew, no less (and perhaps more) profoundly than when seen from the serious standpoint. Therefore, laughter is just as admissible in great literature, posing universal problems, as seriousness. Certain essential aspects of the world are accessible only to laughter. (Bakhtin 1984, p. 66)

This sort of "carnival consciousness" is an important element for freeing human thought and fostering "imagination for new potentialities" (Bakhtin 1981, p. 49). Laughter "purifies" from dogmatic thinking, bringing new ways of seeing and liberating from "fear and intimidation, from the single meaning" (Bakhtin 1984, p. 123). Carnival humor, then, can provide agency and power, especially when the "victory of laughter" (Bakhtin 1984, p. 90) clarifies consciousness and gives "a new outlook on life" (Bakhtin 1984, p. 91) that leaves behind "oppression and guilt related to all that is consecrated" (Bakhtin 1984, p. 94). Carnival created a "space for participants to design interactions of their own invention and creation" (Shepard

2005, pp. 456–457). Carnival consciousness "enables" agency while stamping out feelings of helplessness (Emerson 1997, p. 103).

We can see more modern examples of carnival as a transformative force in the performance of stand-up comedy. Bruce, who reinvented the genre in the 1950s and 1960s, challenged sacred middle-class values— ideas of race and religion—and pushed the limits of freedom of speech. For this he was banned, repeatedly arrested, and eventually convicted of obscenity, to which he reversed the legal logic in clever fashion: "I didn't do it, man, I only said it" (quoted in Casper 2014, p. 351). Other well-known comedians have usedthe carnivalesque onstage to challenge and reverse social values: Margaret Cho, Eddie Izzard, Dick Gregory, and George Carlin are several of many. Pryor challenged the US political and racial landscapes, bringing both mundane and serious aspects of African American life to white audiences in ways they had not previously experienced (Thomas 2012). He did so by creating ambivalence in the audience, using characters such as Super Nigger (a critique of superheroes) and Mudbone (a wise fool). Both explorations modeled a culturally specific wisdom that previously went unappreciated by the dominant culture (Thomas 2012). Soon after the Islamophobic backlash that followed September 11, Muslim stand-up comedians used the stage to challenge common understandings of race, religion, and gender (Amarasingam 2010). These examples of carnival humor—from Carlin's "7 Things You Cannot Say on Television" to the more recent political satire of Jon Stewart—are popular precisely because they subvert dominant cultural values. More importantly, these ideas have not simply entered into the US consciousness; they have helped to engage the critical consciousness of many (Brewer, Young, and Morreale 2013; Thomas 2012).

Beyond more well-known comedic personalities, carnivalesque protest, critique, and activism can be found in many other places, including nonviolent resistance to oppression. The Serbian Otpor movement (translated from Serbian as "resistance"), which played an important role in organizing against Slobodan Milosevic, used humor as a central strategy. Members of the movement parodied various aspects of the government through video and art. Their work not only facilitated a culture of resistance, in carnival-like fashion, but it also turned the oppression upside down (Sorensen 2008). The United States has its own versions of political humor activists. The Raging Grannies have a network of social justice activist groups across the United States and Canada. Cloaking themselves in stereotypical granny garb, they pose as older women and engage in collective resistance against economic injustice and war. Their performance involves satirical songs and the representation of the granny as the wise fool (Roy 2006). Their work drew the covert attention of the California National Guard, which spied on the Raging Grannies after an antiwar rally.

Another group, the Yes Men, engage in "identity correction" by posing as multinational corporate and development representatives and speaking in parodied roles on television and at international economic development conferences. Their main strategy involves the carnivalesque method of telling the truth as a way to unveil lies. They are culture jammers who use the tools of capitalism and international development to parody the system. Similarly, the Clandestine Insurgent Clown Army uses clowning as carnival to ridicule, confuse, contradict, and dissent. Their work includes protesting war in full military regalia (dressed as clowns) and "Carnival Against Capitalism" demonstrations. Weaponry often includes water guns, housecleaning tools (such as dusters), and a symbolic mix of pink and camouflage. Another example is the carnival created by Rev. Billy and the Church of Life After Shopping who use a preacher-revival format to protest overconsumption and speak to issues of economic justice and militarism. With choir in tow, Rev. Billy guerrilla preaches at Disney Stores, Starbucks, and malls across North America (and other continents). The ridiculousness created by these contradictions not only draws attention to the activists, but it sets up a context in which any harsh response by authorities is made to appear unwarranted and absurd because of the buffoonery of the activists. These examples of carnival humor demonstrate the subversive potential of humor and laughter as activist and conscientizing tools—as conflict forms of humor.

Disability Humor: Enabling Social Action in a Politically Correct World

These central elements of carnival humor provide perhaps the most appropriate entry point for the topics of this book: subversion, openness to diversity, agency, and creativity. Disability humor, in contrast to disabling humor, enables a form of activism. It is a tool and an arena in which individuals can "disrupt popular accounts or depictions," disorder shared meaning, and provide counternarratives that redefine disability (Reid, Stoughton, and Smith 2006, p. 637). On the stage, for example, humor can provide alternative images and counternarratives that shake up worldviews by revealing cultural incongruities (Reid, Stoughton, and Smith 2006) and, in carnivalesque fashion, give voice to other perspectives. Nina G., a comedian we interviewed for this project, talks about the unique possibilities comedians have to create alternative narratives of disability. She says that she feels fortunate to be a stage performer because, unlike many disabled people, she can tell her story in her own way.

As we show in subsequent chapters, these counternarratives and cultural incongruities surface when comedians with disabilities use humor as an engaging sociological tool for unveiling hidden structures, norms, behavior, and institutions relevant to their everyday lives and the disability experience: use of public transportation, sexuality and dating, and the demeaning ways people talk to them in everyday interaction. This form of comic relief lays bare the obscured social forces that shape our interpretations of impairment and disability. All of the comedians we interviewed, for example, use the stage to examine everyday social responses to their disability. Josh Blue builds several routines around stories of people mistaking him for a drunk or homeless man. Onstage he recounts that some people have said to him, "I want what you're on, man," to which he responds incredulously, "You mean you want some of my seizure medication?!?" Alan Shain, who also has cerebral palsy, jokes about the narrow-mindedness of friends who limit their suggestions for his potential dates to wheelchair users. Liz Carr, a wheelchair user, and Nina G., who stutters, sarcastically share with audiences the absurdity of being told how inspirational they are when disability happens to be prominent in the media. For Liz Carr, this happened during the Paralympics; for Nina G., it coincided with the release of *The King's Speech* (2010).

We spoke in detail with these comedians about their aims and objectives in telling these stories as well as their own perceptions of how audiences receive them. We were particularly interested in their ideas on humor as a tool that might empower, raise consciousness, and, in the carnival sense, foster a new open-mindedness. In the second half of this book, we focus specifically on this type of disability humor, which exemplifies a carnivalesque mix of laughter with the taboo (and even feared), and creates a space of freedom for social inquiry and action. In the comedic arena, the "problems" of disability can be interpreted, broken down, and reconstructed in new ways, especially when humor transforms the frame from individual problems to collective issues of social injustice (Shepard 2005, p. 447).

Yet these carnivalesque acts of resistance take place in a broader context. Comedy and humor continue to be widely accepted arenas for disabling stereotypes, at the individual and public level. The use of the word "retard" as an insult, for example, remains as popular on playgrounds as it does in films. But the notion of political correctness has certainly impacted how disability is discussed. To some, disability and humor should never mix. If the two are not seen as mutually exclusive, the combination may be somewhat discomfiting, or embarrassing. In a world that equates disability with individual tragedy, any mix of humor and disability may seem cruel. Disability humor, however, can be used as a tool to simultaneously highlight and challenge the prevailing notion that disability is solely individual and necessarily tragic. All of the comedians we interviewed create this type of (intended) ambivalence. Tanyalee Davis, a professional comedian and little person, for example, says at the beginning of one of her routines: "I know I am different, it's okay, I am bi-racial. I'm a white girl." Then she turns around and shakes her rear and says, "I am a black girl"—playing on her prominent buttocks, which is both a common feature of her kind of dwarfism and also a racial stereotype (Davis 2006). As comedians with disabilities these performers have license to playfully cross the line of political correctness and traverse areas of ambivalence and uncertainty. Indeed, to the extent that their work is activism, they exploit this line to both comfort and discomfit the audience, keeping the crowd with them but leading them to new places at the same time.

Uncertainty and ambivalence are more evident in comedic representations of disability on film (R. J. Berger 2013). For example, in 2008, British film censors put a warning label on the comedy *Special People* for its "disability themes," implying that audiences might have unease with disability as a topic in general and that many would feel uncomfortable laughing at disability issues. The 2006 film *The Ringer* featured Johnny Knoxville (of *Jackass* fame) as a con man who fakes a disability so he can enter the Special Olympics (Bauer 2005). The movie was produced by the Farrelly Brothers, whose prior portrayals of disability in their comedies have also been scrutinized (*Dumb and Dumber, Shallow Hal,* and *Me, Myself & Irene*). But *The Ringer* did feature over 150 disabled actors, more than any other film has included. And several of these had prominent roles, demonstrating keen wit and agency of their own. Perhaps more surprising is that Timothy Shriver, Special Olympics president and chairman, was executive producer of the film. The movie garnered support from several disability rights groups, including the American Association of People with Disabilities.

Conundrum Entertainment produced *The Ringer,* which is a fitting name since the movie as well as the other examples above conjure a number of discomfiting questions about the link between humor, disability, and taste: What is funny, and who should be laughing? What makes a joke about disability funny? Do you have to have an impairment to joke about disability? Is it okay for someone with a disability to joke about himself or herself, or does the humor have to turn the gun on everyone else? And what of "crip humor"? Should all humor be subject to political correctness or censorship? While some disabled comedians have faced a backlash from the disability community, those arguing for additional political correctness are often framed as too serious or having no sense of humor at all. We take up these issues in Chapter 6 of this book.

Getting Serious About Humor

It is important, however, to emphasize that humor research is significant in our overall understanding of the environment, both sociocultural and natural,

and of ourselves as part of it. The phenomena we label "humor" is universal
and also one of the most complex.   —*Mahadev Apte (1988, p. 7)*

Before we move on to the historical inquiry, however, a defense of humor
scholarship is in order. It has been argued, quite seriously, that academic
inquiry takes the fun out of humor (E. White 2000; Marx 1959). Consider
the case of E. B. White, the humorist, essayist, and novelist who set the
standard of writing at the *New Yorker* in the twentieth century. He mounted
a more damning case against humor "autopsy" than Groucho Marx:
"Humor can be dissected, as a frog can, but the thing dies in the process
and the innards are discouraging to any but the pure scientific mind" (E.
White 2000, p. 243). For years White wrote humorous essays and cele-
brated stories known for well-crafted and sardonic prose. Yet among college students, White is probably more well known for his own literal dis-
section of the English language through the ubiquitous composition text,
The Elements of Style, which has sold millions of copies. He once wrote,
"Commas in *The New Yorker* fall with the precision of knives in a circus
act, outlining the victim" (White, as quoted in *Paris Review Interviews IV*
2009, p. 142). The irony, of course, is that words were White's tools of
humor, and he was a carver of language who parsed, cut, and cleaved language like a master surgeon. And with this skilled understanding of his
craft, White used his writing to entertain, educate, provoke, and become, in
his words: "philosopher, scold, jester, raconteur, confidant, pundit, devil's
advocate, enthusiast" (E. White 1977, p. vii).

Though not a social scientist, White took on all of these other roles.
His own career and words make an interesting case for the interdisciplinary
nature of humor, and for our need to understand and examine it (despite his
protests). Consider again humor's multiple dimensions: it involves language, both formal and informal, embodiment (physical comedy), and a
physical reaction (laughter). Some aspects of humor are spontaneous, which
makes it both entertaining and an enigma in the academic realm. Much of
comedic writing, though, is a craft that requires specifically planned language and wordplay. Comedic performance requires an understanding of
timing and the ability to read an audience to anticipate and know their
experiences, what might make them laugh, and how far they can be pushed.
Countering both White and Groucho Marx, since we must, requires no
apologetics. Like the comedians who people the pages of this book, White
was a humorist and a critic. His style of humor did its own unveiling, but
even his serious talk of humor unmasked realities: "Whatever else an American believes or disbelieves about himself, he is absolutely sure he has a
sense of humor" (E. White 2000, p. 245).

Humor is often used as a mask but, in the process, it unmasks everything else. Our efforts here to dissect humor, as White would describe it
(2000), parallel attempts of others to understand what makes a novel great,

or a piece of art moving, and how these cultural objects can inform our understanding of social life. This type of humanistic inquiry is essential for making sense of everyday experience. After all, we have spent much time as a culture and as individuals figuring out what makes us sad, or why we cry. Why should our laughter be any different?

In the next chapter, we trace the complex historical relationship between humor and disability, from the Greco-Roman era and jesters of the Middle Ages through vaudeville and the twenty-first century. We specifically focus on how this relationship has paralleled larger political and social changes in approaching disability, and how humor can be used as an index of attitudes toward disability over time.

3

Disability and Humor in Historical Context

When Maysoon Zayid, an American woman of Palestinian descent who has cerebral palsy (CP), takes the stage, she begins with a concerted effort to "get the CP out of the way." She has important messages to get across to audiences and only some of these messages have to do with the experience of disability. Turning her rapier wit on political issues of the day—particularly issues having to do with global conflict and misrepresentations of the Arab world—she wants the audience to accompany her on a journey to places they've never been before but, more importantly, she wants to use humor to open the eyes of her audience to what she sees as abuses of power on a national and global scale. She has several purposes; using humor to renarrate the disability experience is one. Using disability and humor to renarrate conflict in the Middle East is another. She uses the stage to do both:

> People go on a journey with me wherever I've taken them. Whether it's the politics, or . . . whatever it is . . . I [have] much more than that one purpose. . . . I obviously use my comedy to discuss a lot of issues in both the Arab culture and the Israeli-Palestinian conflict plus now the wider Arab world conflict. . . . To vent frustration and to recontextualize things that I've seen misinterpreted in the media.

Zayid's comedy is designed to make her audience laugh while also infusing their experience with a critical perspective on global politics, to which they may never before have been exposed. Comedian Terry Galloway, who has been deaf since early childhood, also has a clear political agenda that adds an edge to her professional work. Like Zayid, it is not just the oppression of people with disabilities that Galloway seeks to change through satiric critique. Rather, she seeks to use humor to combat oppression and xenophobic attitudes on all fronts. She says, "This world doesn't make it easy to be disabled. Nor does it make it easy to be queer or anything that's in any way different. There's a xenophobia inherent in being human that's just dreadful and must be overcome." Zayid's and Galloway's combination of disability with humor that has a critical edge are modern examples of a phenomenon that has deep roots and an interesting, though circuitous, history.

In this chapter, we explore the historical connections between humor and disability as a backdrop to the stage on which Zayid, Galloway, and other twenty-first-century comedians ply their trade. We also explore how disability humor evolved in tandem with changes in the lenses through which disability is commonly viewed, paying particular attention to the ways in which people with disabilities have used humor as a form of social critique within different social and historical contexts. We specifically look at how the relationship between disability and humor changed as public understandings of the problem of disability shifted from moral or religious inferiority through personal tragedy or a medical problem to social inequality, discrimination, and beyond. We use the term *lens* here to denote a widely circulating public narrative about disability and to differentiate these beliefs from more formal models or theories used in academic scholarship. For decades, scholars have argued that narratives are critical to individual identity construction and meaning making (Loseke 2007; Mishler 1995). Individuals tell stories to themselves and others to make sense of the vagaries of everyday individual and collective experience. The stories individuals tell about themselves, however, are not free of cultural, institutional, or organizational influence (Loseke 2007). Individual narratives are judged by others. "Good" stories must be perceived to be believable and important (Loseke 2007). To be believable, personal stories must resonate with widely circulating cultural narratives or formula stories. While cultural narratives can help individuals make sense of their own experience and that of others, they can also place constraints on the kinds of stories one can tell and the kinds of people to whom one can tell them (Loseke 2007). Personal stories that run counter to widely circulating formula stories can, however, serve as resistance narratives and may over time have an impact on wider public understandings. Scholarly models and theories can also influence cultural narratives through social activism; institutional policies and practices; and artistic, literary, and media portrayals—including humor.

We provide a brief, necessarily oversimplified, introduction to the three lenses that have dominated public understandings of disability as a background to our historical analysis. Viewed through a *moral or religious lens,* disability is seen as an individual state of worthiness or human value. Individuals with impairments may be scorned, shunned, or killed because of the belief that they are morally impure, debase, or valueless. In rarer instances, they may be seen as people imbued with special gifts that set them apart from others (Bragg 1997). The cause of impairment may be attributed to divine punishment (or favor), witchcraft, or other supernatural sources. People with impairments (or their families) may be blamed for previous behavior that is assumed to have caused the impairment. When viewed through a *medical or tragedy lens,* on the other hand, disability is equated with illness and considered to be an individual medical problem. The problem of disability is equated with the existence of a biological difference or impairment. Rather than moral blame or favor, people with impairments are often pitied for the tragedy of their affliction. Viewed through a *social oppression or discrimination lens,* disability is neither an individual issue nor synonymous with impairment or bodily difference. Rather, it is synonymous with social oppression and discrimination. Like other marginalized minority groups, people with impairments are disabled by structural barriers and attitudinal constraints. Disability is thus viewed as a socially constructed phenomenon and can be eradicated by the removal of these barriers and constraints.

The social oppression or discrimination lens has gained traction within the community of people with disabilities and their advocates. Decades of work by social activists has resulted in changes in legislation, policy, and programs that are beginning to have an impact on wider public understanding and a shifting cultural narrative of disability. This transition, however, is far from complete and the medical or tragedy lens remains dominate in the minds of many people who lack direct lived experience with disability as well as some who have this experience (Darling 2013). Remnants of the moral lens on disability also remain. As we show in the sections that follow (and in Chapter 5), each disability lens has provided opportunities for various types of humor. The lens through which disability is viewed by the general public (or a particular audience) affects the kind of humor deemed acceptable and funny. In many cases, too, humor has helped to solidify the predominance of a particular disability lens, turning that lens into a formula story of disability within a particular social time and place.

This historical context is important for understanding today's comedians addressing disability. In the contemporary landscape of political correctness, and the continuing dominance of the medical or tragedy lens, comedy and disability might seem strange and uncomfortable bedfellows. How, after all, can it possibly be okay to laugh at the personal tragedy of others? Today it is unlikely that the popular 1980s stand-up comedian and actor Bobcat Goldthwait, who feigned stuttering and mental disability onstage, would garner the same approval from audiences that he did in the *Police Academy* movies or when appearing on *The Arsenio Hall Show.* The 1990s brought shifts in sensitivity as well as definitions of appropriateness, which have certainly impacted how willing studios and production companies are to risk using disabling ridicule for ratings. Strange bedfellows or not, however, disability and comedy (of both the disabling and disability variety) have a long, complex relationship that spans centuries. Consider the 2011 production of *All the King's Fools,* which took place on the River Thames in Henry VIII's palace as a collaboration between Foolscap and the Misfits Theatre. Aiming for historical accuracy, the theater companies commissioned the work of University of East Anglia historian Suzannah Lipscom, a scholar of Henry VIII and early Tudor court culture. The result was a production where the actors had something in common with many of the fools and jesters of the Middle Ages: disability. In an interview for *The Guardian,* the show's director (and former European Jester of the Year), Peet Cooper, stated that "comedy owes a debt to disabled performers" and that disabilities, including learning disabilities, are "deep in comedy's DNA [deoxyribonucleic acid]" (Cooper, as quoted in Logan 2011).

We begin our exploration of this DNA in the Greco-Roman era, where early links between ideas of tragedy and comedy, vis-à-vis disability, can be found. We then examine the important emergence of the jester in the Middle Ages, and the evolution of this role during the Renaissance and the Enlightenment. In that section, we give particular attention to the ways in which *folly*—often a spectacle of physical abnormality, dress, or psychic aberration (Willeford 1969)—came to be associated with disability and madness, particularly a lack of reason. We also examine the unique critical function of the *mask of folly,* or so-called artificial fools who took on the guise of the fool as a shield for entertainment and critique. Our subsequent examination of the vaudeville era traces parallels between the broader capitalist values and individualism with the near exclusion of disability from the comedy scene as well as the enduring influence of vaudeville on definitions of comedy. We conclude with the advent of stand-up comedy in the late 1950s and the emergence of socially conscious, cerebral, nihilist, and commodified forms of disability comedy.

We must mention a few caveats. We cover several important time periods here, but certainly not all of them. Our aim is to provide some historical background for our exploration of the work of modern comedians with disabilities, rather than to provide an exhaustive history. In addition, there is certainly disagreement over general responses to impairment during these times. We do not intend to settle these larger debates, but suggest that humor can help to shed light on some of the ambiguity. Finally, the history of the ties between disability and comedy is not necessarily one of continual progress. So, there certainly are cases of historical regression where the active power of humor as it relates to disability has been squelched over time. But this should not be a complete surprise since the interdisciplinary nature of both disability and humor subjects them to constant reinterpretation through the lenses of economics, medicine, and shifts in authority among these and other cultural institutions.

Greco-Romans: Impairment as Ridicule-ous Comedy

In deformity and bodily disfigurement there is good material for making jokes, though here as elsewhere one has to know the limit.
—*Cicero (On Oratory 239, as quoted in Garland 1995, p. 76)*

In ancient Greece, physical impairment was likely common, and could result from a range of causes: war, birth defects, accidents, disease, plague, and malnutrition. But the Greeks held no fixed definition of disability equivalent to our twenty-first-century understanding, so its meaning depended on both context and the individual (Edwards 1997). They did, though, have clear ideals about beauty. Physical beauty, for example, was a sign of divine favor while congenital impairments were seen as a result of moral failure, illegitimacy, and punishment from the gods (Garland 1995). The moral or religious lens was a dominant way of interpreting impairment, with individuals judged on moral grounds and often receiving different moral valuations based on the nature of their impairments. But response to impairment depended on the cause (Edwards 1997; Garland 1995). Since military service was highly valued, impairments sustained during battle could bring status or respect. Congenital impairments, on the other hand, might result in infanticide, which was practiced in both Sparta and Athens (Lenfant 1999). There is some disagreement, though, over the general social response to impairment in Greek society. Martha Edwards (1997) argues that impairment did not necessarily prevent individuals from carrying out certain social and economic roles and that participation in society was possible. Robert Garland (1995) believes that Greeks took a harsher view of impairment, viewing this group with disdain as useless burdens on society—often leaving them to fend for themselves. More recent scholarship (Rose 2007) has pointed out that, given the lack of evidence, it is unproductive to superimpose modern ideas of health, economy, and impairment on ancient societies.

While it is difficult to know the specifics of response to impairment, we do have some potential indicators. Aristotle and Plato both had clear thoughts on the topic:

With regard to the choice between abandoning an infant or rearing it, let there be a law that no crippled child be reared. (Aristotle 1992, p. 443)

This then is the kind of medical and judicial provision for which you will legislate in your state. It will provide treatment for those of your citizens whose physical and psychological constitution is good; as for the others, it will leave the unhealthy to die, and those whose psychological constitution is incurably corrupt it will put to death. That seems to be the best thing for both the individual sufferer and for society. (Plato 1974, p. 74)

There is no evidence that this was formally or categorically practiced by the Greeks, but the more militaristic Roman society actually codified such ideas. Roman treatment of impairment in general was harsher than that of the Greeks, but again response depended on the impairment and context. Table IV of the law code of the Twelve Tables (450–449 BCE), which was abandoned by the second century, allowed family members to quickly kill a "dreadfully deformed" child. Even when such laws were not enforced, it seems evident that in a culture where oral debate and language were synonymous with intelligence and achievement (Gracer 2003), disability was likely seen as less than ideal. One city, Athens, did provide a safety net for those with impairments (which required a yearly inspection), but it is likely that people with severe impairments were forced to rely on begging or the charity of others (Garland 1995).

In the midst of uncertainty or debates about specific responses to impairment in the Greco-Roman era, humor can actually provide important insight. In some contexts, it is clear that comedy was created from the moral inferiority associated with impairment. As Garland points out, the philosophers of the ancient world "accorded disablement a central place in their theoretical explanations of laughter" (1995, p. 74). Cicero's words from *On Oratory,* for example, provide relevant insight into the relationship between comedy and impairment during this Greco-Roman era: "Laughter has its foundation in some kind of deformity and baseness" (2.236, as quoted in Garland 1995, p. 74). Likewise, Plato, Socrates, and Aristotle all wrote that laughter resulted from the perceived inferiority of others. Laughter and humor, they believed, evoked superiority, derision, and malice. (We examine their philosophy of humor in more detail in Chapter 5.) Aristotle, for example, argued that comedy is an imitation (mimesis) of others, and specifically meant to represent ignoble humans (1984, p. 2319):

> As for Comedy, it is (as has been observed) an imitation of men worse than the average; worse, however, not as regards any and every sort of fault, but only as regards one particular kind, the Ridiculous, which is a species of the Ugly. The Ridiculous may be defined as a mistake or deformity not productive of pain or harm to others; the mask, for instance, that excites laughter, is something ugly and distorted without causing pain. (1984, p. 2319)

It is likely that, by suggesting that the ugly and distorted create laughter (rather than pain), Aristotle is referring to the audience and not the individual who was the object of the joke. After all, he did state in the *Nicomachean Ethics* that jokes are "a kind of abuse" (2000, p. 77). Aristotle did not like this, but he did believe it was reality.

These philosophical interpretations of humor have clear parallels to what is known about the relationship between disability and humor in the Greco-Roman era. While the blind poet seer in the Greco-Roman period was afforded status, other physical impairments could be fodder for disabling humor in the form of ridicule, especially during the Hellenistic era when slaves with impairments became more popular forms of entertainment for the wealthy. Physical impairment and pain did generate laughter and a sense of superiority in some Greco-Roman circles, as humiliation of impairment became a form of comic entertainment. Indeed, despite the ridicule, individuals with impairments were afforded some level of survival within the comic arena. For example, there is evidence to suggest that dwarfs and people with kyphosis (a humped back) were in demand as singers, dancers, mimes, and other performers (Garland 1995). Comic theater and drinking parties were prime locations in which derisive humor was directed toward those with impairments, with the latter a place where guests could witness people with impairments and bodily difference on display and as entertainment (juggling, dancing, etc.). Watching, laughing, and mocking the struggle and pain of others presumed to be morally inferior boosted the guests' self-image (Garland 1995). (This is demonstrated in the *Iliad,* where the gods laugh and mock Hephaistos, portrayed as lame or crippled, as he meanders through the banquet hall filling their cups with wine.) Such mockery, which even evolved into an art of trading insults, served several functions, according to Garland (1995, p. 75): cohesion (among the nondisabled), catharsis, and pathological aggression. Laughter released tension (brought on by fear of people with disabilities), but also brought out a concealed aggression (especially with the addition of alcohol).

While it is difficult to know specific details of responses to impairment, it does seem clear that comedic interpretations of impairment were made through the lenses of religion, ideals of beauty, perceptions of usefulness, and, likely, fear. To the extent that impairments diverged from idealized views of nature and physical beauty, they functioned as legitimized sources of amusement. Often this amusement took the form of degrading disabling humor. The discomfort of others, whether disabled or not, was a "constant source of merriment" (Garland 1995, p. 76), which can be seen from the works of Homer to Corinthian pottery that depicts dwarfs, people with kyphosis, and other people with impairments dancing and juggling (Garland 1995, p. 84). These known responses relate to some of our first formal attempts at theorizing humor, which emanate from superiority, fear, and aggression. (This will be addressed in more detail in Chapter 5.) These forms of humor typically functioned for the pleasure of the audience at the expense of people with impairments—a cruel form of disabling humor and individual critique. Yet later in the Middle Ages, disability and humor would be linked in new ways to allow some individuals with impairments and bodily differences to move from the position of spectacle to that of spectator armed with a critical perspective of his or her own.

From the Middle Ages to the Enlightenment:
Jesters and Fools

> The fool knows the truth because he is a social outcast, and spectators see
> most of the game. —*Chinese proverb (as quoted in Otto 2001, p. 100)*

The emergence of the fool and jester in the Middle Ages and Renaissance
cultures linked disability and humor together in new ways. Beyond simply
conjoining humor with individual critique and ridicule (disabling humor),
the folly of the jester evolved into a fusion of the outsider, the fool, and the
subversive into one persona that could serve important critical social functions. Jesters and fools countered social norms by crossing boundaries with
their humor—and sometimes with their bodies. Natural fools, also referred
to as innocents, were so called because of physical or mental impairments,
typically from birth (Otto 2001, p. 32). Others adopted the fool's guise to
engage in foolish activity. The words "jester" and "fool" are often used
interchangeably, but William Willeford explains their differences:

> The Fool is often a "private person" who gives symbolic expression to the
> problems of human individuality in its relation to rational norms and to what
> exceeds them. "Jester" on the other hand, can be any kind of merrymaker but
> is usually maintained in a prince's court or nobleman's household; he is thus
> a domesticated form of the fool who in other forms is lawless. (1969, p. 13)

While jesters might have had some physical abnormalities, they did not typically have intellectual impairments (Otto 2001). The role of the fool came
with a range of statuses depending on the individual and the context: innocent soul and mouthpiece of God (Otto 2001), depraved moral degenerate,
sage fool or "foolosopher" (Otto 2001, p. 35), subversive critic and professional entertainer (McDonagh 2008), the embodiment of the mysterious and
unknown (Zijderveld 1982), and workers of the devil's will. A person
known as an "artificial" though was a performer, or a "fool actor" who
stood "somewhere between the reality, possibly horrible, of idiocy or madness and its character as a show, something to be entertained by and, if
taken seriously, loved rather than despised" (Willeford 1969, p. 10). Within
the role of entertainer, the functions of the fool and jester evolved to
include one who subverts reality, a licensed truth teller, a mimesis, and a
perpetual reminder that things are not always what they seem. This rise in
popularity and status of the fool, especially in the later Middle Ages, would
also intersect with the emergence of disability as a social category.

   Up until the fifteenth century, the church in Western Europe had
viewed those with disabilities with mixed reactions, based on a moral or
religious lens. Sympathy—viewing them as innocents, natural fools, or sim-
pletons—was actually part of church theology through the sixteenth century

(Billington 1984; Stainton 2004). This made charity in the early Middle Ages more open, without categorizations of impairments, while charitable acts were viewed as spiritually beneficial for those who gave (Metzler 2011). Some individuals with impairments (or certain kinds of impairments) were exempted from common moral expectations (e.g., natural fools and innocents), others were revered as the bearers of special moral authority (e.g., holy fools and God's children). More commonly though, when viewed through this lens, disability was interpreted as moral failing. Causes of impairment were often attributed to divine punishment, witchcraft, or other supernatural sources. Alternately, they (or their families) were blamed for previous behavior that was assumed to have caused the impairment (Mackelprang and Salsgiver 2009). But even though the moral model of disability undoubtedly led to socially condoned abuses (including tolerance of cruel jokes at the expense of individuals with impairments), this view of disability also paradoxically opened opportunities for disability to be used as the basis for humorous, and powerful, social critique.

Reason, Folly, and Disability: The Emergence of the Medical Lens

Michel Foucault (1964) extensively examined the ways that European cultural shifts in values, beginning in the Renaissance, reshaped interpretations of madness. But these shifts, especially a focus on reason and rationalism, are also important for understanding transformations of cultural notions of foolishness, which gave rise to the disabled body as a site of folly and depravity (Stainton 2004). The role of the fool and folly's cultural functions changed in the latter part of the fifteenth and in the sixteenth century, particularly because rationalism replaced folly's "magico-religious" function (Stainton 2004, p. 227). The fool emerged as a popular secular figure in the process. However, the focus on the rational individual also necessitated "the definition and particularization of the 'Other' and thus benign metaphors of folly that had been associated with the abstract idea of *everyman* become, in a very brief period, inscribed on the bodies of those people who would be constructed as reason's 'Other': the idiot, the blind and the disabled" (Stainton 2004, p. 226; emphasis in original). Simultaneously, then, a "drive to define categories of reason and unreason" was responsible for the definition of disability in opposition to reason (Stainton 2004, p. 241). The fool was a symbolic expression of this. The result was a more blatant association of disability with folly, which would soon be found onstage, in court, and in other depictions, including art. Willeford points out that the fool's physical and mental difference "impairs the functioning of his *will*" and creates difficulties "central to the spectacle" of fool actors (1969, p. 9; emphasis in original). A bundling and association of physical and mental impairment then became intertwined with folly:

> Signs of mental deficiency and, for example, of schizophrenia are mixed at random as materials of the fool show. . . . [T]he scientifically differentiated symptoms, syndromes, and illnesses that now provide the means of describing various kinds of psychopathology have in many times and places been conceived as expressions of something diffuse but unitary. Folly is one name for it. (Willeford 1969, p. 23)

But as folly was being redefined and reinterpreted, so too was disability. These shifts in the values and social institutions brought on by the Northern Renaissance had far-reaching effects for the construction of disability as a more concrete category. New roles and responses would soon evolve with these new values and institutions.

As a gradual focus on definition and categorization emerged during the Renaissance, the relationship between madness and reason was altered. Physicians started to medicalize the body and institutions, formal almshouses and asylums became more prominent, and broader ideas of charity toward people with impairments began to shift. Those with disabilities were viewed as sick patients, and pity became a more accepted social response than derision. At times this resulted in people with impairments being "tested" for their "suitability" to determine if they were deserving of pity and support (Metzler 2011, p. 51). Soon, definitions of need shifted as laws were passed restricting begging and vagrancy, charitable institutions developed restrictions on who deserved assistance, and skepticism of faking physical impairment arose (Metzler 2011). Connections between impairment and poverty increased during this time.

New debates also emerged. Was it possible to distinguish between a fool and madman and other types of impairment (Chakravarti 2011)? Should people with disabilities be able to own property? What resulted were new taxonomies and laws to examine these differences. Earlier laws transferred control of persons labeled mentally unstable and their property to the local lord, but during the rule of Henry III (1216–1272) the law differentiated between being an "idiot" (in which case the king could profit from the individual's property) and being "lunatic" or "insane" (which required the king to return property to the individual's family) (Smedley, Rose, and Rose 1845, p. 599). The sixteenth century brought more formal procedures of inquiry into a person's sanity. In 1540 during King Henry VIII's reign, Parliament established the Court of Wards and Liberties, which among other things administered intelligence testing to determine transition of property to family. The process, known as "De idiota inquierendo," was sometimes abused and court jesters could be obtained this way, which is where the phrase "beg him for a fool" originated (Otto 2001, p. 35). However, it took until the classical period (seventeenth and eighteenth centuries) before these shifts were fully entrenched in social institutions (Foucault 2006). In the meantime, folly and disability were intertwined in ways that provided entertainment, truth, critique, and sometimes social change.

Folly as Aesthetic: Incongruity and Violation

The Renaissance did usher in humanist ideals of human dignity, but these did not always apply to people with impairments and bodily differences. The natural fool was still considered other than human, and many individuals with disabilities remained alienated (Chakravarti 2011). What did shift dramatically was a widespread use of folly and intellectual disability as a metaphorical mask to critique authority and subvert social order, including the church. The persona of the fool was appropriated as a symbolic tool and method of challenging what was sacred and powerful (McDonagh 2008). Behind this mask of folly, which had at times either an authentic or feigned connection to disability, was an outsider who had a license to challenge intellectual, political, and social orthodoxies with impunity (Chakravarti 2011). Whether feigned or real, madness, disability, and folly were combined into an allegorical unity—a trope—that was as ironic as it was complex. Thus emerged the fool and jester, who stepped forward in the Renaissance to "assume one of the main roles in life's drama" and give "articulation to the doubts and uncertainties of one of the great ideological upheavals in human history" (Kaiser 1964, p. 11).

Paradox was central to the use of impairment and bodily difference as trope, for both fools and audiences. For example, the fact that amusement was caused by "mental deficiencies or physical deformities which deprive" fools of "rights and responsibilities" put the fool in a position of "outlawry combined with utter dependence on the support of the social group to which he belongs" (Welsford 1968, p. 55). Not unlike freak show audiences of the early twentieth century, observers were both repelled and attracted by the spectacle as well as the positive and negative qualities of the fool:

> The use of physical freaks as jesters is surely in part the expression of an ambivalence that also results in the relegation of such people to the margins of human society; grotesques have both positive and negative powers; they are hideously attractive; they should be approached and avoided, abused and placated. The grotesque jester, like other kinds of fools, is a mascot who maintains a relationship with the ordered world and the chaos excluded by it. This, as we shall see is a complex function, and the ways in which the fool fulfills it are complex. (Willeford 1969, p. 15)

The functions that Willeford references are paradoxical themselves. Often, the fool operated as a masked sage, a role that is illustrated ironically through the widely used modern term *oxymoron,* where Oxus translates as "sharp" and moros as "fool" (Gentili 1988, p. 14). These types of incongruities were the weapons of the jester, and they came in many forms. Physical impairment or bodily difference, style of dress, and psychic difference were all elements of the jester's spectacle of incongruity (Willeford 1969). What is more, he was a constant reminder that ideals, norms, and expectations could never be fixed:

> The fool is a great disturber of designs in appearance, manner and speech. He is a reminder not only that the design is imperfect but that it can never be perfected and for that he has, at times and places, been persecuted and repressed. This constant awareness of human frailty frequently positions the fool as the antagonist of authority; the enemy of the grand design. (Prentki 2011, p. 9)

The jester's violation of the human image often included both the mental and the physical. Indeed, as Willeford (1969) points out, the forerunners of the jester include "cripples, blind, paralytics, amputees" (p. 14) and a "range of individuals who violate the human image and who come to a modus vivendi with society by making a show of that violation" (p. 13).

Though jesters were common in cultures across the globe, Europe had a higher proportion of naturals, and a wider range of jesters with deformities. Not all jesters had physical impairments but, among those who did, dwarfs and people with kyphosis were common. Beatrice Otto believes that the dwarf may have been "singled out for his distinctive appearance," which might have given him "a perspective on the world, literally as well as figurative, that is different from that of most people around him" (2001, p. 27). She goes on to point out that in China, dwarf (*zhuru*) could be synonymous with jester (*youren*), and it was common for this figure to give humorously indirect advice (Otto 2001, p. 27). Dwarfs became popular during the Middle Ages in Europe, especially within the upper class. But as far back as the Sixth Dynasty of the Old Kingdom of Egypt (2323–2150 BCE) dwarfs were used in royal court. They were in demand in Rome among Patrician women (Southworth 1998), where they served more as a dwarf fool. Dwarfs were used in royal courts by nobles around the world, including Turkey, Russia, Spain, and China, as well as for Cardinal Vitelli in Rome (1566). Many did function as jesters, but not all. Often, a more mystical quality was associated with them. Celtic dwarfs, for example, held an association with learning and the creative arts, rather than folly (Southworth 1998). Demand in Europe was so high that even stunting children, a practice originating in Rome, was allegedly attempted.

The Jester Analytic: Subversive Outsider

Beyond the physical, natural or feigned, the jester's aesthetic and performances included verbal paradoxes, attention to the taboo and unexpected veiled meaning, and social critique from an outsider observing from a detached position. This type of folly innately created confrontation by turning conventional wisdom on its head. Indeed, it has been argued that the fool could not exist in a society without sacraments or sacred values (McDonagh 2008). Tim Prentki argues that "the poetics of folly operate at the heart of the body politic, questioning the cherished orthodoxies of correctness and peering around the edges of our most deep-rooted myths" (2011, p. 1). By poking fun at the human condition, the fool and his opinions are placed in opposition to the dominant discourses; yet in this form of critique, the fool can express sharp opinions in a way that often escapes counterdiscourse (Prentki 2011, p. 1). Indeed, he is among the few with license to challenge dominant modes of thought since everyone else could simply rest on the idea that his words were those of a fool (Prentki 2011). The mask of folly—whether real or feigned—was an essential tool for the success of such challenges. Often, it was the rare avenue for such speech to take place: "Given the madness of a world driven by egotism, folly is the only possible mask to adopt in order to get a hearing" (Prentki 2011, p. 14).

The mask of folly, particularly for the fool and jester, also held license to speak the truth, an open door to unmask and unsettle both certainties and ideals. At times, then, the fool functioned as mimesis—he could become, metaphorically or literally, a mirror of social life by pointing out hypocrisy, abuse of power, and inequality. Sometimes such truth telling could serve a protective function for royals and monarchs by providing advice and warnings about public opinion in palatable form:

> The king's need for truth, especially of the unpalatable kind, and the fool's ability to communicate it in a uniquely acceptable form as humour, was a crucial factor in the relations between them from which the fool derived much of his raison d'être. . . . The innocent speaks the truth because he can do no other. He blurts it out and (more often than not) escapes retribution because of his transparent honesty. It was not so much for his folly as for his "wisdom"—that special gift he possessed for hitting the nail of truth on the head—that the innocent was so greatly valued in the medieval and Tudor periods. (Southworth 1998, pp. 24–25)

Whether or not they possessed a special gift, fools typically held a unique perspective that came from a detached outsider status. This might have been more the case if the jester had physical or mental impairments. Indeed, bad news or criticism was likely to feel less threatening coming from a dwarf or a person with kyphosis, who could not "look down" on the king (Otto 2001, p. 31). Jesters were seen as different from other members of court because these other "functionaries cooked up the king's facts for him before delivery" while the "jester delivered them raw" (Nock 1928, p. 481).

In other words, they occupied a paradoxically privileged position at court precisely because they were viewed as Others and, thus, held to different standards. At times, their words were known to change the minds of those in power (Otto 2001).

If fools and jesters aimed to spawn a "transformation of consciousness in the interest of truth" (Willeford 1969, p. 25), the task began with the foolish wisdom that things are not what they seem. And the method to this (sometimes literal) madness involved subversion and inversion: "The jester can turn the world on its head, making people see the ultimate insignificance of many of the things they hold dear, perhaps showing them their priorities from a different angle or a wider perspective . . . much of his humor is based on upsetting and inverting the accepted logic" (Otto 2001, p. 99). One of the dominant forms of inversion entailed asking who the fool really was by satirizing others, or in some way dissolving the distinctions between the fool and the nonfool (Willeford 1969). The juxtaposition may have been more apparent if the fool had a mental or physical impairment. Madness (real or feigned), for example, provided an ironic vessel for this type of inversion, where the jester might conduct a conversation with himself or a bauble that was capped with a small head. This seemingly schizophrenic discussion might mirror the ideas or behaviors of another person or some element of social life, also providing a visual and aural challenge for the audience to consider how things are not always what they seem. In this way, the fool operated as a grotesque and burlesque mirror, one of the reasons that a popular depiction of the fool is with mirror in hand. This act of calling into question society's categorization of fools is perhaps best illustrated by the official motto of the Ifanterie Dijonnaise, a popular medieval society: "anyone who did not wish to see a fool should smash his mirror" (Otto 2001, p. 98). In many cases, disability was central to folly's inversion of social order, functioning as mask and mirror. And in many cases, it was used to demonstrate to some that the detached are the most clear-sighted (Otto 2001).

This activity, though, did not simply apply to specific individuals. We referenced Russian critic Mikhail Bakhtin's concept of carnival in Chapter 2. An appreciation of the value of folly's inversion is illustrated in his work, particularly his general belief that "truth is restored by reducing the lie to an absurdity" (Bakhtin 1981, p. 309). Bakhtin's writing on carnival and folly, particularly the Feast of Fools, demonstrates not simply how folly subverted (under the mask of the natural fool), but specifically how folly functioned as resistance and transformation even if temporarily. The Feast of Fools and Feast of Innocents were medieval festival celebrations that inverted power, status, and social norms by burlesquing what was sacred and turning over authority to those with little power.

The Praise of Folly (and Bodily Differences)

> Doesn't the happiest group of people comprise those popularly called idiots,
> fools, nitwits and simpletons, all splendid names to my away of thinking . . .
> they are the only ones who speak frankly and tell the truth.
> —*Stultia, goddess of Folly (Erasmus, The Praise of Folly,*
> *1511, cited in McDonagh 2008, p. 129)*

Centuries before Bakhtin, however, folly was taking form in the literary
realm. Desiderius Erasmus cemented the legitimacy of literary folly
through his satirical work *The Praise of Folly* (1511). Erasmus was a priest
and theologian, but he was also a known social critic and Renaissance
humanist, who advocated religious tolerance. His book mocked the "wise
and powerful," especially the Catholic Church, its abuse of power, and its
pious doctrines. Despite some criticism, the book was popular in Europe
during Erasmus's lifetime and became a work of satire with far-reaching
influence, especially in setting the stage for the Protestant Reformation.
Erasmus's use of folly is significant for several reasons. First, he was one
of the first writers to give folly a voice (McDonagh 2008), especially one
that inverted our notions of the meaning of "fool" by satirizing those in
power (Willeford 1969). Second, in his celebration of folly, he employed
disability as an allegorical and a representational tool, particularly in ways
that celebrate physical difference as a central aspect of folly; his work fused
folly with the natural fool (McDonagh 2008; Stainton 2004).

Similar to carnival, Erasmus's celebration of folly encourages readers
to value difference, with particular attention to madness or insanity, which
were central to his ideas of folly. He wrote about two different types of
madness. One form was sinister, the other a "happy mental aberration" that
"frees the soul from its anxious cares and at the same time restores it by
the addition of manifold delights" (Erasmus 1973, p. 121). Folly and madness, then, are blessings that invert traditional notions of normality.
According to Willeford, difference became a vessel for new ways of looking at the world:

> Erasmus' notion of madness as folly, and as a blessing, is crucial to his whole
> enterprise of ironic praise. The notion entails a rhetorical trick. . . . Some-
> times he regards such madness, satirically, as equivalent to vanity and self-
> delusion; and at other times he regards it as analogous to a transformation of
> consciousness that would allow us to see things more truly. . . . His truth
> telling is not necessarily central. It is more or less interchangeable with ex-
> pressions of stupidity, madness and freakishness. This amounts to a confu-
> sion between what has value (truth of whatever kind) and what has none
> (nonsense); it is this confusion that is central. . . . What Erasmus finds desir-
> able is an aberration of sense and understanding sufficient to effect a qualita-
> tive difference from the normal human condition, a difference like that be-

tween a dwarf or other grotesque and a normal person. This change, which opens the way to new relations between subject and object, occurs through the constellation of an archetype, that of folly. . . . What are for us symptoms, syndromes, and disease entities are symbolic of the diffuse but unitary, potentially healing power of folly. (1969 pp. 25–26, 29)

Similar to Bakhtin's interpretation of carnival, Erasmus's folly draws on physical and mental difference as a method of critique, satire, and confusion and as a way to open us up to other ways of seeing and relating. In both of these examples, carnival and *The Praise of Folly*, the innocent natural plays a prominent role, at times symbolic and at other times representational, as the device of folly. These are not only active, and even political, roles for folly, but the implicit aims have sociologically informed implications. This madness often had a purpose: to provide "confusion between what has value (truth of whatever kind) and what has none (nonsense)" (Willeford 1969, p. 26) in ways that allowed audiences "to find and affirm our individual destinies within the frame of society and of nature" (p. 47). In many ways, this perspective can be seen as a precursor to the emerging perspective of crip theory, which challenges binary notions of ability and disability (McRuer 2006).

Authentic Narratives of Disability?
The Disabled Jester as Voice

The connection between folly and disability is not simply academic, nor is it relevant to only a few royal courts in Europe. Two particular jesters known to have disabilities profoundly influenced the role, function, and understanding of the jester worldwide. They also shaped important literary uses of the fool as a model for such characters as William Shakespeare's Fool in *King Lear*. (Shakespeare, it should be noted, used fools as characters in more than twenty of his works.) William Somer (d. 1560), who served as court fool to King Henry VIII, King Edward VI, Queen Mary, and Queen Elizabeth I, is perhaps the most well-known jester. Somer referred to King Henry as "Uncle" and was depicted in one of the king's family portraits. His wit has been well documented, as has his influence:

> His specialty was verbal wit more than physical antics, though he could mug funny faces and bizarre gestures. In centering his humor on clever play with language and extemporaneous versifying, he can be considered at the very least the first notable comedian of the English Renaissance, a jokester for the humanist age. He was also the first whose fame greatly outlasted his own lifetime. (Janik and Nelson 1998, p. 406)

Somer was depicted in drama and literature of the sixteenth and seventeenth centuries and, more recently, in episodes of HBO's *The Tudors*.

There is debate over whether Somer was an artificial or a natural. His contemporaries, such as Robert Armin (1563–1615) and Thomas Wilson, depict Somer as a natural. And while the popular understanding is that he was an artificial, some modern scholars believe that he was the last of the famous natural fools and a simple, kindhearted man who exercised a beneficent influence on his royal patron (Southworth 1998, p. 143). There is written evidence to indicate that money was paid to someone appointed as a regular attendant to Somer, suggesting he may have needed assistance because of an impairment of some kind (Southworth 1998, pp. 143–144). It was after his death that there was a "fundamental twist" of his reputation "from wise innocent to witty jester" (Southworth 1998, p. 78). Despite the debate, though, there are enough depictions, visually and in writing, to know that Somer walked with a significant stoop and was "deformed about the neck and shoulders" (Southworth 1998, p. 147). In several stories published after his death, he is also depicted as being narcoleptic (Southworth 1998).

A second influential figure was Robert Armin, an actor who replaced William Kempe in Shakespeare's comedy troupe at the turn of the seventeenth century. Armin became well known for fool roles such as Touchstone in *As You Like It* (1599), Feste in *Twelfth Night* (1600), and the Fool in *King Lear* (1605). Based on his own understanding and observations, Armin played both natural and artificial fools. It is known that Armin was short in stature, but there is also evidence that he may have had other bodily differences associated with dwarfism:

> Armin's physique determines the particular character of his clowning. The pompous or parodic utterances of a man with total vocal control are counterpointed by a deformed body. . . . As Johnson explains elsewhere, dwarves are popular "for pleasing imitation of greater men's actions, in a ridiculous fashion" . . . [Armin's] lines are written on the assumption that body and voice are set in opposition and speak, as it were, different languages. (Wiles 1987, p. 150)

His performance was informed by the fact that Armin was also a serious scholar and biographer of fools. His *Foole upon Fools* (1600) and *Nest of Ninnies,* where he defined the differences between natural and artificial fools, were based on his own observations of natural fools and his historical understanding of the fool role. This insight most certainly influenced the way Shakespeare used fools as a trope onstage since Shakespeare wrote with Armin's strengths in mind. Armin is recognized as "a pioneering realist in his study of how fools actually behaved" (Wiles 1987, p. 158), which enabled Shakespeare to exploit the medieval dramatic tradition where "vice reveals vice to be folly" (Wiles 1987, p. 158). In fact, Armin's arrival brought a shift in the way that Shakespeare used the fool, from more of a clown based on the common man (with Kempe playing the roles) to a wittier and wiser foolosopher.

But beginning in the seventeenth century, a number of changes brought the end of the popularity of jesters and fools. Folly became redefined and eventually confined. The political climate that swept in the closing of the public theaters in 1642 under Oliver Cromwell's Interregnum (the Puritan crackdown on all things vainglorious and raucous), along with the rise of print, decreased the demand for stage and performance jesters. Eighteen years later, when the theaters reopened during the Restoration, the effects of the Enlightenment were expanding. The moral or religious lens on disability was largely eclipsed by the medical lens, as the problem of disability became fully equated with biological difference or impairment. Solutions to the problem of disability therefore were also individual (and medical) in nature. People with impairments were expected to adopt the role of compliant patient in search of medical cure for their tragic individual conditions. When no cure could be found, medical practitioners and other service providers sought to help patients adapt to and cope effectively with the limitations imposed by their impairments, chronic illnesses, or bodily differences. People who refused the patient role or the proposed adaptive strategies were considered to be non-compliant or in denial about their conditions (Beckett 2006; Oliver 1983; Priestley 2003). As this view expanded, an increasing differentiation between reason and the Other became institutionalized (Foucault 2006) through formal asylums and new laws governing the disabled body and charity, as well as economic evaluations of disability. Newer ethical views of poverty and unemployment, along with scientific interest in impairment emerged, as Foucault's "great confinement" (2006, p. 44) began during the mid-seventeenth century and soon spread through Europe. This brought a more objectified view of madness and was part of a larger shift in views of difference, mental and physical. As this more medicalized perception of disability emerged, it dissipated even the small and inconsistent value accorded people with impairments during the Renaissance, when disability was associated with folly's critical lens. Disability soon became serious business. Rather than being given license to critique society by "acting out," disabled bodies became objects to be "acted upon" by medical and allied industries (Albrecht 1992).

The Vaudeville Era

During the previous eras explored in this chapter, cultural interpretations of disability had clear links to humor and folly. But at the turn of the twentieth century in the United States, definitions of disability were increasingly connected to an expansion of capitalist values. An increasingly standardized and mechanized workforce omitted disabled people as an economic liability. As global competition on the capitalist market arose, emphasis shifted to concern for the physical and mental fitness of the nation to compete against other countries. These shifts hardened a range of "aesthetic, episte-mological, and ethical values inherent in early-twentieth-century" into for-mal eugenics campaigns and policies (Pernick 1997, p. 89). At the same time, new interpretations of Charles Darwin's theory of evolution gave rise to the eugenics movement—larger cultural concerns, campaigns, and laws to decrease "contamination" of the gene pool (Carey 2009). Medical insti-tutions gained significant power to define and respond to disability. Segre-gation and even sterilization became formal policies, as politicians, news-papers (e.g., *New York Times*), films (e.g., *The Black Stork*), and, surprisingly, even some figures with disabilities such as Helen Keller advo-cated the ideas that informed eugenic policies (Pernick 1997). In the midst of this burgeoning industrial society, cultural beliefs in the links between hard work, opportunity, and mobility not only attracted immigrants, but also were becoming naturalized into mass culture.

To remain productive, though, the industrial worker did require some leisure. So, these same economic forces created a new stage for the per-formance of humor as a commodity for the mass consumer. Collectively, these thousands of stages across the United States were known as vaude-ville. Although vaudeville spanned a short time period (1880s–1930s), it deserves consideration here for several reasons. There is no doubt that the vaudeville stage was known for its mass appeal and clean, family-style atmosphere, especially due to its association with the popular celebrities who got their start there: George Burns, William "Bud" Abbott and Lou Costello, Don Ameche, Gene Kelly, Ginger Rogers, and Buster Keaton. However, vaudeville certainly had historical links to disability, primarily through its roots in minstrel shows, circus acts, and freak shows (Garland-Thomson 1997). Vaudeville also arrived at a time when notions of the United States as a land of opportunity and the idea of staunch individualism were taking a stronghold. Vaudeville figures, many of whom came from meager backgrounds, reinforced notions that hard work, individual effort, and sheer talent were routes to success and acceptance in the United States. Ideas of disability certainly were reinterpreted within this larger bootstrap cultural context. Vaudeville acts generally avoided engaging social issues, so as not to offend paying audience members. Accordingly, vaudeville com-edy is known to be more slapstick than subversive. There were, however, some well-known acts that represented disability, a few in more transgres-sive ways than might be expected.

Vaudeville theaters provided an outlet for the bustling industrial life with a variety of acts that appealed to a mass audience at an affordable price (Dimeglio 1973). Tony Pastor, one of the early promoters of vaude-ville, took his experience as a circus ringmaster and borrowed the variety of acts from minstrel shows to create a unique hybrid form of entertainment in the 1880s. By this time, the minstrel shows had been widely popular for several decades in the United States. The minstrel show originated with Thomas Rice, who came up with a song and dance routine in which he imitated an old black slave with physical impairments named Jim Cuff or Jim Crow. Rice allegedly bought the man's clothes, learned the dance routine, and then succeeded in staging a show that exploited racist stereotypes about the language and behavior of slaves. The show typically included several white characters in blackface, performing music, dance, and stump speeches. Vaudeville fused aspects of the minstrel show (and its racist and ethnocentric comedy) with elements of circus freak show entertainment (as long as they were not too risqué). A typical bill at most theaters included at least eight acts such as comedians, dancers, singers, magicians, and mind readers.

Pastor was central in creating a vaudeville that censored the bawdy and raucous humor that might be found in a saloon or riverboat. At its height, there were about 2,000 vaudeville theaters across the United States, but the mecca of the tour was in New York City. One of the most famous theaters of the early 1900s was the Victoria, owned by Oscar and William Hammerstein. The Victoria Theater, considered a nut or freak vaudeville house by some (Gilbert 1963, p. 246), booked a broad range of acts, including Sober Sue. Audiences were challenged to make her laugh (without knowing that her face muscles were paralyzed). Others included Motogirl, who learned to control every muscle in her body, and Hadji Ali, who would regurgitate objects. The staunch censorship and focus on family entertainment did not preclude the exploitation of bodily differences in this and other vaudeville venues. A number of vaudeville acts featured little people in a variety of musical, comedy, and dance skits. Lowe, Hite, and Stanley, slapstick comedians who also danced, featured seven-foot-seven-inch Henry Hite (whose real name was Henry Mullins); Stanley Ross, an average-sized man; and Lowe, a little person (whose real name was Roland Picaro). Several troupes of little people left circus and fair shows to tour vaudeville stages. (Some of these later went on to do movies.) Rose's Royal Midgets[1] included twenty-five little people from the United States, Europe, and India who danced, sang, did impersonations, juggled, and told jokes. Leo Singer, whose Singer Midgets went on to star in *The Wizard of Oz,* recruited little people from Europe to be in his musical comedy performances. Most of them left behind poverty and family to join Singer. The Hans Kasemann Troupe, from Germany, also became a popular act on the vaudeville circuit. They were known for their dance and comedy skits, some of which satirized contemporary news stories. As was the case with many acts involving little people, they were recruited and managed by an average-sized man who booked them across the United States to perform. This kind of economic exploitation of people with bodily differences by the able-bodied is controversial. These performances were a source of livelihood for people who may otherwise have been unable to find work due to discrimination and stigma (Bogdan 1988; Garland-Thomson 1997), but the freak show nature of the entertainment is likely to have contributed to further stigma and discrimination in the long run (Davies 2005). It has been argued that the word "midget" took on negative connotations within the community of little people because of its overexposure during this era of exploitation. Other groups with similar performances included the Klinkhart Midgets and Henry Kramer's Hollywood Midgets. The Rossow Brothers were a boxing act in which brothers of short stature performed a three-round battle to evoke laughter, followed by one of the brothers reappearing after the fight dressed in girl's clothing performing songs. Other novelty performers who walked the line between exploitation of the freak show spectacle and performance art included Carl Unthan. Born without arms, he did card tricks, poured drinks, and played the violin with his feet.

Vaudeville had a profound influence on the US comedy scene of the twentieth century. For decades after its demise, it continued to shape the expectations of audiences as well as the content and performance styles of later comedians and comedic formats. While opportunities for disabled performers were limited on the vaudeville circuit, comedians who did make it in vaudeville set the stage for the modern stand-up comedians with disabilities, who are the focus of this book. Perhaps the most prominent disabled vaudeville comedian was Marshall P. Wilder, described by the *Encyclopedia of Vaudeville* as a "hunchback dwarf" (Slide 1994, p. 555) and by the *Atlanta Constitution* as the "greatest one man or 'one half' company on the road" (as quoted in Schweik 2010). Jane Addams referred to Wilder as "one of the world's greatest comedians" (as quoted in Schweik 2010). His monologues offered a rare dose of social reality and social analysis on the vaudeville stage. Wilder had a successful career before vaudeville, already holding celebrity status by the time he hit the vaudeville stage for the first time. His monologue act seems to have been the only one that follows in the line of the subversive jester legacy of the Renaissance, a connection that Wilder himself acknowledged:

> As far back as history goes you will find the jest, also the jester. Some kings more powerful than any European sovereign is to-day are remembered now only by what their jesters said. . . . [A]ll these jesters are said to have been little people. . . . It is easier to knock a man out with a joke than a fist blow, especially if you haven't much height and weight behind your fist. Tis the better way, too, for the joke doesn't hurt. (Wilder 1905, pp. 24–26)

According to Susan Schweik (2010), one of the few academics who has written about Wilder, he used humor to discomfit and to articulate a social model of disability. Wilder did this in several ways. First, he marshaled US individualism onstage, which allowed him to challenge US ableism (Schweik 2010). By representing his own individualism—discussing his world travels, mobility, well-known friends, and world audiences—he engaged in identity management on the stage, which opened the door for other topics. Second, Wilder subverted the discourse about dwarfism (Schweik 2010). Cheerfulness has long been an assumed innate trait of dwarfism, so Wilder used his own "sunshine" as a weapon to examine real differences between nature and cultural expectations. Finally, he pulled back the veil on confinement and medical institutions. He described his own institutionalization as a child, critiquing the notion of cure. In other words, if he was expected to be the sunshine, Schweik (2010) argues, Wilder articulated a social model of the "shade." He performed in almshouses and penitentiaries (for which he was paid by Cornelius Vanderbilt) and aligned himself with other oppressed groups, including criminals. In doing so, Wilder turned the audience's attention from the physical to the social, but he managed to do it with a vaudeville flair.

Another successful act representing disability on vaudeville stages across the country was Helen Keller and Anne Sullivan Macy, which ran from 1920 to 1924. Though not a comedy show, Keller was recognized by newspaper critics for her use of wit and humor during the twenty-minute show, which included a brief review of her biography and accomplishments, a demonstration of finger spelling, an inspiring speech, and a question and answer session. A playbill from the Palace Theatre in New York billed the performance as "a remarkable portrayal of the triumph of life over the greatest obstacles that ever confronted a human being" (quoted in Crutchfield 2005). Her act did include humor, though it was not a dominant theme. Jokes did come out during the question and answer session, though it is not entirely clear from the handwritten notes of these Q&A sessions if these jokes were rehearsed or impromptu (see Crutchfield 2005):

> QUESTION: Have you thought of any way out of our current troubles?
> ANSWER: Have you thought about divorce?

This infused (and recognized) humor and wit, some of which was scripted, demonstrated that people with disabilities possessed a sense of humor, but notions of overcoming impairment were also dominant. Susan Crutchfield argues that the performance was more like a "thinly veiled *sideshow act*" that "appealed to audiences" for many of the reasons that freak shows appealed to them (2005; emphasis in original). Freak shows toured the country from the mid-nineteenth to the mid–twentieth centuries, and audiences flocked to them (Bogdan 1988). The continuing appeal of this kind of exploitive entertainment might explain the successful four-year run of

Keller's vaudeville show (with breaks). Keller's own words, though, seem to acknowledge the paradox of representing disability on the vaudeville stage. In a letter to her mother, Keller wrote, "Although I love the people, I don't care much about the sort of audiences one gets on the Vaudeville, they appear so superficial. They are peculiar in that you must say a good thing in your first sentence, or they won't listen, much less laugh. Still, they have shown us such friendliness, I'm grateful to them" (Keller, as quoted in Case 2011).

There are also a few cases of figures, such as Billy Barty, who used their fame to engage in disability advocacy offstage. Barty is best known to contemporary audiences for his roles in films (*Legend, Willow, UHF*) and television (Sid and Marty Kroft's *Sigmund and the Sea Monsters*). But before his screen success, he spent seven years playing vaudeville, where he performed impressions and played drums as part of "Billy Barty and His Sisters." He remains an important figure in the little people's movement. Before there was a unified disability rights movement, Barty founded the Little People of America in 1957 by first initiating a gathering of people with dwarfism in Reno, Nevada (Kennedy 2005; Dedman 2007). What began as twenty people spending a week with Barty sharing ideas and experiences has grown into a North American organization with thousands of members. Today the organization has a medical advisory board; holds an annual conference; and provides information on education, parenting, medical issues, and disability rights (see http://www.lpaonline.org/about-lpa). Unlike figures such as Wilder and Keller, Barty's advocacy took place far from the entertainment stage. But it is unlikely that his intense advocacy would have been successful without his celebrity status, which raised his profile as he helped to build a disability rights movement for individuals with dwarfism.

As is the case in much humor with disability content, it is sometimes difficult to draw the line between vaudeville humor that was disabling and humor that might have served to humanize the disability experience for audiences steeped in the medical or personal tragedy view of disability. For example, one popular vaudeville skit, which was also filmed under the title *Pity the Blind No. 2* (1904), began with a young boy leading a man with a cane and dark glasses onto the stage. The boy then puts a sign around the man's neck that reads "Pity the Blind" and leaves the stage. First, a man with a cigar passes, reads the sign, and puts money in the hat. Then, two women also pass and give the man money. While they are walking away, one of the women adjusts her dress, raising it slightly. The blind man pulls his glasses down to look at the woman's leg. As women leave, the blind man grins widely. While this certainly could be criticized for playing to the audience members' preconceived notions that the practice of faking disability is widespread, it also subtly challenges the idea that legitimately blind people should be targets of pity. It could also be interpreted as a critique of an economic system that puts people in the position of needing to resort to faking disability as a means of survival. The point here is that the difference between humor that disables and disability humor that has the capacity to challenge preconceived notions of disability often lies in the intent of the humorist and the meaning attached by the audience. Were this skit to be performed by a comedian with a disability, for example, the meanings attached by both parties might be different than those attached when it is performed by an able-bodied actor. Similar examples of equivocal meaning can be found in the following jokes collected by minor comedian Ed Lowry during his vaudeville time:

> I know a fellow who is deaf and dumb, but he has a speech impediment: his little finger is broken. (Lowry 2006, p. 90)

> MAZIE: I'm in love with a deaf and dumb guy. He makes love to me with both hands.
> DAISY: Say, he may be deaf, but he ain't dumb. (Lowry 2006, p. 90)

> QUESTION: Did you ever attend a school for stuttering?
> ANSWER: N-no, I j-j-just p-picked it up. (Lowry 2006, p. 250)

In vaudeville, as on the stages of comedy clubs today, intended and received meanings matter. In the next chapters, we examine jokes that are not radically different from the vaudeville jokes above, yet they are written and performed by comedians with disabilities who use their insider positionality to help clarify meaning and intent and who have specific functions in mind for these jokes within their larger performance.

Market forces eventually brought an end to vaudeville in the 1930s. Theaters increasingly partnered with cinemas as movie tickets became more affordable. This effectively weakened the large tour base of vaudeville theaters, making national tours unsustainable. The mass production of radio, the emergence of talkies, and the Great Depression effectively ended the vaudeville era altogether.

Despite its ancestral roots in the minstrel and freak show, vaudeville employed a family-friendly model of comedy aimed at making money. To this end, serious discussion of social issues was generally avoided, and authentic disability appeared chiefly in ways that enchanted the audience, rather than challenging them. There are some cases where people with disabilities demonstrated for audiences that they had a sense of humor and wit. But perhaps more important than these anomalies is the fact that the aesthetic of vaudeville itself—the sink or swim format—points to a larger individualist and bootstrap notion of success and mobility. Where disability once could use folly to speak in powerfully humorous ways, now it was excluded not only from the workplace, but also from play. This exclusion is significant because vaudeville, which was once called an "intellectual wasteland" (Dimeglio 1973, p. 6), influenced decades of sketch comedy, sit-coms, stand-up comedy, film, television, and stage. It was not until the 1960s that some comedians broke from this mold to tackle serious social issues. The links between folly, critique, and disability, which were broken during the Renaissance era, would not again be firmly connected until well into the twenty-first century.

The vaudeville era helps illustrate how a more individualized medical lens of disability (that dominated views of disability in Western capitalist countries from the Enlightenment through the late 1970s and still exerts powerful influence today) had a clear impact on the relationship between disability and humor. Medicalization not only permeated the general view of disability, but it dominated scholarly discourse on disability for centuries. Disability was constructed as an individual problem; and a "disability business" built up around medical and rehabilitative solutions to the problem of disability (Albrecht 1992; Fleischer and Zames 2000). As the medical or tragedy lens solidified, it became less socially acceptable to laugh at individuals with impairments who were presumed to have suffered a medical tragedy. While this was in some ways an improvement over the association of disability with moral inferiority, with pity came a presumed lack of agency. With presumed helplessness came the loss of legitimized subversive power to critique. As Rosemarie Garland-Thomson puts it, "The extraordinary body moved from portent to pathology" (1997, p. 58). However, the links between folly, legitimized social critique, and disability that were broken in the Renaissance era would again be connected later in the twenty-first century in the form of countercultural stand-up comedy.

The Rise of Stand-up

The arrival of a mass radio audience did help to bring an end to vaudeville but the monologue format of narrative joke telling, which emerged from the minstrel show and evolved on the vaudeville stage, did not die out as the theaters closed. Between the 1940s and the 1960s, stand-up comedy emerged as a revamped art form in nightclubs and resorts. Over the next twenty years, stand-up entrenched itself into popular culture through album sales, new comedy clubs, and an increased television presence. By the 1980s there was a wide swath of comedy clubs across the United States that hosted professional comedians seven nights a week, and stand-up comedians had starring roles in some of the highest-rated television shows (*The Cosby Show, Roseanne,* and *America's Funniest Home Videos*). This rise of stand-up, from a marginal form of entertainment to a central and ubiquitous aspect of US culture, might be attributed to the fact that many comedians had their fingers on the pulse of broader social changes that were occurring. During the 1960s and 1970s, a number of comedians became popular by creating critical social satire and parody that reflected broader countercultural ideologies. When a cultural shift toward political correctness arrived in the late 1980s and early 1990s, a number of popular comedians tapped into the backlash through hate humor. But while gender, race, and politics were standard fare onstage, few comedians addressed issues of disability. Even when they did, audiences were more often drawn to its use as spectacle or a cheap hook by comedians such as Jerry Lewis and Goldthwait. These acts tended to overshadow the work of pioneering comedians who were authentically representing disability as stand-up comedians in the late 1970s. As we discuss later in this chapter, this is partly because stand-up became such a popular art form that, like vaudeville, its commodification often led to a less critical form of humor.

Most stand-up comedy routines prior to the mid-1960s filled time as minor acts during burlesque shows or between orchestra and band sets at nightclubs. But the second half of the twentieth century brought an evolution of the art form and an explosion of stand-up into the US imagination and popular culture. Comedians such as Mort Sahl, Lenny Bruce, and Dick Gregory, who rose to popularity in the late 1950s and 1960s, incorporated a more countercultural ideology in their routines by challenging and deconstructing traditional norms of decency and race. Some, such as George Carlin and Bruce, went to jail for these transgressions. As debate over civil rights became more prominent, black comedians such as Redd Foxx, Dick Gregory, and Richard Pryor spoke candidly to white audiences about race and racism in the United States. Other comedians, such as Bob Newhart and Bill Cosby, succeeded by reflecting less controversial content. As stand-up gained popularity, demand created new outlets and venues. Most of these comedians seized on the opportunity to record comedy albums, which brought their stand-up to broader audiences than would have been possible through the few comedy clubs that existed at the time in New York and Los Angeles. Sahl, the first comedian to record an album (and appear on the cover of *Time* magazine), was also the first non-musician to be awarded a Grammy for his work. A number of successful albums followed, including work by Cosby and Newhart that would top music album sales on the Billboard charts. By the 1970s, comedy albums were a mainstay of record sales. Steve Martin's *Let's Get Small* became the first comedy album to be certified platinum. The cult following of albums by Cheech and Chong (Richard "Cheech" Marin and Tommy Chong) translated into the film *Up in Smoke* (1978), which grossed over $100 million. The success of these albums helped to build a larger fan base and a demand for comedy clubs to appear in cities other than New York or Los Angeles, including Boston and Chicago.

Comedians had already been appearing on television throughout the 1950s (e.g., *The Ed Sullivan Show*) and the 1960s (e.g., *The Tonight Show* hosted by Jack Parr), but the 1970s was the breakout decade for stand-up on broadcast television. The sketch comedy of *Saturday Night Live* and *Laugh-In* regularly featured comedians, as did *The Tonight Show Starring Johnny Carson,* which became a launching ground for innovative stand-up. These outlets stoked the demand for stand-up comedy. The popularity of cable television in the 1980s brought new exposure, especially for uncensored stand-up that was not a fit for broadcast shows such as *The Tonight Show.* Media outlets such as HBO, MTV, and its sister station VH1 fed a demand for comedy clubs across the nation, which were often more affordable and novel than seeing a live musical act. Hundreds of clubs had sprung up by the late 1980s, including chains such as the Comedy Strip and the Comedy Factory.

Although a significant number of earlier stand-up comedians had used their comedy to critique social life, the new comedy of Jerry Seinfeld and others moved away from politics altogether: "Pryor and Bruce talked dirty to make you hear astringent comic truths. Fueling their attacks on almost everything square was a righteous rage—a hipster morality that, for all its darkness, did dare to hope for a better world" (Hirshey 1989, p. 229). What took its place, according to Gerri Hirshey, was the work of Eddie Murphy's "mass market misogyny" (1989, p. 229) and other rock star comedians who were now selling out large venues. One of the most popular comedic acts of the 1990s was Andrew Dice Clay, whose verbal attacks on the homeless, immigrants, gay men, and women tapped into a broader cultural backlash against progressive cultural changes. In fact, this rise in hate comedy is actually reflected in research conducted on the increased acceptance among young Americans of humor directed at women (Carroll 1989). As the ubiquity of stand-up grew, cable television and other commercial interests came calling. Soon comedy was being used in corporate boardroom training sessions and in commercials selling everything from long-distance phone services to lite beer.

This massive dose of stand-up via cable, comedy clubs, radio, and other forms of mass communication eventually led to its decline. Stand-up comedy became so commonplace that, by the mid-1990s, the media and even academia reported on its decline (Holden 1992; P. Lewis 1993). Many comedy clubs began to close, which forced the more successful stand-up comedians to look toward television shows. (Many of these sitcoms, such as *Seinfeld,* centered on the mundane rather than the political.) Sketch comedy, though, hung on during the 1990s through the new Comedy Central channel and the success of shows such as *In Living Color, The Kids in the Hall,* and the established brand of *Saturday Night Live.* It would be the Internet and the reemergence of satire and political comedy, though, that would revitalize an interest in stand-up comedy. During the first years of the twenty-first century, stand-up comedians Dave Chappelle and Jon Stewart skyrocketed to fame on Comedy Central with their politically sharp humor, thereby raising the profile of stand-up comedians and of politically oriented comedy on television. Comedian Stephen Colbert developed his own successful show following his success on Stewart's *The Daily Show,* and Lewis Black, who also appeared on *The Daily Show,* used his success on the show to mount tours, specials, and a comedy album. Bill Maher launched *Real Time with Bill Maher* on HBO. All of these comedians infused a more critical, intellectual, and political aesthetic into their comedy, which met with significant ratings and massive financial success for themselves. (When Chappelle infamously quit doing his show in 2005, he was halfway through a two-year $50 million contract with the production company.) The critical and political aesthetic of stand-up had returned and proven that it could be one of the most commercially viable forms of entertainment.

From Jerry's Kids to Cousin Geri

The fact that many early stand-up comedians were countercultural, and often used satire and other forms of humor to incorporate a civil rights aesthetic, should come as no surprise. Stand-up grew into the public zeitgeist just as the civil rights movements of the 1960s were gaining popularity. As a result, race, gender, and critiques of social norms made their way onstage, just as they did on screen. Disability, though, was not presented in these ways until nearly twenty years after Bruce and Gregory rattled the US value system. So, if some stand-up comedians were progressively pushing the envelope on these other issues, where was representation of disability? Certainly, for comedy to play onstage, people have to laugh. In a society where segregation of individuals with disabilities was rampant through forced institutionalization, and widespread lack of accessibility in education, the workforce, and public spaces, it is likely that few audience members were ready to laugh about an issue that evoked just the opposite of laughter— pity, fear, and sadness. This dubious silence in public discussions masked a more complex and bleak reality behind the doors of institutions across the United States that housed individuals with disabilities. Robert Kennedy's 1965 description of one of these institutions in New York, Willowbrook, succinctly described most, if not all of them: a "snake pit" (as quoted in Castellani 2005, p. 117). The civil rights of people with disabilities in these decades still lagged behind other minority groups. Activists, however, were beginning to mobilize while learning from the success of other civil rights groups in the 1960s (Scotch 2001).

Given the personal connection that President John F. Kennedy had to issues of disability, and the number of returning veterans with disabilities who were viewed as heroes and deserving of services, some positive political moves were made during the 1960s. President Kennedy instituted the President's Committee on Mental Retardation and made formal calls for deinstitutionalization. Medicare and Medicaid began providing benefits to people with disabilities. The Vocational Rehabilitation Amendments of 1965 and the Architectural Barriers Act of 1968 attempted to reform structural barriers to independent living and accessibility. Despite these new policies, though, medicalized approaches to disability, which neglected structure and societal barriers, still dominated entitlement programs in the United States. Steeped in the Enlightenment ideas of using expert knowledge and science to solve individual problems, policy approaches to disability continued to be heavily medically based (Dudley-Marling 2004; Fisher and Goodley 2007). The President's Committee on Mental Retardation was composed mostly of medical professionals. Government programs, including social security, employed a medical model approach to understanding and responding to disability. Culturally, disability continued to be seen as an individual medical condition rather than a social problem—a tragedy that was neither topically funny, nor a social issue related to discrimination.

Reacting against these entrenched individualized and medicalized approaches, disability rights activists built on lessons learned from the civil rights movements of the 1960s (Scotch 2001). Initially, advocacy groups representing a range of disabilities functioned independently of each other, without much coherency as a larger movement. But soon, stronger and more widespread arguments for deinstitutionalization and reform in rehabilitation arrived as part of the independent living movement in the 1970s, which championed a philosophy of individual autonomy, accessibility, and social integration for individuals with disabilities. The independent living movement helped to galvanize a broader social activism amid diversity of disability (Crewe and Zola 1983; DeJong 1983). Independent living centers, often staffed by people with disabilities, also provided central public spaces for advocacy by providing benefits counseling, social support, and grounds for strategizing. Soon activist groups began to appear across the United States: the Rolling Quads; the Physically Disabled Students Program and the Disabled Women's Coalition (University of California, Berkeley); Disabled in Action (Long Island University); the Centers for Independent Living in Houston, Chicago, Los Angeles, and Boston; the American Coalition of Citizens with Disabilities (ACCD); Disabled in Action; Disability Rights Center; and American Disabled for Public Transit.

These groups and others pushed for the legal and political changes that would come over the next decade (Scotch 2001). Some of the most prominent included the *Parc vs. Pennsylvania* court case, which ruled that all children are entitled to a free and appropriate education; *Haldermann vs.*

Pennhurst, a ruling which gave impetus to the deinstitutionalization movement; and the landmark Rehabilitation Act of 1973, which protected people with disabilities from discrimination. When President Richard Nixon's veto and congressional political stalling created a four-year lag in approving the regulations of Section 504 of the Rehabilitation Act of 1973, disability activist groups launched a visible campaign that was broadcast around the world, using such tactics as crawling up the stairs of the Capitol in Washington, DC, taking over federal buildings, and chaining wheelchairs together once inside. At this point, the movement had cultural and political traction (Scotch 2001). In the United Kingdom and the United States, these shifts in thinking about the nature of the problem of disability had their roots in the work of social activists and academics—many of whom were living with biological differences. The field of disability studies and social movements on both continents was born of their work (Beckett 2006; Crewe and Zola 1983; DeJong 1983; Oliver 1983; Priestley 2003; Shakespeare 2006; UPIAS 1976). Disability activists and scholars in the United States made similar arguments, articulating what later became the independent living movement. Central to academic and activist arguments on both continents was the separation of biological impairment from disability (Barnes and Mercer 2005). In this view, disability is synonymous with social oppression. People are disabled by structural barriers and attitudinal constraints. Disability is, thus, a socially constructed phenomenon and can be eradicated by removing these barriers and constraints.

Despite this progress, though, a large shadow dominated comedic and tragic interpretations of disability during the 1960s and 1970s. Jerry Lewis rose to megastardom as part of the Martin and Lewis (Dean Martin and Jerry Lewis) team, and with a Jim Carrey-esque talent for inverting "acceptable standards for governing the body, maturity and masculinity" and "grostesquery" (Krutnik 1994, p. 13). Lewis's work in movies such as *The Errand Boy* and *The Disorderly Orderly* have been called "burlesque of an idiot" (Crowther 1949). In *The Patsy,* Lewis is described on the movie poster as a "dumb-like-a-fox bellhop." What has been called the "genius" of his "craft" stemmed from his ability to stutter, stammer, and contort himself, losing control of his body and language in ways that amused an audience (Krutnik 1994, p. 17). Even as some of his characters represent a fragile form of masculinity, or triumph, many of the films include a "spectacle of maladjustment" (Krutnik 1994, p. 20). Lewis's comic genius has garnered him millions of dollars and recognition as one of the most recognized comedians of all time as well as an influential force on later generations of comedic actors.

But later generations know Lewis more for his advocacy and fundraising on behalf of the Muscular Dystrophy Association. His long-running *Jerry Lewis Labor Day Telethon* began as a Thanksgiving party fund-raiser in the 1950s. But in 1966 it became a full-fledged telethon media event, featuring a twenty-two-hour variety show of "patient profiles," the "love network" of television stations that carry the event, and celebrities such as Frank Sinatra, Dean Martin, co-host Ed McMahon, and Celine Dion. (Fittingly, for many years, the show was based out of Las Vegas.) The telethon has raised over $2 billion, but for the past three decades it has been criticized for relying on a combination of pity, paternalism, slick production, and celebration of celebrity to raise funds. Lewis's paternalistic name for the children he represents—"Jerry's Kids"—not only has drawn charges of old-fashioned paternalism, but it has become a moniker used by comedians and others to describe people with disabilities. Frank Krutnik argues that, if Jerry Lewis's body no longer functioned as "a signifying simulation of disability" on screen (1994, p. 25), the telethon certainly did. And it did so in ways that attempted "to generate capital via the exhibition of different bodies" (Smit 2003, p. 688). Paradoxically, Lewis made millions as a buffoon and idiot contortionist whose body was a spectacle and punch line, but he generated billions by drawing the opposite emotions of pity and tragedy from the images and lives of real people with disabilities whom he was claiming to help.

By the end of the 1970s, the cultural climate had shifted. Criticism of Lewis was beginning to mount, and the regulations for the Rehabilitation Act of 1973 were finally signed (four years after the bill passed). New comic representations of disability also began to emerge. Between 1977 and 1978, a small number of disabled comedians began bringing disability to the comedy stage, and later to television and movies, in more authentic and sophisticated ways. Geri Jewell, who has cerebral palsy, is best known for her role on *The Facts of Life* as Cousin Geri, but she began as a stand-up comic in the 1970s, making her first appearance at the Comedy Store in 1978. Jewell got into comedy after meeting fellow comic Alex Valdez in college. Valdez, who is blind, convinced Jewell to try stand-up while they were talking inside the Disability Support Services at Fullerton Junior College. Both worked comedy clubs in the late 1970s. Jewell was noticed by Norman Lear, the producer of *The Facts of Life,* which led to her move to television. Valdez's and Jewell's routines were groundbreaking for their time. They invoked their own disabilities onstage, merging self-effacing humor with authentic insight into their daily lives that simply had not been presented onstage. The fine line that they walked between activism and entertainment is captured in clever fashion in this joke by Jewell: "We have to fight . . . for the right to be stared at" (1982). Jewell became the first regularly appearing television character with a disability in *The Facts of Life* and went on to appear in *The Young and the Restless, 21 Jump Street,* and *Deadwood.* Valdez, who began doing stand-up at the Comedy Store (Westwood) a year before Jewell, proceeded to become the emcee at the Laff

Stop (Newport Beach) and a partner with Jim O'Brien doing musical and sketch comedy material on blindness, ethnicity, and "comedy in the dark." Valdez and O'Brien have worked in clubs across the United States and have appeared on *An Evening at the Improv* and Comedy Clubs Network on Showtime. (Both Jewell and Valdez also speak regularly on disability issues to government and nonprofit organizations as well as corporations.)

If the arrival of comedians such as Jewell onstage and in television was remotely beginning to reflect broader social changes—such as the International Year of Disabled Persons (1981), the Gallaudet University Deaf President Now campaign, and the mobilization and drafting of the Americans with Disabilities Act—traditional disabling depictions of disability remained prominent in comedy. Perhaps the most popular act came from Bobcat Goldthwait, who embodied (contrived) aspects of disability in his stand-up routine, from the mid-1980s to the mid-1990s. Goldthwait began performing his stand-up persona in between his punk band's musical sets. The character he created for the stage, and later on film (*Police Academy 2, 3,* and *4,* and *One Crazy Summer*), stuttered, screeched in a high-pitched voice, huffed, and neurotically paced in a manner described as *The Muppets* Animal on heroin or a deranged version of Pee-wee Herman. Kathryn Bishop of the *New York Times* news service called Goldthwait "a caricature of an overgrown, emotionally damaged child . . . not unlike watching a mental patient with strong political opinions going through primal scream therapy" (1986, p. 74). Onstage, he moved back and forth between anger and vulnerable fright. In some ways, his adoption of this persona as a mask parallels the role of traditional jester described earlier in this chapter: he used the spectacle and unpredictability of the persona, randomly moving between anger and innocence, to draw and keep audience attention. While he may have used the mask as a hook, or a way to open the crowd up to what he had to say, it did nothing to shake up traditional ideas of disability.

To be fair, some of Goldthwait's stand-up work did have a critical bent, even if the presentation was misguided. In between mad rants such as "my toaster is possessed by the devil," he would squeeze in humorous critique of right-wing icons such as Ronald Reagan (who fired union air traffic controllers in 1987), the National Rifle Association, and militias. He questioned why representatives of *The Tonight Show with Jay Leno* did not want him to make his noises or scream during his appearance on the show. In this sense, it could be argued that he was somewhat transgressive for putting this embodiment onstage, as inauthentic as it was, and coupling it with clever insight. But in the end, spectacle overshadowed substance, and it did little to challenge traditional notions of disability. However, film studios seized on the popularity and novelty of Goldthwait's act. He was cast in three of the *Police Academy* movies and other comedies such as *One Crazy Summer*. These films took simply the mask of Goldthwait's persona, without any of the content. (Goldthwait has, however, gone on to make critically acclaimed independent films.)

This type of stand-up comedy appeared to have run its course in the years following the passing and signing of the Americans with Disabilities Act. By then a small cadre of comedians with disabilities were touring widely, including J. D. England, Chris "Crazy Legs" Fonseca, Brett Leak, Kathy Buckley, and Steady Eddie (Christopher Widdows). These comedians would lay the groundwork for a full-fledged renaissance that would follow at the beginning of the twenty-first century (Haller 2003). By 2005, a range of comedy troupes and stand-up comedians with disabilities was regularly appearing in comedy clubs across the United States, Canada, the United Kingdom, and Australia and on college campuses around the world. Josh Blue's win of NBC's *Last Comic Standing* in 2006 might be considered the commercial breakthrough proving that comedy addressing issues of disability could be successful and thought-provoking stand-up material. By professional comedy standards, many of these comedians have had successful careers. Most have appeared on television, performing stand-up on late night shows (the *Late Show with David Letterman* and *The Tonight Show with Jay Leno*), and acting. Some have been the feature of documentaries (*Look Who's Laughing*) and have opened for major rock groups.

While these comedians have found an audience for disability comedy, there are certainly remnants of disabling humor on and off the stage. Though not specifically stand-up comedy, a number of FM radio shock jocks have also provided a venue for disabling humor over the past few decades. Howard Stern, for example, featured the Wack Pack on his show, which he insisted had nothing to do with their appearance but the fact that they had no perception of why they were funny. Members included Beetlejuice (a little person with microcephaly), Speech Impediment Man, Wendy the Retard, Eric the Midget, Hank the Angry Dwarf, and John the Stutterer. Until recently, the show of a local radio personality in our own hometown, Mike "Cowhead" Calta, featured a segment called "Retarded News" that recently was stopped due to complaints. The show also frequently featured a member called Tongueless Brett. However, with radio audiences on the decline, shows that incorporate this type of content risk alienating audiences, and these shows face competition with new media technologies that provide more choice for listeners, such as podcasts, and the ability to stream television and movies.

The emergence of newer outlets and a more stylist approach to cable programming have brought increasingly nuanced and paradoxical portrayals of disability using humor as a lens. From *South Park* to *Glee*, disability is more regularly addressed on mainstream television, often in ways that question traditional norms, while also poking fun at political correctness. The recent mockumentary television series *Life's Too Short*, starring Warwick Davis and written by Ricky Gervais, exemplifies this shift. Gervais describes it as a show about "the life of a showbiz dwarf" who is arrogant and manipulative. Yet the show highlights the social obstacles that Davis's character faces, including the reactions of other people around him. Clearly, a new way of embodying and giving voice to disability has emerged through comedy, from television and Internet mediums to the comedy club. These newer forums for publicly discussing disability allow individuals with impairments or bodily differences to write and tell stories about disability and culture and to engage in their own forms of social critique. Some might argue that, in an oversaturated market with thousands of programming choices, disabled identity and difference have themselves become a commodity. However, the critical and commercial success of many of these stories does put discussion of disability into the public realm in ways that have never been done, and it certainly pushes audiences while also reflecting broader tastes.

Disability Humor and Emerging Views of Disability

In addition to humor, we have traced the historical development of various lenses through which disability has been viewed. While these lenses developed in a particular historical sequence, moral or religious, medical or tragedy, and social or cultural views of the disability experience are all evident today. The social or cultural model and emerging models being developed from it may dominate scholarship in disability studies and the sociology of disability in the twenty-first century, but individuals living with impairments are likely to be viewed through all of these lenses at some point in their lives. In fact, while many individuals with impairments have adopted a disability identity consistent with the social model, others have rejected this identity (Darling 2013). There is a gathering of sentiment around the idea that the disability experience is neither solely individual nor solely social in nature and, thus, cannot be fully understood using a single lens such as the medical or social model. Viewed through this emerging perspective, disability "is both individual and social; both biological and cultural. It is a complex, nuanced, embodied and socially contextualized experience in which social and cultural oppression interacts with bodily experiences" (Green, Darling, and Wilbers 2013, p. 160). Tom Shakespeare (2006) argues that the removal of oppressive barriers and negative public attitudes would not entirely remove the problems associated with the disability experience. For some people, part of the problem resides in the bodily experience itself, including pain, illness, and incapacity. These problems are, however, severely exacerbated by social and cultural constraints; and, for many (perhaps most) people, the constraints are far more problematic than the bodily experiences. At present, this emerging view lacks a standardized nomenclature. Following others, for the purposes of our analysis, we call this interactive view of the disability experience "critical realism" (Shakespeare 2014).

Crip theory is another new perspective on disability that is emerging at the intersection of disability studies and feminist queer theory (Kafer 2013; McRuer 2006). This postmodern perspective challenges the binary distinction between bodies that are deemed normal and those deemed impaired or disabled. This perspective is purposefully transgressive and attempts to problematize and destabilize the very idea of normality as a fixed concept. This is not to say that crip theory argues that everyone is disabled. In fact, proponents of crip theory recognize that distinct disadvantages accrue to people whose bodies are deemed abnormal (McRuer 2006). Robert McRuer, whose work on compulsory able-bodiedness is often credited as the foundation of crip theory, calls attention to the ways in which the significance of disability is created through discourse (McRuer 2013)—particularly discourse embedded in the power relationships associated with industrial capitalism.

Consistent with both critical realism and crip theory, various types of humor are being used by disabled comedians today to reframe, reconstruct, and reorder what have been the dominant narratives of disability. As we show in the next chapters, a sophisticated multidimensional treatment of disability that challenges traditional expectations of what it means to live with bodily difference is being brought to the stage with clever wit by a number of comedic artists in the twenty-first century.

Common DNA

We have attempted to delve into the *common DNA* of disability and comedy, to return to the director Peet Cooper's term. Beyond simply demonstrating that context shapes what is funny as much as it shapes ideals of the body, we argued that ideals of humor and disability share an overlapping and related path, often shaped by the same (re)interpretive lenses. Rather than focus on specific arguments of causality, we directed our attention to the ways that humor can illuminate broader ideals, especially ideals about the body, and how these indicators change over time. In the Greco-Roman era, morality and religion were the common evaluative lenses, with individual ridicule as a common outcome of humor. Tragedy and comedy were related, as impairment was a form of amusement. In the Middle Ages and Renaissance, folly, disability, and madness were intertwined, and a more active and critical comedy emerged. Folly was an aesthetic that involved subversion, paradox, and the taboo, and at times the disabled body actually had a voice through the jester role. As the Enlightenment emerged, though, notions of medicine redefined disability and folly in new ways. Folly was confined as it was redefined. When the Industrial Revolution arrived, both capitalism and medicine emerged as dominant forces that marginalized the disabled body, which was all but banished from the workplace, school, and public area as an economic liability and pitiful spectacle. This marginalization not only secluded the disabled body within institutions, it also obscured it in other aspects of daily life: work, school, and public spaces. Along with physical representation and presence, more abstract representations, such as humor, were impacted. Disability moved from being more central to European court humor to an association with misery and pity, which were not congruent with laughter.

With the emergence of stand-up as a specific medium, however, comedy once again became an active and activist force, returning somewhat to the critical aesthetic of the jester. It is no coincidence, of course, that this was happening as the civil rights era began to usher in reinterpretations of race and gender, and a more revolutionary culture was evolving. When the disability rights movement gained its own momentum, ideas of humor shifted again, reflecting and challenging dominant ideas of disability. All of these shifts help illustrate how humor and disability are each defined in relation to many other institutions and structures: moral, religious, medical, and economic. But such historical analysis also demonstrates how humor can function as an indicator and an agent of social change, which does not always follow a progressive linear path.

If these historical examinations illustrate how humor can be used as a social index of attitudes over time, though, such analysis takes us only so far. Who are the comedians who take the enormous risk of bringing disability comedy to the modern stage? What are their aims and motivations? What strategies do they employ, and what obstacles have they faced? These are the topics to which we turn our attention in the next chapter.

Note

1. Many little people prefer that the word "midget" not be used to describe them because of its historical use in hate speech and bullying. We use it only in quotations and titles. Otherwise we use the words "dwarf" or "little people," which are currently preferred, though still somewhat contested. See Leonard Sawisch's essay at http://the-m-word.blogspot.ca/. See also Adelson (2005) for a helpful historical review.

4

A Twenty-First-Century Cast of Comic Characters

There's something about humor. . . . You can't dismiss it. You can't feel superior to it. . . . Tragedy . . . , you can [feel] all . . . sad . . . and just walk on away from it. Humor, not really . . . you simply can't. . . . It affects you in a very different way. —*Terry Galloway*

Canadian comedian Tanyalee Davis stands three foot six, but her confidence is towering when you meet her. Onstage she is clearly comfortable with her body, referencing the benefits of her height (curves) and talking candidly about sex in her comedy routine. As a child, though, teasing led her to use humor to try to circumvent the negative attitudes of others: "I always tried to be the life of the party or tried to be very friendly . . . so that people would like me, but you know [how] kids are . . . I got bullied big time." Like other performers we interviewed, some of Davis's stand-up draws on these negative childhood experiences as a source of material:

> It was weird because . . . the first time I ever did comedy I had a rolodex of things in my head like of shit that happened when I was a kid and I thought: "This will come in handy someday." . . . I think my opening line . . . the first time I went onstage [was]: "Hey, did you guys know that there is a midget here? Uh, no? I walked in and they were like: 'Hey, look at the midget.' And I was like: 'Where?'" It did get a good laugh because I disarmed people and they didn't see that coming.

During a stint in community theater, Davis got the lead in her first production—as Perry the Penguin in a play for children—a role that some might consider patronizing, but one that ironically lead her to a successful career on the very adult comedy stage.

Spend even a small amount of time with Davis and it is clear that performing remains an important part of her life—not only professionally, but also personally:

> If I haven't been onstage for a couple of months, I am an absolute bitch, more than usual, and it really affects me. It seems . . . there's some sort of endorphin release. . . . I've been so sick . . . before I go onstage, and I get up there, and I'm able to do a set. . . . Then, as soon as I get offstage, . . . I practically collapse. . . . I [found] out my sixteen-year-old cousin died. She got crushed by a car and I had to go onstage that night and was devastated, but I had one of the best shows ever. . . . Emotionally, I was just on the brink, but . . . I put that into my show and people are like "Wow! That's the best we've seen you," and I was like "Yea, well, I just had a lot of built up emotion and it came out in my show—not in tears, but with energy."

Beyond these individual benefits of the stand-up stage, though, Davis's aims as a comedian are varied—bringing honesty, personal life, embodied experience, and even shock to the stage in a narrative of the disability experience that challenges the idea that disability is personal tragedy.

In this chapter, we take a look at the lives, work, and professional aims of Davis and the nine other modern comedians who consented to share their stories with us through in-depth interviews. Consistent with interpretive methods, the first step in the analyses presented in this chapter and elsewhere was to immerse ourselves in the typed transcripts. Our goal was to engage with each transcript as an intact story before extracting themes or using theories of humor or models of disability as templates in our analysis (Green 2015). In this first step of the analysis, we made a concerted effort to hear the story that each participant wanted to tell—bracketing our own experiences as family members of people with disabilities as well as our scholarly interests. In the later stages of the analysis, we identified themes in the transcripts that relate to the purposes of the various chapters of this book. In this chapter, we discuss common themes related to the social positionality of the comedians we interviewed, the intersection of humor and disability in their everyday lives, and the delicate dance of creating new narratives of disability through professional comedic performance.

Setting the Stage: The Cast of Characters in Social Context

The biographical sketches that are included in the Appendix clearly suggest that the lives and the professional careers of these performers are very individual. As noted in Chapter 1, they vary in terms of a number of social positions including: sex and gender; marriage, partnership, and singleness; parenthood; and sexual identities. The stories they told during their interviews exemplify a variety of perspectives on the lived experience of disability and on the roles that disabling and disability humor can play in this lived experience. Some commonalities are also evident in these stories, however. For one thing, this group of ten comedians is relatively homogenous in terms of race, class, and educational opportunities. Most of them bring to their experience the privileges associated with a white middle-class family background in the context of Western capitalism—specifically in Canada, the United Kingdom, and the United States. There is some diversity in terms of ethnic identity. Nina G. describes herself as a woman of "white, Italian American descent." Maysoon Zayid, whose parents are first-generation immigrants from the Middle East, is the only comedian who describes herself as a person of color and talks about the experience of juggling identities at the intersection of disability and minority ethnic status. In her interview, Zayid describes her complex set of identities: "I always say I fit into several different minorities, because I am a woman. I'm of color . . . but the defining minority is . . . disability. . . . It's something I address every single day and I think the biggest challenge in my entire life is the fact that I have been denied jobs due to my disability." While she did not feel the sting of ethnic discrimination as a child, Zayid has found that her identities as a Muslim woman and a disabled comedian intersect in ways that sometimes create complicated layers of disadvantage and discrimination:

> I actually missed out on several opportunities because I'm not a hijabi [someone who wears the scarf]. Because I do not wear a hijab (scarf), they do not consider me a Muslim. . . . They did Muslim comics on CBS. It was a big deal. They wanted two performers—a guy and a girl. . . . They . . . didn't know I was Muslim. . . . Are you kidding me? I say it in every interview and performance. . . . They say: "Well, you know, you are not a practicing Muslim" and I'm like: "What does that mean? . . . I am!" . . . They don't understand that you can wear a hijab and not practice, or not wear a hijab and practice.

For most of our other participants, disability was the main source of social disadvantage that they experienced. In seeking to challenge the disadvantages of living in a disabling world, several mentioned that they look to the civil rights movement and critical race activists for inspiration. They see the fight against racism as an example of how ableism might be resisted and contested in their lives and work.

In most cases, the comedians we interviewed for this project came from families that place high value on education and educational experiences—in and out of the classroom. Liz Carr, for example, says that her parents valued education "hugely," and Davis says that her mother pushed her to "go to university and get a real job." In addition, most of the comedians we interviewed spent the majority of their school years in regular, as opposed to special, educational settings. Zayid's family, for example, was adamant that she receive a good education and fought for her right to attend mainstream schools rather than a special education center.

I was mainstreamed as a child. My father sued the New Jersey school system in 1980 to get me into the public school system. They wanted to send me to the school for children with like Down syndrome . . . which would send me on a completely different road. I mean, I never would've been functioning at the level I do if those were my school surroundings. So they sued the school . . . and I went to a mainstream school.

As adults, these particular professional comedians also tend to share fairly similar positions with respect to disability pride and activism. In her recent book on disability identity in the Lynne Rienner Disability in Society series, Rosalyn Benjamin Darling (2013) proposes a typology of disability identities with five distinct types. Individuals are categorized into types based on three variables (degree of integration into mainstream society; acceptance of the idea of disability pride; and participation in disability activism or disability culture). Darling calls the five categories: *normative typicality* (integrated into mainstream society, rejects the idea of disability pride, and does not participate in disability activism or disability culture); *affirmative typicality* (integrated into mainstream society, accepts the idea of disability pride, and does not participate in disability activism or disability culture); *affirmative activism* (integrated into mainstream society, accepts the idea of disability pride, and participates in disability activism, disability culture, or both); *personal activism* (excluded from mainstream society, accepts the idea of disability pride, and participates in disability activism, disability culture, or both); and *resignation* (excluded from mainstream society, rejects the idea of disability pride, and does not participate in disability activism or disability culture). These categories, of course, are ideal types and real people are rarely completely aligned with any one of them. A person's position in the typology may also shift over time. At the time of our interviews, the ten performers who participated in this project seemed most closely aligned with the affirmative activism category. While several may have begun life in one of the other categories, most expressed disability pride and had been, or were currently, at least somewhat active in disability groups and mainstream society.

Darling's (2013) research indicates that disability identity category membership tends to vary with severity of impairment, age of impairment acquisition (lifelong impairment vs. acquired impairment), and current age (or perhaps age cohort membership). For example, those in the two typicality categories tend to be younger and have less severe impairments than those in the two activism categories and the resignation category. Those in the affirmative typicality, affirmative activism, and personal activism categories are more likely than those in the normative typicality and resignation categories to have lifelong rather than more recently acquired impairments. Individuals in the resignation category tend to be older than those in the other groups. Darling argues that her findings suggest that activism tends to be associated with disability pride. However, a positive view of one's disability seems to be most strongly associated with time of disability acquisition: people with lifelong disabilities tend to have higher levels of pride than those who have acquired their disabilities later in life. Exclusion from mainstream society seems to be an impetus to activism for some (the personal activists), but other activists (the affirmative activists) seem to be motivated by strong ties to the disability rights movement. . . . Those with less disabling conditions who are able to participate in mainstream society seem to avoid associating with disability-related organizations, whether or not they reject an identity of disability pride. (2013, p. 147)

While our participants varied considerably in terms of age and the severity of their impairments, all acquired these impairments at birth or in early childhood. They may, however, differ in important ways from people with lifelong disabilities who are educated in less inclusive settings during early childhood. Several of the comedians we interviewed told us that, although the inclusive educational experience they had during their early school years had tremendous advantages, it also served to limit their exposure to other children and adults with disabilities and delayed the development of a strong, positive disability identity—an identity they now value as adults and as performers. In many cases, these comedians came to their disability activism (as well as their positive disability identity) as a result of contact with other people with impairments outside of school. For Terry Galloway, this extracurricular contact came early in her life, when she was sent to a camp for children with a variety of impairments. As an adult, Galloway places a high value on the disability identity she developed as a result of this experience and continues her interactions with people with a variety of impairments through her work with a performance group called the Mickee Faust Club:

I look for it in the intimate connection. I want that connection. . . . As a deaf child . . . , it was of paramount importance. . . . I want that to be of paramount importance until the day I die. . . . Right now, some of the most important work for me is the work I do . . . with the Mickee Faust Club. . . . About 40 percent of the people are self-identified as disabled.

For other comedians we interviewed, contact with other people with impairments was delayed until early adulthood, when they had contact with disability groups in college or through their work as performers. In a number of cases, these performers developed or solidified an affirmative activist identity when they had to fight as adults for rights that they had taken for granted as children. For example, Zayid (who has cerebral palsy) says, "In my first phase, until I was eighteen, I didn't realize I was disabled, and in my second phase, it was all people ever talked about." This identity transition began when she was accepted to Arizona State University:

I wanted to be a dancer. Because I grew up dancing. I wanted to be an actress on Broadway. I applied to Arizona State University as a prelaw dance major. . . . When I got to college, people didn't know me my whole life. . . . People thought that because I had a physical disability, I also had a mental disability. I went into my first dance class and they were like, "Do you think this is realistic?" And I was like, "Yeah, I totally think it's realistic." And they were like, "This is not realistic." And I'm like, "Yeah it is." And so I kept doing the dance thing, and then one of my requirements was to take an acting class. . . . I was like "I love this! I'm going to become an actor." So I actually switched my major to women's studies and acting . . . ended up with an epic acting future.

In summary, while there are individual differences, in general this group of comedians brings to the lived experience of disability a relatively homogeneous advantage in terms of race, class, and educational background. They have taken different paths to a positive disability identity and participate in disability activism in different ways. As a group, however, they tend to meet criteria for membership in the affirmative activism category in Darling's (2013) typology. In the next section of this chapter, we look at themes related to the role humor plays in the everyday lives of these particular affirmative activists.

The Intersection of Humor and Disability in Everyday Life

In this section, we describe six overarching themes related to humor in everyday life that emerged from our open coding of the interview transcripts: (1) humor as a natural trait; (2) humor as a tool for emotion management; (3) humor as a path to social inclusion; (4) differences between disabling and empowering humor; (5) deploying humor as a weapon against ableism; and (6) personal catharsis through public comedic performance.

Humor as a Natural Trait

I don't plan on being funny, it just comes out. —*Josh Blue*

Like Josh Blue, the other comedians we interviewed tend to think of humor as a natural talent—something that is as much a part of who they are as is their disability (and, in some cases, predates their disability identity). They began using humor at an early age and see it as an essential part of their interactive style. As noted in the introduction to this chapter, Carr wanted to be sure we understood that, although she didn't begin to perform as a comedian until she was in her thirties, she was funny long before that. Davis, tells us that she "was always a bit of a cornball." Several comedians credit their impairments as one source of their humorous material. Blue speculates that the obstacles imposed by his cerebral palsy might actually make him a better observer, which in turn makes him a better comic writer and performer. He says, "I don't know if it has to do with my disability or just the brain I was given . . . but if you don't have any hindrances . . . you might not see the thing you're going to trip over." Similarly, Nina G. sees a direct link between her learning disability and her humor. "I think people who have LD/ADHD [Learning Disabilities/Attention Deficit Hyperactivity Disorder] will see the world in a slightly . . . skewed way because we don't pr-process information the same way as everyone else and oftentimes that is where the humor comes from."

While these comedians tend to talk about their natural proclivity for humor, most also told us that they came from families in which humor is used as a tool to encounter and interpret experiences. Their natural tendencies were nurtured in environments in which humor was appreciated. Davis, for example, says that she gets her humor "from my father's side of my family." Carr says that members of her family "laugh a lot . . . and probably laugh . . . to hide emotions." Galloway tells us that she and her two sisters were raised by parents who were "wonderful, sweet, funny, complicated people who didn't hesitate to talk about the complications or difficulties of life."

Humor as a Tool for Emotion Management

This world doesn't make it easy to be disabled. —*Terry Galloway*

In their seminal work on emotion management among wheelchair users in public places, Spencer Cahill and Robin Eggleston (1994) argue that wheelchair users bear an unusually burdensome responsibility to manage not only their own emotions, but also those of nondisabled individuals they encounter in public places. They are often faced with embarrassing situations caused by environmental barriers or the awkward embarrassment and sometimes hostile incivility of others. To get on with life, they have to find ways to encounter and manage their own emotional responses to these frustrating experiences and encounters. They also have to find ways to help others get past their anxiety to facilitate even rudimentary interaction. Based on their interviews, autoethnographic analysis (by Eggleston), and participant observation (by Cahill), they suggest:

> Wheelchair users commonly resolve the emotional dilemmas of their public lives in this way. They expressively mask their own emotions so as to manage others. They cover their embarrassment with good humor, relieving witnesses' emotional discomfort. They hide resentment behind calm graciousness. . . . Even when wheelchair users feel fully justified in their emotional

reactions, their public expression often contrasts sharply with their private feelings. (Cahill and Eggleston 1994, p. 304)

Like the wheelchair users interviewed by Cahill and Eggleston, several comedians who participated in our study told us that both they and their families used humor as a way to encounter and reframe frustrations associated with the experience of living with impairments and bodily differences. Galloway, for example, says,

> One of the ways that we [she and her family] always approached tragedy is that there was always this kind of dry, you know, disbelief to be alive. . . . And even in the middle of things, we found things to laugh about because . . . it relieves the tension but it's also a way to say, "What in God's name are we doing in this world? How did we get here, and isn't it hysterical?"

Steve Danner provides us with another example of humor that builds from a place of frustration, but works eventually into a catharsis and reframing. For Danner, shopping for clothes was a frustrating experience, and the outcome was often embarrassing: "It took me a long time to say that I wear kid shoes . . . kids' shoes suck. I wore a pair of [adult] tennis shoes for the longest time, and I always got a size eight. As I wore 'em more, the toes would kind of curl up. And a little person walking around in shoes with curled toes . . . it didn't look good." Eventually, he found comedy to be a healthy way to process and reframe these experiences, particularly through articulating them to other people: "I wasn't angry at the world, I just didn't know how to use my own voice to kind of tell people about my frustration with things like that . . . [now] I speak my mind very clearly."

While Galloway, Danner, and others use humor as a way to encounter and reprocess personal frustrations associated with living with an impairment, they also use humor to deal with the frustrations of living in a disabling world. Galloway says that humor has "allowed me to make light" of living with the difficult predicament of being different in a xenophobic world. She also encourages other individuals with impairments to use humor as a way of reframing and reprocessing the all-too-common negative consequences of environmental barriers and ableist public attitudes. In writing and performance workshops, Galloway has helped other people with impairments and health conditions to construct and tell their stories in humorous ways that engage others in their disabling encounters with the world:

> I want to give an example of something. When I first started doing these workshops called "Actual Lives" [workshops for people to write and perform], . . one of the very first people we interviewed was a woman named Terry, and she was in a chair and I think she had MS [multiple sclerosis]. And

her husband at the time was in very ill health. And she came in and she was telling a very sad story about how her wheelchair had gone to Boston without her. And she's telling this story and I start laughing. I think it's the funniest thing I had ever heard in my life! And I said, "Oh my God you have got to write this," and she looked at me and . . . she said: "It is funny!" And so, . . . she wrote that and it became one of the pieces that we do. . . . The people in these workshops would write about the most humiliating and terrible things that seemed like awful tragedies. But we were all just laughing.

Galloway argues that using humor to make light of a situation brings a less serious approach to dealing with the frustrations of the daily indignities imposed on people with impairments by an unhelpful and often intolerant world.

Sometimes dignity is different, you have to redefine dignity, you know. And so these are horrible stories. And we are saying, "No. They're funny." So we are not these tragedy queens. . . . Let's look at the stories differently. And I'm telling you, I hate the word "empowering," but why? I mean there's nothing more empowering than getting on top of something that could humiliate you and turning it upside down and making it funny. You get a grip on it. You know and so, I love that and that helped me. . . . I didn't have to be quite Tragedy Anne about my own humiliations.

Making light can be read in another way—as in shining light or providing a new perspective. As Galloway points out, the outcome of this type of reframing empowers by providing agency and control over the situation, a notion echoed by Blue, "You know, cuz if you're in control of humor you can control a lot of situations." Nina G. says that "humor opens a door that otherwise may not be open in terms of communicating the message." Galloway tells us that another value of humor is that it allows her to gain control of the narrative of her own life—turning the tragedy narrative of disability on its head: "I think it's a way of redefining myself. Of taking a hold of my own personal narrative. . . . I take my narrative and I talk about it in ways I want to talk about it. And I use humor to do that. And so I become a figure more of fun and wit than a figure to be pitied. You know, or to be mocked or scorned or anything like that, so humor is the way that I do that." For Galloway, humor that reframes horrible stories and tragic encounters becomes a tool of agency. Similarly, Danner says,

That's comedy to me, when you take the tragedy and formulate it into something you laugh about. It has a lot of truth to it, but at the same time, it's tragedy delivered in a humorous fashion. I think that's why people with disabilities have such a niche for comedy. 'Cause, you know, they deal with tragedy, they've got to have a level head on their shoulders. 'Cause we laugh about it one minute, we're annoyed by it the next.

Humor as a Path to Social Inclusion

I always tried to be the life of the party. —*Tanyalee Davis*

In addition to using humor as a way to encounter and reframe frustrating experiences, these comedians clearly value humor as one way to ease social tensions and make friends. Danner says, "You know, people . . . have a lot of questions that they wanna ask, but they . . . usually stick their foot in their mouths trying. . . . I offset [that] with a joke or two. . . . I try not to look at people as 'they're trying to hurt my feelings.' I'm just trying to get by just like they are. . . . Most people want to know the truth about you." Kim Kilpatrick agrees and says that "people want to know and they're curious . . . and they want to talk to you about how you perceive things. . . . I also find a lot of funny things happen to you and a lot of funny conversations."

As children, most of these comedians used humor to try to gain social acceptance. Galloway says, for example, "I also was a ham as a kid. I just loved to perform. . . . That was the way I made friends. . . . I had little comedy routines that I would work. . . . People thought they were funny and that was my way in." As adults, they also use humor as a way to deal with the peculiar (often frustrating) actions of others in public places in a way that doesn't hamper the flow of social interaction. Like the wheelchair users interviewed by Cahill and Eggleston (1994), Kilpatrick finds that she is often treated as an "open person" (Goffman 1963, p. 126): "People . . . feel that they can ask you whatever they want. . . . You can be on a bus and someone can say: 'So, how did you get blind?' . . . I don't think they'd ask some nondisabled person: 'Like, how did you get fat?' [*laughs*] They decide that this is alright to ask you, or to give you advice like: 'Oh, your dog should be wearing boots.'"

The comedians we interviewed often make a conscious choice to use humor to diffuse such awkward public encounters rather than reacting with anger. Zayid says, "I have done . . . that . . . since I was like five years old. . . . People say some stuff to me and I would just you know immediately respond back and it's how I deal with the disability now." Nina G. says that disability is a minority experience, and she and the other comedians we interviewed feel that humor can help lighten the load of living in an ableist world. Kilpatrick gives an example:

> Humor has saved me. . . . You just kind of have to find it funny because it sort of is funny. [*laughs*] . . . You'll be in a hotel room and someone will change the order of the bottles you put them in . . . and you wash your hair with like lotion or something . . . and it's all like sticking out and I mean what can you do? Right? [*laughs*] If . . . anyone . . . has no humor [laughs] about the disability . . . , I think that's harder. I think it's harder on the public and I think it's really harder on the . . . person with the disability. . . . I think it helps other people when you . . . really laugh about something. . . .

It's huge. . . . I think it really helps people feel comfortable and you lighten up a bit. . . . You feel relaxed when you think of a joke. . . . It really works. . . . The disabled people I've seen who don't use it at all and just get agitated and get angry . . . have a harder time in life. . . . People aren't as helpful to them . . . because they're not as fun. [*laughs*] . . . It's not right, but it just feels like I get better public service.

In general, in relatively benign (though awkward and frustrating) situations like these, the comedians we interviewed are willing to give others the benefit of the doubt and use humor to smooth over the rough edges of social interactions to get on with life.

These comedians also sometimes use humor to directly contest disabling assumptions of others because they feel they can make the point that needs to be made more successfully through humorous rebuke than angry retaliation. Nina G. gives an example of her use of humor as a corrective measure when a wheelchair user was having trouble escaping from the unwanted and persistent attentions of a stranger:

I was hanging out with my friend who uses a wheelchair and we were walking around B-B-Berkeley and some guy . . . went up to her and said . . . "Do you know Olivia?" . . . and she was trying t-to get away from him. . . . I said . . . "N-not everybody in a wheelchair kn-kn-knows each other." . . . There's just situations when you have a disability or when you hang out with others . . . that that will happen and I kind of made an agreement with myself a couple y-y-years ago that I was going to say something. . . . Whether it's me or disabled people that that I'm around, I will always say something whether it is a little joke or talking sh-shit back. . . . That guy did a microagression to my friend in a wheelchair. I could have gone a-a-after him in a really bitchy way and gone o-o-off on him. . . . I kind of did it in a more teasing and flirty way so . . . he knew what I was getting at. [*laughs*] . . . To joke about it . . . is just a way to put it through some other avenue. . . . People aren't going to want to hear otherwise.

Differences Between Disabling and Empowering Humor

That's not humor, that's bullying. —*Terry Galloway*

No matter how naturally predisposed they feel to using humor in everyday encounters, however, the comedians we interviewed draw a clear line between humor that disables and humor that serves to facilitate interactions with others. They are willing to give people the benefit of the doubt and use humor to manage their own frustrations and awkward social encounters to facilitate social interaction as long as they perceive that others mean well. They aren't willing to tolerate behavior, humorous or otherwise, that is used with the intent to do harm. As Galloway puts it, "It's the tone that gets me. It's the intention of the joke." In making the distinction between humor from others that is harmful and disabling and humor that is acceptable and potentially empowering, they tend to use several common criteria including: the power differential between the person using the humor and its target, the intent of the person using the humor, the sophistication of the humor, and the degree to which humorous treatment of the disability experience gets it right.

Several of the comedians pointed out that the line between humor and bullying often has to do with power—specifically how powerful the target is and how much they risk losing through the humorous interchange. Galloway, for example, says, "You know when someone is the brunt, it's never a joke. And it's not humor. You know I don't regard that as humor. There's a light touch in humor. . . . And there's also, I believe, a weird compassionate underpinning in humor. . . . I do not believe it's humor . . . if anyone that is in a position that is weaker than yours. . . . That's not humor, that's bullying."

The comedians we interviewed also report assessing the intent of the person with whom they are interacting before deciding to set them at ease through humor. Kilpatrick, for example, says, "If they're really nasty . . . or not wanting to learn about disability and just assuming you're stupid . . . , I don't think I would use humor. . . . I don't engage with them." These comedians with disabilities have become skilled in assessing the intent behind the joke, and they react accordingly.

For humor about disability to be funny, the person using the humor also has to get it right. Jokes that miss the mark fall flat and are irritating. Kilpatrick says, for example, "I don't like jokes that make blind people look really incapable . . . really inept. . . . I don't like some of the standard jokes about . . . 'How did Helen Keller burn her hands? Trying to read the waffle iron.' . . . I find that stupid." Similarly, Danner differentiates between humor that gets it right and failed attempts:

> I knew I wasn't dressing very well. I was kind of frumpy and I thought I wanted to up my . . . fashion game. So I asked my female friend to take me shopping. I said, "I'm horrible at this. Can you help me get some nice looking clothes?" . . . She sees one of those Big & Tall shops and she thinks she's being funny and goes, "Well, there you go. We'll go in there." And I'm like, "Now that's a stretch. You just stretched it too far. It's not even funny. . . . When you have something funny, get back to me." Thirty seconds later we're still walking and she goes, "That's more your style," and so I look over at the Kid's Gap. And I just looked at her and said, "Now, see, there you go." Like I said . . . it has to be relevant. When my friend looked at the Big & Tall store and said, "ha ha ha" you know, I was like, "That's just a bad comparison . . . not even funny." But then she saw Kid's Gap, and I gotta admit, I found that funny.

While Danner and others we interviewed are tolerant of well-intentioned humor and will try to help others get it right through the kind of gentle corrective he describes in this story, there is a tipping point beyond which they lose patience: "Some people I can say a joke to about it and . . . now I'm getting joke after joke [from them]. . . . For myself, it only makes it weird when somebody just won't let it go. I think that's the worst part. It's like, you know okay, it was amazing at first, but after four hours, oh geez." Like Danner, Kilpatrick is also frustrated by others who get hung up on something that's not really very funny to begin with and then run it into the ground. She says, "If . . . I use words like 'Oh, see you later,' some people are like . . . 'you can't!' . . . they get all involved in that . . . which is stupid because, what am I supposed to say, 'I'll hear you later?' . . . I use the words that we use . . . and they think that's kind of funny . . . I don't." This doesn't mean that she finds all humor about blind people inappropriate. She says that she and her family laughed at a standard joke about Helen because it resonated with their own experience. "I mean the one about Helen Keller when they said 'What did her parents [do] when she was bad? They rearranged the furniture.' . . . That one's kind of funny because, actually, my parents, not when I was bad, but they would move things and I would come home and whack! . . . 'Oh, sorry Kim, we moved the couch.'" In this case, the joke gets it right and is seen as funny rather than demeaning.

Another major factor in determining whether or not something is considered funny rather than inappropriate is how sophisticated the humor is. If the humor is too easy or simplistic, it is not something they find humorous. Instead, they see it as lazy, irrelevant, or simply mean. Much disabling humor involves simplistic mimicry or cheap shots that require little creativity, according to our interviews. Carr, for example, points out that this type of tired humor is overused and too obvious:

> When they make fun is when they use it as an easy punch line, and when they use it and just say the word "cripple" at the end of it, [they think] it should get a laugh. I think that is lazy. I don't think it's clever. They do it with gay stuff. They might call me "gay" or "queer" or whatever. You know, or "stupid." It's common . . . but . . . I don't think it's acceptable.

Punch lines that play off the low-lying fruit are unimpressive. Jokes told by others that have real-life relevance and clever incongruity, though, are sometimes appreciated and may be used later as fodder for stand-up routines by these comedians. Danner says, for example, "If you're gonna pick on me, it better be funny. . . . It has to be somewhat relevant."

Deploying Humor as a Weapon Against Ableism

People and their nonsense. —*Nina G.*

While the comedians we interviewed can and do use humor to smooth the waters of social interaction, they also can and do deploy their rapier wits as weapons against ill-intentioned others. Blue says, for example, "If you can say something funny while someone's trying to be cruel, they just look like an idiot." Knowing when to use which edge of the sword is, of course, key. Nina G. uses humor in complex and nuanced ways to set well-meaning people at ease while challenging the nonsense of others. In some situations, she uses humor to try to circumvent potential awkwardness and make people comfortable in situations in which the personal stakes for her are high. She says, for example, that she has used humor to circumvent potential discrimination when applying for a job (see Chapter 2). She tells us that this "was a really good way to introduce them and to put them a-a-a-at ease." In her role as a disability educator, she also uses humor as a gentle tool. "When I do disability e-education I'm very soft and . . . I use humor as a way to make people c-comfortable." When she's not in her role as educator and she's faced with demeaning behavior on the part of others, however, she often uses the sharper side of humor's sword to combat "people and their nonsense." As is the case when deciding if the humor of others is funny or disabling, these comedians assess in the moment the worthiness of their opponent and decide whether to be kind or cruel. Kilpatrick, for example, finds public reactions to be mixed—some more troublesome than others. "People are very curious and very friendly to me in a way too . . . and you get into some really interesting conversations with people. . . . There's really weird interaction, but there's also really great interaction."

Personal Catharsis Through Public Comedic Performance

> I think I'm . . . an exhibitionist. I think I'm equally insecure. I think I enjoy the power of being onstage. —*Liz Carr*

As Carr suggests, for the comedians we interviewed, stage performance is more than a way to make a living. The public performance of humor also serves as a tool for the management of personal emotions in a disempowering and disabling world. Davis provides some powerful examples of the personal benefits of stage performance in the introduction to this chapter. Similarly, Zayid tells us,

> Comedy is a great way to get over whatever is bothering you. . . . I always say I have a great job because . . . no matter how down I get, when I jump up onstage, I'm making people laugh. It's interesting. . . . I could be sick, I could be upset. I could have lost my cat and I'll be onstage. . . . The only time I ever did step off the stage was in June . . . after my father passed away.

In addition to Davis's earlier examples of personal catharsis, she told this story in her interview: "Last year was a bit of a rough year for me. . . . I went through a divorce. . . . I had . . . anxiety issues that I never had before and . . . probably a little bit of . . . depression as well, but my stand-up's what pretty much got me out . . . of the funk and kept me going and that's why I've chosen now to just be constantly on the road." Danner also sees his stand-up performance as a cathartic platform through which he can speak his mind and express his frustrations. He feels, however, that he had to be both mentally and emotionally prepared for this very public kind of "speaking out."

> When I was younger, I was angry . . . it was probably about my early . . . twenties when I started accepting being a little person and mid-twenties when I stopped being angry. . . . I had to be a comedian to kind of overcome that step. . . . I have a lot of people saying "Wish you would've been a comedian earlier in life." I have to say "No, because I wasn't emotionally and mentally prepared."

In summary, humor has played an important role in the everyday lives of the comedians we interviewed. They describe themselves as natural humorists, but most were also raised in families in which humor was appreciated and encouraged. They are willing to use humor to set others at ease to engage in positive social interaction, but only when they perceive that others are well intentioned and open to learning about disability. Even when this is the case, their patience is not inexhaustible. Jokes that are repetitive, rely on clichés about disability, and generally reflect an unsophisticated understanding of the disability experience are a source of irritation. Again, however, if the intent is perceived to be good, they will meet these irritating attempts with their own humorous response and help guide the jokester to a more sophisticated disability humor that gets it right. What they do not tolerate is a joke told with the intent to harm, belittle, or bully. Hate speech is hate speech, and they have no difficulty recognizing it when wrapped in humorous packaging. Using nuanced skills honed over a lifetime of experience, they make in-the-moment distinctions between humorous attempts that disable and humor that has the possibility of forging human connections. The power differential between jokester and target, the intent of the person telling the joke and the tone with which it is delivered, and the sophistication of the humor and the degree to which it accurately portrays something about the disability experience are all factors in the acceptability of humorous treatment of disability in everyday interactions. These comedians use their humor in encounters with others to manage their own emotions and those of well-meaning folks. When the intent is not so positive, but there is hope that a lesson might be learned, they use humor as a corrective measure—sometimes gentle and sometimes less so, depending on their own level of frustration as well as the seriousness of the infraction. In using humor in their everyday lives, they consciously attempt to counter the tragedy narrative of disability with a humorous narrative that helps others see the humanity of the disability experience in all its complexity as well as the complexity of the human experience that includes disability and impairment. They also take this humorous narrative of disability and humanity to the stage.

The Delicate Dance of Creating New Perspectives on Disability Through Comedic Performance

In addition to discussing the complex role of humor in their everyday lives, the comedians we interviewed also told us about the delicate dance required to combine the sometimes incompatible goals of activism and performance. The sketches give us a glimpse of the professional aims of these ten comedians, particularly how they deploy humor as a tool to create ambivalence and new perspectives on disability for audiences—often by disarming, discomforting, and shocking people into a recognition that disability is not always and only a medical tragedy. In the remainder of this chapter, we describe five themes related to this delicate dance that emerged from our open coding of the interview transcripts of our ten participants: (1) first, you have to make them laugh; (2) breaking through the fifth wall; (3) making the personal very public; (4) the uneasy alliance of performance and activism; and (5) challenges of representation.

First, You Have to Make Them Laugh

Eliciting laughter while entertaining, of course, was the primary motive mentioned by all performers. For many, making people laugh has tremendous intrinsic rewards. As Danner puts it, "I like the rush of the stage, be a performer, get up there and make a whole crowd of people laugh." It's not just about personal enjoyment, however, these are professional comedians whose job it is to entertain. He goes on to say,

> We are comedians first, you know? We are here to make people laugh. If I was just up there talking about how great . . . [it] was to get through my hardships and everything like that, I would just be a motivational speaker, not a comedian, you know? So I always say I am a comedian first. But it is great to be a part of this . . . we are really like reaching out and kind of touching people.

To touch people and change preconceived notions of what disability is, professional comedians also have to be cognizant of the bottom line. Club owners expect them to draw and entertain crowds—to make money for the venue. Simon Minty says that, during the early days of the formation of Abnormally Funny People, "there was a frustration with the same crowd of people—they wanted a larger crowd. The ones we need to attract are the nondisabled people. Plus, to sustain it financially, you can't just get the same eight people." To draw crowds and make money, comedians with disabilities have to keep people laughing and, with nondisabled audiences who are steeped in the tragedy model of disability, this can be a challenge. Several of our interviewees talked at length about having to quickly make people comfortable enough with the unfamiliar territory of disability to laugh. Nina G. calls this "breaking through the fifth wall."

Breaking Through the Fifth Wall

Getting a nondisabled audience to see disability as something familiar requires that comedians walk the audience through potentially uncomfortable or awkward territory. Nina G. describes this complex process this way:

> I have to work at making them comfortable . . . and I've had to learn, and I'm still getting used to the fact, that people will laugh at how I'm saying it instead of what I'm saying and that's why I try to write really well to over sh-shadow any-any-anything that they might laugh at just because of my speech. . . . I don't want to be a sellout or to be laughed at just because of my d-disability. . . . Then there's also people thinking . . . that if they laugh at me that then they're bad people, but I'm the stand-up c-comic. . . . There's like kind of that "white guilt" kind of thing. . . . "I can't laugh at this because that would mean that I'm a bad person." Well, it's like if you don't laugh at it you're also a bad p-p-p-person. The audience makes this transition within the first few minutes. . . . People don't want to laugh at someone that you pity and so there's this weird balance where you have to make an audience not pity you. They've been conditioned all of their frickin' lives to pity you because that's the only time they've ever seen someone who i-is like you. So in that first m-minute and a half, I have to fight every single fucking st-stereotype that they've ever had o-on stuttering to get them to a point where they can hear me, hear my jokes . . . that's a profound thing that I just said.

A number of the comedians we interviewed have acknowledged this fifth wall, either during our interview or in their stage routine. Like Nina G., Zayid forces audiences to acknowledge her disability up front: "First of all, when I get onstage . . . the first thing to deal with is the audience. . . . If they don't know I have CP, they're either going to think I'm drunk or nervous. . . . I like to get the CP out of the way. And by halfway through the routine, I don't think anyone even remembers it's there."

Davis takes a similar approach. She begins by surprising (perhaps shocking) the audience by joking about her short stature and other bodily aspects of dwarfism. This is aimed to relax the audience, but also to set them up by providing a framework, focusing the audience on the comedian's unique perspective, context, and experience. She is prepping them to partake in a novel perspective and viewpoint, and attempting to distract them from wanting to categorize or decipher. Audiences of comedy often want their own values reinforced, but they also want novelty and incongruity in a performance. By acknowledging disability up front, these comedians make it an important point of departure for the content of their routine. As Nina G. points out, audiences have been trained not to publicly acknowledge physical differences, and certainly not to laugh at them. Based on the interviewees' own experiences as individuals with disabilities, as well as their keen observations as comedians, they know very well that many audience members become distracted by their discomfort with the physical difference they see onstage.

Carr believes that if you're a disabled comedian, you have to get audience members past their discomfort "more so than any comedian." So, early on, she choreographs discomfort as part of the joke. By addressing disability early in the routine, these comedians are able to guide the audience members to a place that loosens the guilt that often chokes off laughter when disability is in the mix. This is an important strategic move. The necessity of this prep work, of course, depends on how well the audience already knows the comedian. Blue, for example, can now spend less time working the audience past their discomfort with his disability:

> I feel like now that I'm an established comic and people come to see me specifically I have less explaining to do. Whereas before if you don't know me, you don't know I have cerebral palsy, I've got a lot of things to explain to you to get you to a point where you're comfortable with laughing at me. Whereas now I can just go up there and be like bam, you know? Just launch into it.

Carr, on the other hand, enjoys playing with the expectations of audience members who are not familiar with her work:

> When an audience . . . sees me wheel onstage they really aren't expecting what they get, and you do get the audience members thinking, "Oh my God, it's charity night or they're raising money for something," you know? . . . You see their discomfort. . . . They're like "Oh my God. She's got to be lifted on the stage. What if she's not funny? Do we have to laugh?" . . . They're scared of not being politically correct. Like "What if she's not funny, will we hurt her feelings?" . . . You feel that in the audience. . . . Then, the fun thing . . . is playing with an audience's expectation. . . . I think we can do that because . . . you don't expect . . . to see somebody that's short or blind or in a wheelchair doing comedy. I mean it's brilliant that we are there. . . . But it's not what people expect and I think if we can play with that, why not?

Pity certainly has no place in the performance and humor of any of these comedians. While many do use self-deprecation, as we show in the next chapter, it is often deftly employed as a tool rather than a quick way to get a cheap laugh. Indeed, they often engage embodiment in raw ways to tap into fears of disability, but their aim is to represent a fearless form of disability in the process. Nina G. poignantly articulates the challenge involved in walking the line: "Comedy is like sex . . . you don't wanna fuck someone that you pity. And people don't want to laugh at someone that that you pity. And so there's this weird balance where you have to make the audience not pity you."

Davis feels that making an audience comfortable with disability not only liberates them to laugh but can also change their perspectives on disability:

> They can see right through my eyes and I make it accessible to them and that's what I think makes me so successful. . . . Nobody can really imagine being disabled right? So, they [are] . . . like "Oh my God, you're so brave. . . ." I'm not brave, I'm just living my life, but because they can't put themselves in your shoes, they can't even imagine coping. . . . They just can't get their heads around it. They can't imagine how we do it, and so my stand-up is all about: "Hey don't feel sorry for me. Look at all the shit I've done!" . . . I'm going to Japan tomorrow. I'm . . . doing all this on my own. . . . People go: "Holy shit. That's amazing!" . . . My stand-up is my life so I need to keep having these experiences to add to my stand-up. . . . I'm not disciplined enough to be sitting there and writing new jokes on a regular basis so I need to have life experiences. otherwise my act doesn't change at all.

Making the Personal Very Public

As Davis points out, like most comedians, comedic performers with disabilities use their own experiences as fuel for their performance. The difference is that, for these performers, personal experience is often inseparable from the most personal aspects of their bodily experience. She puts it,

> My stand-up is so honest. . . . It is my life. . . . It's so personal. . . . I talk about my personal experiences and the adventures I have, . . . but I'm also very physical onstage even though I'm so tiny. . . . You know, move these short arms, funny hands. . . . We all like watching people that don't look like us move. . . . It's fascinating. . . . In some people's eyes, [I] talk too much about being a midget. I don't talk too much about being a midget. I'm talking about me.

The need to make audiences comfortable with disability while also drawing on personal experience as fuel for comedy can create a difficult tension for comedians who want to be accepted for who they are, but do not want to be known primarily because of their bodily difference. Danner says, for example,

> Unfortunately, right now, about 90 percent of my content is all related to [disability]. Being a comedian, you want to develop. You want to develop yourself as more than that. Do you want to be the little person comedian or . . .

the comedian who happens to be a little person? So, I mean, I'm very fortunate . . . to get down with some "midge." . . . I see the average white person get up there and try to make jokes and I think: "Man, I'm glad I'm a little person." . . . I can tell a little person joke and . . . I listen to the crowd . . . and they'll be cracking up. . . . My biggest thing lately is trying to write the material in between the little person stuff.

All of the comedians with whom we spoke discussed the connections between humor, boundary work, and specific reasons for discussing disability. When this boundary work is successful, audiences connect with the comedian and begin to see disability as another aspect of the human experience. While successful comedians tell stories from a specific point of view, the stories they tell resonate with audience members with and without disabilities. Blue is a Paralympian, father of two, and married to a woman from Japan who is a nurse. Carr has a BBC radio podcast, studied law at Nottingham University, and has starred on BBC's crime show *Silent Witness*. Even as they speak to unique experiences and circumstances that involve the intersection of disability and humor, they touch on broader issues in ways that engage a larger audience, as Carr points out:

> I guess I talk a lot about disability because it's who I am, and it's a big part of my life, and my observations of the silliness of life from my perspective is what I want to share. . . . Sometimes I'm criticized for talking too much about disability . . . but it's not like there's fuckin' hundreds of us out there doing it. . . . I don't think . . . people should put it down because it's not necessarily about disability. When you asked me is my stuff mostly about disability or is it not, I paused and the reason was I think that sometimes my jokes may appear to be about disability and they are. But I think there is a huge resonance for other people. I think you kinda go, "The world is a crazy place."

In Galloway's performances as well as the workshops she conducts with other performers, she seeks to provide a refuge from disabling humor and other forms of mistreatment in an atmosphere that values human difference and also sees the humor in the human condition:

> I want to represent the human condition and part of that is disability and queerness and all of these things, but it doesn't have to be exclusively that and for me it's never been. . . . A lot of humor is political because the personal is political. . . . It doesn't have to necessarily have a political agenda, but [it] has a political attitude and it's always, always a liberalism. . . . I'm not going to force it, I'm not interested in that, but I want to be out there. I want to be part of the conversation. . . . I think it's so important that disabled people now become part of that. . . . A lot of people with disabilities have . . . a great deal to say. . . . We can look at our body and we can use it in funny and comic ways that . . . aren't predicated on us being in . . . normal bodies . . . and we can say: "Okay, my body is set up a little strange. . . . Here is how I'm going to use it. . . . Behold the Glory. This is me!"

Just as audiences vary in how they interpret and react to this humor, the comedians' views on these topics are not homogeneous. Danner indicated that when the Comedians with Disabilities Act perform together, some members sometimes call others out for going too far with disability content in their routines. Across the pond, Carr describes a similar diversity of opinion among performers in the group Abnormally Funny People:

> Chris McClausland is a blind comic but he doesn't do blind. He doesn't like to fall back on it. . . . I came in talking about "disability, disability, disability," and he was like, "fuckin' shut up about it!" We never . . . agreed . . . on our different approaches. There was . . . conflict amongst the group in terms of disability and comedy and that's quite interesting as well.

Minty, director of the Abnormally Funny People lineup, sums up the fine line that these comedians traverse. They must balance efforts to surprise (and perhaps shock) with consideration of how others will interpret the humor, particularly in relation to their association with a larger group of people with similar disabilities:

> Yes, there is a responsibility that we do not cheapen disability, we do not sell our souls, we stay this side of the social model, but we wouldn't restrict an act unless it was bad. . . . I know when I was doing the stand-up myself, I felt a huge responsibility toward other short people, I couldn't get away from it. I remember some of my friends who were short who came. I was desperate for their nod afterwards for them to say, "You were alright. You didn't compromise us; you didn't sell out; you didn't make a cheap gag for the sake of it."

The Uneasy Alliance of Performance and Activism

All of our interviewees hope that their artistic endeavors help to challenge misconceptions about disability and view their work as a way to advance the goals of the disability movement. However, they vary in terms of just how tight they tie the knot between performance and disability rights activism. Minty says, for example, "I've never said to myself 'keep in mind the social model.' How do I prepare a joke like that?" He goes on to say, however, that "things like charity or medical [model], if a comedian did a lot of those jokes, . . . I think we would probably go, 'Are you demeaning yourself here for the sake of the laugh?'"

Nina G. is perhaps the most direct in her activist aims: "I feel that I am an activist first no matter what I do and . . . [that] just happens to be c-c-comedy. . . . So, I come at it in that way." Some referred to this aspect of their performance as social critique. Others, like Galloway, see it as an underlying political attitude. Several of our participants say that "educating" the audience about disability is one of the goals of their performance work. Blue, for example, says,

> All my siblings and my dad, they're all teachers. They all teach language of some sort. My mom's a librarian, but people are always like, "Oh, they're all teachers. You didn't get into that." And I'm like, "Well, I kinda did just without the label." I've always said . . . "When you come to my show, you're gonna leave with a different perspective of disability whether you know it or not." . . . "The best professor I had in college he was great because he was entertaining and funny." . . . I just kinda take that and apply it to a worldview. You know it's also really up to you whether you want to learn something from what I say. I'm never gonna be like, "This is how it is." 'Cause I'm turned off by that sort of thing.

All of the comedians we interviewed, including Nina G., however, are careful to separate the act of performance, especially comedic performance, from more pedantic forms of disability training—in which several are also engaged. Carr, for example, explains the ways in which what she does onstage differs from a training session:

> I came from a world . . . of what we call disability quality training . . . "awareness training.". . . I think I've probably achieved as much by doing a ten- to twenty-minute comedy slot as I did in a whole day of training. I think people can hear a lot more when its comedy and . . . I think it softens the blow. I think it makes it a lot more humane. I think . . . it breaks down people not knowing how to relate to you. . . . In any situation, people always don't know how to relate to me, or they talk patronizingly to you. So, you're there on the stage and you have the power. You've got the stage . . . and you see what you can do with that. . . . I think humor becomes the way that you communicate and you go, "It's OK, I know you don't know what to make of me." I'm gonna make you think, you know? I'm gonna make you laugh and if you think maybe that's a bonus, but I just want you to laugh and get my jokes." . . . Humor and being on the stage with humor gives you a position of power and then I think you sideswipe them with the comedy and you get in there and you break down some of those barriers.

Part of the reason that it is not a training session is that these comedians are not, as Blue points out, telling the audience "how it is" by laying out a hard and fixed reality. They are engaging humor in ways that create ambivalence in the audience—creating situations of oppositional possibilities: they comfort through laughter, but they discomfort (and possibly shock) by addressing the taboo onstage. Rather than disability as spectacle, they use humor to situate the disabled body as a producer of knowledge (Thomas 2012). They bring together what James Thomas defines as the "presence of two equally intense but diametrically opposed feelings, such as pleasure and pain; enjoyment and outrage; or sadness and hope" (2012, p. 321). As humor entertains, it can disarm—which not only opens up the audience to being more comfortable with the disabled comedian as an individual, but also with entertaining a new perspective on disability altogether. This approach brings the nuances of the disability experience to the forefront while also allowing comedians to process their own individual experiences and reach audiences with their messages. As described by Nina G., "We can get really angry or we can make fun of it. . . . Personally when I work on a lot of my jokes the first couple of weeks I'm really angry . . . and no one laughs. And I eventually have to work the anger off of it . . . and work off the edge so that the audience can then respond."

Several comedians spoke of humor as a mechanism that shocks audience members into a new perspective. Carr notes the intersection between honesty and the bite of humor:

> I like it to have some bite and make people go "whoa" and I think I like to disarm people. . . . I don't even have to try to be honest. . . . The thing about me as a disabled person is I do look like I'm ill or have been ill. I don't just look like, um, a regular person sitting down. . . . I'm four foot six because of the effect of drugs. . . . I have been ill in my life and I think I wear that in my body and what that means is that when I wheel onstage I look quite frail, you know? . . . One of the things I do [is] I ask if there's any social workers in the audience and quick look around and hopefully there aren't any . . . but regardless of that . . . I say, "Thank God, because otherwise I'd have to do my act like this" and I sit there and . . . I start to dribble.

This physical humor, though shocking to some, makes a poignant point. Carr goes on to explain that, at that moment in the UK, holding a microphone might put her in jeopardy of losing her disability benefits because these are only secure for folks who are "on death's door." Any indication of a successful life is a threat to these benefits. Galloway takes a similar approach. She believes that humor is a way to "shock the recognition many times." This jolt moves the audience from the known to the unfamiliar: "They want something that's familiar . . . that's what conservatism is about . . . you want what's familiar—and they are not willing to take the risk and see . . . 'Oh! This could become familiar.'"

Challenges of Representation

The comedians we interviewed wanted to contest stereotypical narratives of the disability experience with the richness and complexity of their own lived experience. Nina G. says, for example, "I think you know part of the reason why I started doing comedy . . . was that I felt that my voice wasn't being reflected . . . in the media . . . or anywhere . . . maybe on . . . the occasional *S-South Park,* but it really wasn't out there and I felt . . . I had a story and I would like to attempt to talk about it." Similarly, Zayid says,

Disabled folks that we see on television fall into one of two categories:
"You can't love me because I'm disabled" or "Heal me, fix me, help me,"
and I'm neither of those. So, if someone wants to give me a surgery or perhaps inject me with botox, which was initially for people with cerebral
palsy. . . . I said, "I don't need you to fix me, I do yoga. I don't want your
medical intervention."

The comedians we interviewed were very aware, however, that their
stories were not the stories that all people with disabilities want to tell.
They are also sensitive to the fact that not all people with disabilities are
comfortable with humorous approaches to the disability experience. Danner
told us,

The humor I use about being a little person, . . . some little people find it
funny, some don't. . . . You know, some people know how to laugh at themselves in the community. A good chunk of them don't. They, you know, take
this very serious. . . . I understand. . . . It's hard being treated always like a
happy person. We're always supposed to be happy and we should be carrying
around candy, giving candy out to everybody. . . . Then you get the "Oh, you
must be Grumpy." . . . So, the humor that is out there, it is rough. I'm a very
fortunate type of little person. . . . Some . . . have a lot of medical needs.

Several of our participants find performing for disability groups to be particularly challenging. On the one hand, there are insider jokes that can be
told in only these specialized settings. Nina G. says, for example,

On May 31st we're doing a show called "Disabled and Proud," which is a
benefit for a disability organization that works with young adults and I am
superexcited about that show because I can do more insider h-humor that I
am not going to be able to do at some of the other shows. . . . One of my jokes
is: "People tell me that that stuttering isn't a real d-disability and I shouldn't
be in the Comedians with Disabilities Act, but the Americans with D-D-Disabilities Act . . . says that a disability is a physical or or mental impairment
that substantially r-r-results in having to deal with assholes."

On the other hand, several performers told us that, when performing for disabled audiences, there is a tremendous pressure to get it right. Carr
describes her feelings about the tensions inherent in performing for disability groups:

It's a very different audience. The great thing is that you can say things that
. . . are . . . shorthand, you don't have to explain. . . . If I'm talking about DLA
. . . the benefit over here called Disability Living Allowance, . . . most self-
respecting disabled people would know that. . . . So, if you're making jokes
about that, . . . there are shorthands you can bring in and jokes you can make
that you can probably only make in that community. The problem is . . . the
"politicized crip" is quite horrific in any country. . . . December 3 is interna-

tional day for disabled people. I've done a lot of gigs on the third of December, but you've got people that have been brought from a [disability] center and you've got people who are friends of yours. They are two different audiences. Doesn't mean the center people won't like you, but they may not like you. . . . Disability is so vast . . . and people are at different stages of their education and who they are. . . . I think probably most of my biggest critics have been disabled people. I remember my nemesis. . . . He's like . . . "What she says isn't funny, it's lazy, it's stereotyped." Maybe it was hurtful because some of it was true, but I think we don't have many disabled comedians in the UK and therefore I think when disabled people come see you they want you to be everything. . . . Do you know what I mean? So, you are then the disabled comedian, and, of course, as I said earlier comedians come in all shapes and sizes. . . . I'm rude. Some people don't like that, but I think that it's the same way whether you're on TV or on the stage or doing comedy. . . . Because there's not enough representation of disabled people, when you get to be in those positions, people want you to be everything and if you're not, you face their criticism. . . . Actually, criticism . . . from my own community is more painful.

Danner describes a conversation he had with Davis, who was performing at a Little People of America conference. Danner says,

"I don't know if I'm ready for that." She goes: "Why not?" and I said "Really I don't know why" and she said "You're in front of an audience of our people and they're looking at you like you're their advocate. . . . You're telling them how we live. So, you've got to get it right" and I was like "Yeah, I think that's it."

Carr also spoke about a double standard that can exist regarding who can speak candidly about disability and about specific disabilities:

Oh there's a double standard. I can say anything. [*laughter*] . . . I can say whatever I want about disabled people. I'm not for censorship. . . . I'm not for going "disabled people can only make jokes about disability." I've heard some brilliant stuff and some brilliantly political stuff done by comedians who aren't disabled. You don't have to be in that group, I think [to talk about disability] . . . but I think it is more acceptable. I can talk about it in a position of understanding and a position of truth.

Carr recognizes the privilege of her position as a person with disability experience and the advantage this position gives her in being able to speak the truth about disability from the stage. However, she does not see the license to speak as a birthright. Nor does she think that only those within the disability community are capable of getting it right in humorous portrayals of disability on the stage. She says, "You know I think I have more understanding and more right to talk about it. But I don't think I have a unique right." As we saw in the case of their humorous portrayals in everyday life, the key to these comedians is getting it right. While they feel that comedians with disabilities are more likely to be able to speak the truth from the stage, they also feel that comedians without disabilities who are talented and especially empathetic can also sometimes get it right. Similarly, they feel that it is quite possible for comedians with one kind of disability to get it wrong about those with another, or about the personal experiences of the same impairment in the lives of others. This is one of the things that makes the public performance of disability so fraught with risk.

In addition to bearing the burden of performing disability in a way that resonates with the lived experience of others in the audience, several of our interviewees also talked about feeling more than a little uncomfortable when they are viewed as an inspiration to others. Blue says, for example, that he doesn't want to be held up as a motivational exemplar:

> Like "if I can do it, you can do it." I really don't think that's true. I don't think you can do what I can do. I really don't. But I also know I can't do what you're good at, you know? So it's more about this is my story, I'm gonna . . . tell it in my way. I've just been fortunate enough where I'm in a position where people pay to hear my story. [*laughs*]

Nina G. feels comfortable being an inspiration for other people who stutter, but draws a sharp distinction between this and being seen as an inspirational comedian in the eyes of nondisabled people: "If you st-stutter I'm an inspiration. If you don't. I'm just an angry bitch. . . . For a stutterer, I don't mind being an inspiration but for everyone else I don't want you to see me in that way . . . because I think that is . . . what disabled p-people are in the media and I want to not represent that." Zayid resolves the issue of representation this way:

> I decided my responsibility to the disabled community is to be like a nonpathetic, no mercy disabled chic. . . . This is who I am. I don't want to change, and I am very OK with it. . . . Which is not to say I don't have days where I can't stand it. Some days, I'm just so tired I just want to be able to like make a cup of soup without it being like a huge production. . . . I'm not invincible, but that's the disabled person that I am onstage. . . . So, when you ask if I am a role model, yes I am a role model to somebody with a disability that wants to be a gladiator. I'm not a role model for someone with a disability that wants you to stop using the word "crippling" of the economy. . . . My battles are very specific and again it comes in the form of being the person I want to be, being like a good mother, a woman that my kids would look back on who I am and how I lived my life and be proud of it. I am invincible. . . . I toured around the world and got married which you know in the Arab world . . . is like the ultimate. . . . So, I think in that way I am a role model.

In summary, we have shown in this chapter that the comedians we interviewed approach their professional aims in autonomous ways and on their own terms. They often use humor, both on and off the stage, in ways that both provide a space in which a shift in power dynamics can occur in favor of people with disabilities and in a way that helps manage the emotions of disability—for themselves and others (Cahill and Eggleston 1994; Francis 1994). Breaking through the fifth wall requires an understanding of where the audience is. It is a performance strategy that can be used on the street corner or the corner bar as well as on the stage. This strategy involves risk and the creative talent to break through the wall. It also requires courage to face the potential consequences of what lies on the other side. The "bite" of humor, as Carr calls it, involves explorations of life in the raw and requires that comedians meet people where they are in order to then lead them over a new edge—toward a place where fluidity is required and absolutist thought is challenged.

We have said little until now about specific theories of humor—why we find something funny, or not—and how these theories of humor might inform our understanding of disability. Are there ways, for example, that humor theories and models of disability overlap, intersect, and correspond with each other? How are various types of humor being used by professional comedians with disabilities to support or subvert various models of disability or lenses through which disability has been historically viewed? In the next chapter, we explore how the creative process reflected in the complex intersection between activism and comedic performance in which these comedians work might help us understand in new ways the connections between theories of humor and models of disability. Through exploration of the common analytical ground between humor theory and disability theory, our analysis gives primary attention to the theory behind comedic action of performance, an element of the literature on humor and disability that is currently lacking. While our analysis thus far has addressed humor as a vessel that carries narratives of disability to the broader public, in the next chapter we go further to focus on humor as a method of (re)constructing, (re)interpreting, and (re)framing particular narratives of disability in private and public performance.

5

Creating New Narratives

Every August for twenty-five days, in over 3,000 different shows, the Edinburgh Fringe Festival (the Fringe) draws over 2 million people to see cabaret, circus, comedy, dance, musical theater, opera, and other artistic performances. The biggest art festival in the world is not juried, giving it an accessible, unstuffy feel. You might see jazz next to jugglers, comedians performing for a crowd of young children (a challenge for comedians who are forced to clean up their acts for the kids), or the next big thing. Rowan Atkinson and members of Monty Python played the Fringe before making it big. If it is possible to become the center of the Fringe, stand-up comedy has done it. In recent years, disabled comedians and disability comedy have become part of that center. In 2005, Simon Minty and coproducer Steve Best assembled a group of comedians to perform at the Fringe in a lineup known as Abnormally Funny People. Tanyalee Davis was already a seasoned comedian when her invitation came. Liz Carr, who was an administrative assistant and amateur actor at the time, was at the beginning of her comedy career. Minty had extensive experience as a disability trainer, but little time on a comedy stage. Chris McCausland was leaving a sales career. Just two days before the group's debut for a test audience, they came together to rehearse for the first time within the brick interior of a British pub. For veteran comedian Davis, it was a chance for some global exposure. The others had a shot to get their voices on the stage for the duration of the festival—a solid twenty-nine-night run. By taking their work to the center of the Fringe and other venues, Abnormally Funny People and the other comedians we interviewed are bringing new narratives of the disability experience to the general public. As Terry Galloway points out, the humorous narratives of disability constructed by these comedians are hard to "just walk away from." They are using the comedy stage to shake up existing narratives of disability and create new ones in their place.

In this chapter, we take an interdisciplinary approach—drawing on theoretical perspectives from humor and disability studies, and our interviews, to analyze humor and comedy as sociocritical tools that can be used to reorder, disorder, question, and reconstruct traditional narratives of disability. We saw in Chapter 3 that the lens through which disability is viewed by the general public (or a particular audience) affects the kind of humor that is deemed acceptable and funny. In many cases, too, humor has helped to solidify the predominance of a particular disability model, working to turn that model into a formula story of disability within a particular social time and place. A *formula story,* or cultural narrative, is a story about types of people doing types of things. These narratives are widely circulated and reinforced by news media, arts and cultural performance, and public policy. They can also be the basis, or the result, of conscious social movement activities (Loseke 2007). In this chapter, we pay particular attention to the moral, medical, and social models of disability because these have evolved over time into contradictory formula stories of disability—circulating widely and influencing public views of what it means to be disabled. We use the term *disability lenses* in this chapter to denote formula stories about disability in order to differentiate these widely circulating public narratives of disability from the more formal models of disability considered by disability scholars. In the sections that follow, we examine the interaction between four theories of what makes something funny (superiority, relief, inferiority, and incongruity) and the moral, medical, and social lenses on disability. We also consider superiority, relief, inferiority, and incongruity as types of humor that can serve as active agents in the creation of new narratives of disability. In other words, just as scholarly models of disability have correlates in the types of formula stories or lenses through which people tend to view disability, scholarly theories about why we laugh are grounded in particular types of humor that occur in everyday life and on the stage.

In this chapter, we make a case for the theoretical complexity of humor by demonstrating how various theories and types of humor can function as *analytical tools of social life.* That is, the very thing that makes something funny can contain its own specific critical and evaluative elements and approaches to social inquiry and activism. Folly, in other words, can function as a form of critical consciousness, providing new understandings of the disability experience. These theories are ideal types and are not mutually exclusive. The types are often merged in real-world instances of humor.

Particular attention is paid here to humor as a form of communication for dispersing new narratives and to the "cultural expertise" of comedians (Francis 1994). We give primacy to two critical contributions that the comedians we interviewed are making: (1) their humor shifts the framing of disability issues from the moral and medical to the social; and (2) they do this in a way that keeps the embodiment of disability front and center, literally. As the social aspects of disability are invoked through humor, the bodily aspects of disability are also related through performance of disability—on and off the stage. Drawing these interdisciplinary links between humor theory and disability, we believe, brings needed attention to the complex theory behind the comedic action of performance. Indeed, there are ways in which these comedians embody theory onstage.

As we saw in Chapter 3, when stories about disability have been told using humor, they have mostly been constructed by people without disabilities—often in disabling ways. Humor narratives carry significant cultural power. Humor can be (and often is) used to oppress. It can, however, also be used to empower and counter the tragedy narrative of disability as well as to resist and fight back against disabling humor. The ability of a marginalized group to tell its own stories through humor presents a critical opportunity for autonomy and action. This is clearly articulated by Nina G., who puts a contemporary voice to the centuries-old problem of representation:

> I'm in a very f-f-fortunate position because I get a chance to tell my st-story, and most people with disabilities do not. Oftentimes people who stutter, their stories get misappropriated by others. Like in *One Flew over the Cuckoo's Nest,* or *My Cousin Vinny,* where we are represented as laugh-laugh-laughing stocks, or incompetent, or we kill ourselves in the end. It was not until I was s-s-sixteen and was watching the Howard Stern Show that I saw someone I could relate to: Stuttering John. And my joke there is when a f-f-feminist with a disability says the only place she saw herself reflected was on the How-How-Howard Stern Show then you know there is a problem in the media.

In the sections that follow, we consider each of the four theories of humor. For each theory, we begin by describing its historical links to a disability lens or lenses. We then use interview data to describe how modern comedic performers employ the particular type of humor described by the theory within the context of twenty-first-century narratives of disability—paying particular attention to how they use the type of humor to resist or contest existing, disabling assumptions about the disability experience. We end this chapter by drawing comparisons between the work of these performers and emerging scholarly models of disability—including critical realism and crip theory. These models are being proposed while the social model is still in the process of becoming a formula story and may influence cultural narratives of disability in the future.

Tired Jokes: Superiority Theory and the Moral and Medical Lens on Disability

As we showed in Chapters 2 and 3, ridicule, especially of those with disabilities, is one of the oldest forms of humor. The idea that humor originates from hostility and aggression, ending with feelings of personal victory, is one of the oldest explanations for why we laugh. The superiority theory of humor has occupied the work of a number of philosophers and social thinkers such as Plato, Aristotle, Thomas Hobbes, Arthur Schopenhauer, and Sigmund Freud. Humor and laughter, according to this theory, are generated from the supposed superiority of those laughing at the inferiority of others. Since it is a form of humor based on ego and downward evaluative comparisons between self and others, it is no surprise that the supposed misfortune of others often plays a key role. This form of humor has strong links to traditional interpretations of disability, especially judgmental interpretations that privilege the able-bodied. For example, Hobbes argued that laughter was caused by "some deformed thing in another, by comparison" resulting in others suddenly "applauding themselves" (Hobbes 1840, p. 125). He believed that the "the passion of laughter is nothing else but a sudden glory arising from some sudden conception of some eminence in ourselves, by comparison with the infirmity of others" (Hobbes 1840, p. 13). This type of humor generally focuses on individuals; it positions the source of blame or liability at the personal level, rather than blaming broader ideals and norms. It often does so with a specific set of evaluative standards or criteria that relate to both moral and physical attributes of the joke's target—thereby putting the target in his or her place while also reinforcing norms and assuring the audience that they, unlike the target, uphold these norms. Henry Bergson (1911) argued that it can even be aimed at correcting our neighbors.

This view on why we laugh has clear links to the moral and medical lenses of disability, but superiority humor is perhaps most unequivocally associated with, and justified by, the moral lens through which impairment is seen as the result of moral failure. People are assumed to be disabled because they, or their parents, have failed to uphold the norms in some way. This view of disability gives license to jokes at the expense of people with disabilities since they are assumed to be morally inferior (or the product of morally inferior parents). While this kind of disabling humor was most common in earlier periods of history, it persists today. The modern use of superiority humor reinforces lingering public perceptions that disability is an inferior state of being. Consider the following joke by Jimmy Carr: "I don't know how to describe it to people who didn't see the Paralympics. It's sort of like a children's book where all of the broken toys have a picnic" (J. Carr 2010). He goes on in this routine to suggest that the British team that won the silver medal in football was beaten out by "some kittens" that won the gold medal. Carr's jokes are deeply rooted in an understanding of disability as inferiority. They serve the ego needs of the joke teller and those who laugh at the joke.

Jimmy Carr is not alone in employing this kind of disabling humor on the modern stage. In 2010 at the Hexagon Theatre in Reading, UK, Scottish comedian Frankie Boyle mocked people with Down syndrome during his stand-up routine. Referring to them as "Mongoloids," he mimicked the way they talk, ridiculed their haircuts and clothing, and argued that they are "destined for an early death" (Boyle, as quoted in West 2010). When disability is viewed through a moral lens and impairment is assumed to be caused by a moral failing, these kinds of disabling jokes can be told with impunity. They may even be seen as a form of moral or social corrective.

Under the assumptions of the medical lens, however, tension around the connection between humor and disability arises from the questionable practice of demeaning people who have suffered a tragedy. While it is generally considered acceptable to feel superior to and make fun of people who are deemed to be morally inferior, many people feel uncomfortable about the idea of making fun of people who have suffered through no fault of their own. The medical lens of disability problematizes superiority humor as applied to disability. This may be the source of the public application of rules of political correctness, which we consider in the next chapter. Of course, nondisabled comedians and members of the general public still make jokes in which disabled people occupy inferior positions, but they don't do so with complete impunity. In Boyle's performance described above, for example, two audience members began whispering to each other about whether they should leave. Boyle called one of them out, asking what they were saying. Sharon Smith replied that her five-year-old daughter had Down syndrome and she was upset by the joke, to which Boyle replied, "Ah, but it's all true, isn't it?" Boyle, whose 2010–2011 tour was called "I Would Happily Punch Every One of You in the Face," later called the interaction with Smith "one of the most excruciating of my career" (Boyle, as quoted in Walker 2010). However, just two years later Boyle took widespread criticism again for Tweeting the following: "I'd love to have the skill and dedication of some of these Paralympians, almost as much as I'd like to have some of their meds" (@frankieboyle, August 29, 2012) and "Things haven't all gone smoothly at the Paralympics. I hear the blind highjump's [*sic*] cancelled after two Labrador's [*sic*] were hanged during training" (@frankieboyle, August 29, 2012). Boyle was later released from a contract with Britain's Channel 4, which was also covering the Paralympic games. Other contemporary comedians have come under similar censure. Ricky Gervais also received harsh criticism in 2011 for his use of the word "mong" in some of his tweets, along with pictures of himself making faces. Gervais initially defended himself, arguing that words change and that "mong" did not have the same meaning anymore. The UK's Daily Mail Reporter (2011) pointed out, however, that *The Oxford English Dictionary* says that the word refers to a person with Down syndrome and that it is "now generally regarded as offensive." Gervais later admitted that his use of the word was "naïve." The examples of Jimmy Carr, Boyle, and Gervais illustrate that superiority humor continues to play a disabling role on the comedy stage, but that the widely circulating formula story of disability as illness and personal tragedy problematizes the practice and limits the degree to which public performers can get away with it.

That these kinds of jokes still get exposure at a time when cultural ideas of disability have progressed to at least some degree (due to the social activist strategies associated with the social model of disability) attests to the lingering temptation to make jokes at the expense of others to bolster feelings of self-worth. This kind of humor is often used to circumvent control by veiling socially unacceptable feelings of superiority in the mask of play. Theorists such as Freud (1928) and Gershon Legman (2006) recognized this function, especially the ways that humor can provide an outlet for aggression. "Under the mask of Humor, our society allows infinite aggressions, by everyone against everyone. . . . In the culminating laugh, by the listener and observer . . . the teller of the joke betrays his hidden hostility and signals his victory" (Legman 2006, p. 9). Such hidden hostility tends to rear its head most when progressive changes threaten the dominant group. Racist, sexist, and ableist jokes often have surfaced as an outlet of backlash, where the last uncontrolled arena of the dominant group—the informal institution of interactional speaking—is the mechanism to exert some control and power. In a changing world, then, this type of humor offers members of the dominant class an escape from challenges to the existing relations of dominance and power from which they have traditionally benefited. They can reinforce their positions of dominance through superiority humor more readily than through rhetorical argument. The power and cultural significance that these jokes carry, as well as their importance as indicators of social attitudes, have received attention within the critical race, gender, and disability studies literatures (Bemiller and Schneider 2010; Coogan 2013; Weaver 2010). In disability studies, there is broad agreement that this kind of humor can be disabling, and the results of our interviews support this agreement. Disabling superiority humor, no doubt, remains prevalent within everyday interactions in the form of ableist, racist, and sexist jokes, or any form of humor at someone else's expense. This is the kind of disabling humor that Galloway decries when she says that it's not humor when you tell a demeaning joke about a person who "is in a position that is weaker than you . . . in that case, you're a bully." As Galloway implies here, most superiority humor is aimed at someone, but it also serves to reinforce lingering notions that people with impairments must in some way deserve their fates. In this chapter, however, we are also interested in ways in which superiority humor is used by disabled comedians to contest, resist, or fight against disabling assumptions through disability humor. While representation and voice remain a significant challenge to the disability community as a whole, we saw in Chapter 4 that most of the comedians with whom we spoke indicated their use of humor as both a sword and a shield—a form of power and a method for defense and advocacy. Indeed, as we explored in Chapter 3, humor has long been used as a vocal chord as well as a sword against the more powerful.

Superiority humor, in particular, provides a much greater spectrum of opportunity for resistance than is evident on the surface. A good illustration of this can be seen in Liz Carr's Superman joke in which she says: "I love my superheroes, I do. My favorite was, of course, Superman. And I was very, very excited when Christopher Reeve became a cripple" (L. Carr 2010). Taken literally, this kind of joke could be seen as an example of superiority humor that would be considered questionable under the assumptions of the medical lens. Liz Carr appears either to be wishing a medical tragedy on Reeve, or poking fun at him for having suffered one. The punch line, however, shows that what she is really doing is much more complex. After letting the audience squirm a bit, she says: "'Save me from this burning building!' He replies [*imitating Superman, breathing heavily*]: 'There's no. lift. Lois. You're. fucked'" (L. Carr 2010). Carr's point is not that Superman is now inferior; rather, she uses hyperbole as a method to get to the second half of her joke in which she powerfully demonstrates that some very real barriers (lack of elevators) can present obstacles even for the "Man of Steel." Carr's joke shows that superiority humor can be used to problematize the medical lens that equates disability with impairment by focusing attention on barriers. In this and other aspects of her work, Carr demonstrates how superiority humor can actually be used in more complex and nuanced ways to reorder, reverse power, give voice to underrepresented perspectives, and focus audience attention on important issues such as accessibility. Attacking the Man of Steel is a way of exploring how disability can be a great leveler of the power hierarchy—exposing previously privileged people to the indignities of living in an inaccessible and stigmatizing world.

Other comedians we interviewed also give examples of using superiority humor to turn the tables by framing not disability itself but traditional able-bodied interpretations of disability as morally inferior. Josh Blue, for example, told us in his interview:

> I take the piss out of myself. Pretty much throughout the show, but by doing that it leaves the door wide open for me to take the piss out of you too. . . . And to point out that you're ignorant about disability or your preconceived ideas or whatever it is. You know, I find the harder you are on yourself, the easier it is to get away with being rough on other people.

When Blue says that he "take[s] the piss out of" himself to be able to "take the piss out of" the audience, he is reversing the usual order of power and dominance that exists in interactions between individuals with and without disability. Nina G., whose online material includes a bit called "Shit Fluent People Say to People Who Stutter," also reverses this order in her work. She says, "Most of my humor points the the finger a-at everyone else." As an example, she describes a joke she often tells in her stage performance in which a man she is meeting for the first time pressures her when she stutters on her name while introducing herself: "If I am in the midst of my 'N-N-N,' what the guy will do is this [*hand motion for 'hurry up'*]. Yeah, this [*hand motion*] fucking helps me . . . this and telling me to 'spit it out.' Those are very helpful things. I'll be like, 'Is that what a girl does when you take your dick out?' You know, 'Where's the rest of it?'" Her use of superiority humor here functions as a mechanism to defend herself from what she calls a "microaggression." This particular joke operated as a form of individual triumph when the interaction was taking place. In this personal encounter, she deftly outmaneuvered the man by turning the joke around so that the final punch line came at his expense, punishment for his cruel impatience. By telling this story to an audience during her stage performance, she illustrates that she is capable of powerfully defending herself with wit. Her public performance also serves as a warning to those who might engage, or have engaged, in the same kind of microaggression toward people who stutter. From the powerful position of the stage, she uses superiority humor to warn others not to behave in this ridiculous and offensive manner.

Relief Theory: Humor as an Outlet, Humor as Liberation

A number of important theorists, including Freud (1928), Herbert Spencer (1860), and Schopenhauer (1964), have addressed the relief functions of humor. Typically, they have written about humor as a tension release mechanism—a way to blow off steam. Relief humor about disability is also directly connected to the medical lens through the assumption that people who experience tragedy use humor as a coping mechanism—they laugh to keep from crying. As we discussed in Chapter 2, humor has most often been considered in the literature as a source of hope and hopefulness, particularly in times of stress (Herth 1993; Vaid 1999; Vilaythong et al. 2003). In both the cultural narrative of disability as tragedy and the literature on coping, the value of humor is framed in opposition to other value-laden words with negative associations such as "struggle," "suffer," and "endure."

Relief humor is also used to blow off steam in disabling ways. For example, in contexts in which political correctness and progressive cultural openness to new groups restricts openly xenophobic sentiments, humor can provide an outlet for these sentiments. In the case of racism and sexism, for example, humor has been used to target certain groups as a scapegoat for aggression and resentment over progressive social change. In the specific case of disability, the joke might become a safe vehicle for the reassertion of ideas about able-bodied superiority associated with the moral and medical lenses of disability. When framed as a harmless form of play, aggression can be shielded from critical reaction. The shield behind which the aggression hides is the argument that these are jokes, after all, and should not be taken seriously. (In these cases, we can see superiority humor and relief humor working in tandem.) The comedians we interviewed, however, indicate that relief humor can also be wielded by individuals with disabilities as a powerful tool. It can be used to put others at ease with the issue of disability in order to get them to move past the impairment to other things (Stebbins 1996). In this way, it is used to counteract pity associated with the tragedy narrative of disability. This may involve making light of difficult situations with humor, or showing a sense of humor as a way to relieve the discomfort of others or the awkwardness of the situation (Cahill and Eggleston 1994). As discussed, in Chapter 4, Kim Kilpatrick says that using humor to relieve awkward situations results in better public treatment from others. As a child, Davis used this kind of humor to gain acceptance in an often hostile world: "I know growing up I got teased so much. . . . I don't know if I had any snappy comebacks or stuff like that, but I think I always tried to be . . . the life of the party or tried to be very friendly . . . so that people would like me." As an adult performer, Davis uses much more sophisticated forms of relief humor to warm her audience up so that they can see past their discomfort with her disability. Used carefully, relief humor can be a catalyst for interactions that might not otherwise take place. It can open doors and break down barriers. But relief humor can also function to put others at ease at the expense of addressing why they are uncomfortable in the first place. Traditional norms can be perpetuated when the dominant group remains comfortable rather than challenged. Using relief humor to put people at ease in ways that empower, rather than further disable, people with disabilities takes skill and experience.

In addition to providing relief from the frustrations of living with impairment (as in humor as a coping mechanism) and putting others at ease, humor can provide an outlet for pent-up frustrations associated with living in an ableist world. In other words, it can be used to cope with the frustrations of the disability experience rather than the frustrations with impairment. Humor can provide relief from stress, anger, and confusion wrought by the actions of others as well as a method to process all of these. Humorous approaches to these frustrations can be converted into material for comedic performance. This is clearly articulated by comedian Nina G.:

> Having a disability is a-a-a minority experience . . . things happen to you and you have to interpret those. The little things that come at you all day long and

they put stress on you. So if you are able-bodied you might not have those the way I do, and I think those add a lot to what you see in the world and how you use that to make humor out of it. And then get others to see it.

Relief humor can relieve stress by providing an interpretive frame for both comedians and audiences. But as Nina G. argues, it also relieves by providing a tool to actively oppose dominant ideals. Or, as John Morreall writes, "To laugh in breaking free of constraint can also be to laugh in scorn at those who have been constraining one" (1983, p. 20). Relief humor can serve as a form of resistance against those who have controlled the school lines and employment lines as well as the punch lines. To the extent that disability humor exposes constraints that are structural and cultural in origin—institutions, norms, rules, built environment, and so forth—it can certainly function as a form of relief. Relief can come from processing, understanding, articulating, and acting against these social constraints, providing an empowering way to encounter social constraints and to resist and act on them. In this way, relief humor can also reinforce the social model perspective of disability.

More than simply an outlet for frustration, though, relief humor has a role to play in the issue of representation invoked earlier in this chapter. Tobin Siebers, for example, has challenged those working in the various areas of disability studies to specifically find new ways to represent pain:

> The greatest stake in disability studies at the present moment is to find ways to represent pain, and to resist current models that blunt the political effectiveness of these representations. I stress the importance of pain not because pain and disability are synonymous but to offer a challenge to current body theory and to expose to what extent its dependence on social constructionism collaborates with the misrepresentation of the disabled body in the political sphere. (2006, p. 177)

Disability humor can provide a forum for the representation of pain—be it physical or emotional—as well as an acceptable outlet for releasing it. For the comedian, as well as audience members, there is relief in being able to articulate and represent the experience of pain. Relief comes from exerting power over pain, particularly through reframing discussion and debate and privileging a new perspective. In this way, relief humor that depicts pain actually bridges an important gap within disability theory: it brings the material body back into critical discussions of disability. If the medical model approach to disability neglects the social by putting too much focus on the individual disabled body, the social model has been critiqued for shifting the focus too far away from the body (Siebers 2006; Shakespeare 2014). A number of disability studies scholars have called for reembodiment within disability theory—a critical approach to society that brings the realities of the corpus back into the discussion (Zola 1991). Disability humor of the relief variety can serve this function. This type of representational relief can bring previously taboo topics into a public arena in ways that confront the audience visually and aurally. Sometimes, as Nina G. explains,

> I once had a woman stand up and say "I-I can't take this" and she walked out, and she yelled it . . . what I said at the time, because in comedy if you can make someone walk it means that you're so offensive. . . . I was like "I'm so gangster at this that I just open my mouth and they walk." So that's how I framed it there but if that ever happens again I'm gonna say . . . "If I could go through m-m-middle school with this, then you can get through the next s-s-seven m-m-minutes."

So, relief humor serves structural and interactional functions. It can provide representational relief by embodying the complexity of disability onstage, but it also operates as a significant tool of navigation and sense-making in everyday interaction. This type of humor can function as an active tool to push back, invert power, mock, satirize, and parody systems and people who act as the oppressor while also providing relief. The knowledge that one possesses this powerful resource can be a source of comfort. In this way, relief humor intersects with a number of the aims of disability studies, particularly as a way of embodying the disability experience through new representational narratives.

Inferiority Theory: The Ironic Power of Self-deprecation and the Sympathetic Imagination

One of the most common themes that arose during our interviews with comedians was the idea that successful comedy tells a story to which audience members can relate. In other words, humor is a relational tool that can help foster a sympathetic imagination through a story. It should not be surprising, then, that when the relationships between humor and disability have previously been examined and acknowledged in social science literature, the analysis has often centered on humor as a method of circulating narratives of what disability means. For decades, scholars have argued that narratives are critical to individual identity construction and meaning making (Loseke 2007; Mishler 1995). Individuals tell stories to themselves and others to make sense of the vagaries of everyday individual and collective experience. As a narrative form, stand-up comedy has the potential to help audience members who lack disability experience to see disability and impairment in new ways. For this to happen, however, comedians must tell stories to which the audience can relate. Careful, skillful, strategic use of inferiority or self-deprecating humor is one way they accomplish this. Maysoon Zayid says that she takes her audience on a journey in which they forget about her disability—relating instead to the other aspects of her life with which they can more easily identify.

This notion that we laugh at the things to which we can relate turns superiority humor on its head (Solomon 2002). Rather than laughing at someone, inferiority humor involves laughing with them. And rather than derision, this theory sees the essence of humor as benevolence (Carlyle 1829). As Galloway put it in her interview: "There is . . . , I believe, a weird compassionate underpinning in humor." While we use the accepted term *inferiority* to discuss this theory, the self-deprecating humor of the comedians we interviewed did not typically involve positioning themselves as inferior to the audience; rather, the laughter stimulus is the performance of modesty and human vulnerability, the ability to see the self and all of humanity as less than ideal. Wedded to this vulnerability is empathy and compassion about the shared human experience. According to Daniel Wickberg, this complexity is part of the evolution of humor over time from chiefly being a method of staking one's status to that of a tool for self-understanding, relating to others, and fostering community:

> Where humor had once referred to the eccentricities of an objective character type, by the early twentieth century it had come to mean, for many, a mode of regarding the self as an objective character, while for others it meant a mode of regarding other as if they were oneself. The sympathetic imagination thus presented a paradox for the meaning of humor. Humor came to mean both a sympathetic laughing at others and a laughing at oneself. The imaginative capacity that could bridge the gap between the observer and the object of his observation, that could bar one from treating other persons as objects, was the very same capacity that allowed one to affect a detachment from the self, and consequently to treat oneself as an object. In the twentieth-century value scheme associated with humor, sympathy with others' mishaps was good; yet, in the common phrase, one shouldn't take oneself too seriously. (1998, p. 68)

Disability humor can provide this imaginative capacity by bridging the gap between performer and audience. Consider this example provided by Galloway:

> We got really tickled one day . . . in the workshop . . . I'm talking to a woman with cerebral palsy, who has . . . difficulty being understood, who is being interpreted by a woman who is blind. . . . We were gonna do a joke about that. . . . We thought it was hilarious [*laughs*] because it's . . . funny the way it gets muddled or garbled. . . . The difficulty of repeating and repeating and repeating . . . [to get] one little thing across.

Galloway considered creating a performance skit based on this interaction because it links disability content to the widely shared human experience of misinterpretation and misunderstanding in chains of communication. In this case the communication breakdown is exaggerated by the added complication of different forms of impairment. The intent here is not to mock people with impairments. Rather, the aim of such a skit would be to encourage the audience to laugh together at something funny about the collective human experience. This is not to suggest that there are no risks in using inferiority humor in a context in which people with disabilities have so often been targets of disabling superiority humor. Galloway went on to point out that even when the intent is good, feelings can be hurt, and she expressed second thoughts about creating this particular skit. She has, in fact, sometimes been criticized by people with disabilities for her work, and she welcomes this type of critique as it opens up important discussions about disability and representation: "This happens sometimes too, and that's just wonderful. That's exactly what you want people to say: 'Wait a minute, that's not me!' We have to rethink. Or we have to redo it. . . . So, there are many interpretations of this." There are many interpretations because of the complex ways that humor appreciation functions. It builds on personal history as well as personality traits (Ruch and Hehl 1998). In the case of disability humor, reception of humor also depends on one's ideas about how disabled performers should publicly represent disability. Add in individual variations in social capital and access to power, and the picture becomes more complicated. While other groups have long histories of self-deprecating humor, the modern disability community that emerged from the civil rights era does not. Inferiority humor, then, walks a fine line. Galloway puts it this way: "I found humor to be extraordinarily complicated. It amazes me that we can even have . . . these collective outbursts of laughter."

Yet if we return to the history of the relationship between disability and humor, we find some important historical connections and functions of this type of humor. In many cases, it is too simplistic to read inferiority humor as pandering or as rejecting part of the self to assimilate into the larger culture:

> The notion that laughing at oneself somehow implies self-abuse or self-effacement is based on a premise of ideal perfection. The implicit assumption underlying such categorization is that the object of humor ideally has no faults at all. . . . Self-effacement, providing that it is not comprehensive, may in fact be consistent with a reality-based self-image and not abusive. (Juni and Katz 2001, p. 139)

As Samuel Juni and Bernard Katz indicate, the victim role of self-deprecating humor has important links to the role of the jester. As we showed in Chapter 3, the jester often used himself to parody the king, so under the surface of what appeared as self-effacement was a more searing critique of those in power. Rather than a defense mechanism, it was an offensive strategy. The jester would lure in the audience with a more comforting style of humor, which put the jester in "control of the 'next move'" (Juni and Katz 2001, p. 139). Then, in a more powerful and aggressive manner, the jester ensnared the conscience. This form of humor, then, is not always about passive assimilation (Juni and Katz 2001).

Might modern self-deprecating humor also be used in a powerful and aggressive manner to set up the audience for comfort and put them at ease, allowing the comedians to then hit them with more searing stuff? Nina G.'s willingness in the first five minutes of her routine to "work the audience through the fifth wall," provides an example of this. This strategy can prepare the audience for what is to come later in the routine. Indeed, while it might seem like various comedy bits are often strung together as unrelated stories, points, themes, or jokes, when taken as a whole routines often are put together purposefully. Most of the comedians we interviewed strategically use self-deprecating humor, often building toward a later joke at the expense of the audience or to point to misperceptions about disability. Blue might throw out jokes like these: "I tried to hail a cab and a pigeon landed. Set it free and now people think I am a magician" (2006a) or "My nickname is the human vibrator" (2006b). As Blue suggests, self-deprecating jokes can either set up the audience for a more searing critique that is forthcoming, or a single joke might begin with self-deprecation but end with Blue looking clever or witty, and often calling out the behaviors of other people, such as this one: "Did anyone make fun of me when I was younger? Um, they're still making fun of me, shit. I've found that self-deprecation, you know, you make fun of someone else before someone else can. And then they do it and they look really dumb. Reverse teasing. Cripple comes out on top!" (2008). This approach exemplifies the arguments made by Juni and Katz (2001) that self-deprecating humor can lure an audience in and prep them for what is to come.

What follows self-deprecation is not always critique, though. Sometimes self-deprecation is used to point out the (incongruous) advantages that come with disability: "There are some real perks to being short. There's a special scheme. We get a cheap taxi. It's really great. I hail the taxi and once it pulls over 17 of my short mates just bundle in" (Minty, as quoted in *Abnormally Funny People* 2006) or "Don't feel sorry for me. I'm 21 years old and I still get into the movies for the kid's price" (B. Williams 2008). At other times, comedians employ self-deprecation in savvy ways to invoke connections between disability and sexuality. Nina G., for example, told us how she uses humor to counter the prevailing and damaging assumption that women who stutter are not sexy. After hearing from other women who stutter that men, but not women, who stutter can be considered sexy by others, she used the power of the stage to contest this belief:

When I heard that I just wanted to cry and it it makes me almost w-w-wanna cry now that these women who are just really smart and wonderful and beautiful don't think of themselves a-as sexy because they grimace a little bit when they talk [*laughs*] because they they repeat the same sound and I wanted to reframe that. . . . One of my jokes is um a-after I do the n-n-n-n-n-n, I say "I-i-isn't that s-s-sexy?" . . . I say "Well I-I think that's kind of sexy. I think I'm kind of a S.T.I.L.F., which is like a M.I.L.F., a-a stutterer I-I'd like to fuck." . . . Stutterers . . . all around the world . . . st-started u-using that . . . I even heard that at the British stuttering convention. They were going around calling me, c-c-calling each other, S.T.I.L.F.s. And to me that was very exciting.

Like Nina G., some of the comedians we interviewed employ self-depreca-tion as a technique to engage and then reframe disability—as clever, sexual, advantageous, or as a bridge into more critical territory. Indeed, self-deprecation can be deftly used as a tool of power and autonomy to navigate, reframe, and engage in emotion management with the audience. Making oneself seem vulnerable can be employed as a strategy for more transgressive activities, though care must be taken not to employ catego-rical inferiority.

Subtle self-deprecating humor that is cleverly and strategically used can also demonstrate to an audience that people with disabilities "are not so fragile as to need constant condescension through political correct-ness" (O'Connor 2002, p. 8). It is the skillful mixing of self-deprecation with sharp wit that shatters stereotypes and reshapes the generalizations that come with traditional understanding of disability, ultimately giving a more complex and relatable understanding of disability (R. J. Berger 2013). While their styles of humor are radically different, inferiority humor can be seen in the work of comedians such as Blue and Liz Carr. Blue cleverly approaches his CP with the following joke: "So I'm not really a religious man, except when I shave. That's my time to talk to God!" (Blue 2006a). Liz Carr regularly addresses the physical realities of her own body, including a joke where she likens herself to Michael Jack-son coming back from the dead, but then moonwalking in her wheelchair. In both cases, these comedians integrate self-described aspects of inferi-ority with strength and cleverness. They speak to their own individual peculiarities, embodying disability onstage while also speaking to larger issues of beauty and insecurity. Rather than categorical inferiority, though, their sets include a range of jokes that portray their own under-standings of themselves and society, astuteness, wit, and the ability to navigate everyday life.

Rather than a medical model attempt to fix disability, inferiority humor, when used with skill and purpose, depicts the diversity and complexity of impairment—Blue's CP impacts his ability to hold a razor, and he links his particular experience of shaving with hands that do not always obey his will with the ordinariness of everyday life to which everyone can relate. Like Geri Jewell's joke about the difficulty of trying to apply mascara with cerebral palsy, Blue pulls the audience into his particular experience by drawing connections to a general experience to which most members of the audience can easily relate. Rather than lumping different groups together into one category called "disabled," or assuming that impairment dominates all other aspects of life, inferiority humor paints a diverse and complex picture of human life—including disability. Yet like relief humor, inferiority humor also functions as a form of embodiment. By naming and bringing attention to impairment and addressing the taboo, these comedians invoke what Tobin Siebers (2008, p. 29) calls "corporealities." As opposed to an approach that focuses only on social structures, this type of humor has the potential to bring the personal experience of impairment back into the discussion. Yet the potential of this type of humor, carefully and consciously used, is not only to paint a complex picture of the personal experience of disability, but also to translate this to the experience of all—to perform the imperfection in the human condition through humor. This ability to focus attention on difference and distinction while also universalizing difference is clearly articulated by Wickberg:

> Humor, however, asked the observer to measure the temperament, the concrete peculiarity and eccentricity of characters, to see in the details of character everything that was odd and peculiar, even incongruous, and then, having established the individualism of difference, to collapse the distinction between observer and observed through an act of abstraction by which those differences were dismissed. Humor both emphasized the differences between persons and acted as a solvent of those differences; it emphasized the distinctive, concrete peculiarities of the unique individual and the universal abstract sameness of all human beings. (1998, p. 68)

The ability to link the personal to the universal is not an aim limited to disability studies; it remains an essential element of the broader sociological imagination. In this way, inferiority humor challenges social ideals that are often used as a measuring stick of human worth. To see oneself as less than ideal not only requires an understanding of the rule, but also the strength and power to name this in a public place and the wit to link specific personal experiences to larger elements of the human experience.

Jokes as Reframing: Incongruity Theory, the Social Model Lens of Disability, and Beyond

The logic behind the incongruity theory of humor begins with the notion that, in any social structure or society, there are widely accepted expectations of order: norms, patterns, rules, forces, responses, and values. When these expectations are not met, hilarity can ensue. As argued by German philosopher Schopenhauer: "The cause of laughter in every case is simply the sudden perception of incongruity between a concept and the real objects which have been thought through it in some relation, and laughter itself is just the expression of this incongruity" (1964, p. 76). The more unexpected the incongruity, Schopenhauer believed, the more intense the laughter would be. With jokes, it is often this unexpected twist that generates the punch line or climax of a joke. Yet often with this type of humor, the twist itself also creates a cognitive shift by pointing out the paradoxical, ironic, or inconsistent aspects of social life. Consider this joke by comedian Nina G., who points out the absurdity of how people respond to her in social situations: "People would come up to me at parties and say, 'I saw *The King's Speech*. . . . I just want you to know that I saw *The King's Speech*.' So I asked my friend who is Chinese American if people were going up to her saying, 'I saw *The Joy Luck Club*.'" Her juxtaposition of these two scenarios creates an ironic incongruity that makes the audience laugh, but also unveils for them the ways in which people with disabilities are subjected to interactions that are not typical in the nondisabled world. This type of humor relies on an understanding of conceptual ideas, social phenomena, and shared popular culture. In this sense, humor based on an incongruous aesthetic entails an innately more analytical and sociological orientation, in comparison to superiority humor, which generally relies on a simple evaluation of the characteristics of an individual. To understand incongruity, we must have a grounded sense of norms in a given social context. Without these standards as a form of comparison, there is no ridiculous, absurd, opposite, or unexpected. We get no surprising twist without a path of widely shared normative expectations. In Nina G.'s example, identity provides a context that shapes the acceptable response: in one case (disability), the response is considered by the general public to be appropriate. In the other (ethnicity), it seems absurd.

If this form of humor is a thinking person's game involving cognitive play and a sociological imagination, then there is much to be learned from incongruity, and even absurdity, revealed through humor's lens. French philosopher Bergson articulated this in his classic essay *Laughter:*

> For the comic spirit has a logic of its own, even in its wildest eccentricities. It has a method in its madness. It dreams, I admit, but it conjures up, in its dreams, visions that are at once accepted and understood by the whole of a social group. Can it then fail to throw light for us on the way human imagination works, and more particularly, social, collective, and popular imagination? Begotten of real life and akin to art, should it not also have something of its own to tell us about art and life? (1911, p. 1)

In this seminal essay, Bergson argued that humor and the social are inextricably bound through incongruity. Whatever light the comic throws on the social depends on observations of incongruity between human ideals and realities—the light must first pass through the lens of incongruity. One of the lessons bound up in humor, particularly humor as a social force, is social correction. Bergson (1911) believed that society requires that individuals have some level of elasticity to be molded to common norms and values. Laugher, then, can restrain the eccentric, or those who might have separatist tendencies. Fear of being laughed at offers powerful restraint.

The type of incongruous humor Bergson wrote about obviously functioned to reinforce dominant social norms, but incongruous humor can also serve the opposite function as a mirror to reflect and invert traditional norms and values and as a form of resistance. In this sense, incongruous humor is still used as a social corrective, but in ways that challenge the values of the dominant group while giving voice and power to the subordinated through incongruity. Consider this joke by comedian Alan Shain: "My brother and I went out to eat, and the waiter asked my brother how many menus we wanted. I answered the question with, 'There's two of us at the table, so I think we'll take 4 menus.' The waiter did, in fact, bring us 4 menus" (Shain, as quoted at Alanshain.com 2012). Shain evokes audience laughter by portraying the unexpected, which is also a window into the unexperienced. In so doing, his joke reframes and provides a cognitive shift in which the indignities of public treatment are laid bare. While the individuals in the encounter about which he jokes, such as the waiter, most likely miss the view through this window, the audience members' laughter is evidence that they process the irony at hand. Shain and the other comedians we interviewed wield incongruity as a reframing tool that evokes laughter while also injecting an element of critical social analysis.

To get a better understanding of the reframing functions of humor—as a lens into the unexpected and unknown elements of the disability experience—consider how the work of these comedians threads incongruity humor and critical theories of disability together onstage. Specifically, these comedians link incongruity humor and a social model lens on disability. From a social model perspective, socially created structures—such as language, architectural barriers, stigma, and ableist assumptions—limit individuals with disabilities much more than impairment does. The work of the comedians we interviewed lies clearly within the social model framework. The medical and individual tragedy views of disability are often targeted by their humorous critique. Nina G., for example, sees her comedic performance as a direct challenge to the medical model. "People assume it's the medical model or the moral. That either we're not trying hard enough or i-it's our own fault. That you just haven't tried these techniques, and if you did, then you would talk like everyone else. . . . I am comfortable with this. This is the way I talk and it's other people that are the issue." Like Nina G., the other comedians we interviewed also draw on incongruity humor to

counter the tragedy narrative embedded in the medical model lens by pointing to the richness of their lives. Robert McRuer says that one of the foun-
dational issues of what he calls "compulsory able-bodiedness" is that
"people with disabilities embody for others an affirmative answer to the
unspoken question, Yes, but in the end, wouldn't you rather be more like
me?" (2013, p. 372). These comedians perform a negative answer to this
question in very public ways. All of our interviewees clearly indicate to
their audiences that they are at home and comfortable in their bodies.

The result of a humor aesthetic that pairs incongruity with the social
model lens on disability is a humor that turns the gun away from any one
individual, instead putting social structures and society itself in the cross-
hairs of analysis. It targets social norms and reactions to examine how artificial our notions of normal or ideal can be. As we show later in the chapter,
this humor depicts incongruity between social ideals of equality for all with
the realities of everyday discrimination against people with disabilities. It
highlights the dysfunction of social service bureaucracies and the incongruities in what society expects of people with disabilities. This type of
humor deconstructs and reframes definitions of normality, and our notions
of opportunity, by poking holes in our ideals of equality and normal. Yet
incongruity humor can also function to invoke specific and personalized
issues of the body in ways that do not fit with traditional views of disability. A number of comedians we interviewed draw on incongruity humor to
embody disability onstage, especially through stories about dating, sexuality, and athletics: topics often assumed to be irrelevant to the disability
experience. Davis describes to her audiences, for example, one of the "fun"
parts of being married to a man who is six feet tall: "My husband's a great
guy, super affectionate, but I like to freak him out. Like this one time, we
were on the city bus, sitting there side by side, my husband wants to give
me some hugs and some kisses . . . so he leans over to give me some hugs
and kisses, and I'm like, 'Daddy, stop it!!'" (T. Davis 2006). Davis's use of
incongruity highlights the physical difference between herself and her husband while also invoking sexuality—offering a challenge to desexualized
stereotypes of disabled bodies. Similarly, Blue uses the often uncontrollable
actions of his right arm in ways that embody the physicality of disability
and are incongruous with what the audience is expecting. In his *7 More
Days in the Tank* (2006a) special, Blue talks about getting into a fight, and
what he calls the "Palsy Punch": "First of all, you don't really know where
it's coming from. Second of all, neither do I!" Later in the show he
announces not only that he voted, but that he voted Republican. After waiting for cheers or groans from the audience, he looks at his right arm and
says, "It wasn't my fault!" Jokes like these illustrate how incongruity
humor can be used as a lens to explore embodiment and physical humor
related to disability onstage. Through the lens of incongruity and the ana-

lytic frames it offers, comedians can traverse areas of ambivalence and uncertainty, and even the taboo. Drawing on the element of surprise and the incongruous, they are able to navigate a fine line between audience comfort and discomfort within the short distance of a sentence or two.

These comedians draw on stereotypical, often disabling, public assumptions about disability to create incongruity that evokes laughter. In the process, they call attention to, and challenge, the very stereotypes on which they draw. Liz Carr says, "I think it's quite easy to do with disability . . . because almost anything you say is incongruous with our image." From performing sketch comedy as a bingo caller doing "disability bingo" (made up of various disability-related phrases) to a podcast on BBC radio called *Ouch!* (www.bbc.co.uk/ouch/podcast), Carr's work certainly challenges audiences to rethink what they think they know about disability. She sometimes draws on disability stereotypes in shocking ways. In her interview with us, she discussed specific examples from her *Ouch!* podcast that offend some, as they expose raw thoughts and ideas about disability in taboo ways. Carr explained during our interview: "We have a quiz called 'Vegetable, Vegetable, Vegetable.' . . . That's when disabled people come up and we have to guess what's wrong with them by asking them questions. . . . The questions are usually quite offensive. . . . 'If you were born today would you be aborted?' 'If I saw you in the street would I know you were disabled?'"

To be sure, the title of the quiz Carr describes above uses loaded terms that, taken out of context, would be highly offensive. However, the podcast in which it is embedded engages humor to challenge important and disabling assumptions about the lived experience of disability—such as what kind of life is worth living—as well as the effects of these assumptions on public policy. Certainly, it remains unclear whether or how the use of these terms impacts listeners, but the autonomy and quick wit of the podcast certainly present disability in a way that is raw, in your face, clever, and a far cry from tragic, helpless, or weak. Carr's live shows might be even more discomforting to some people with and without disabilities than her podcast. As we have already shown in other chapters, she incorporates taboo elements of embodiment into her routine. She pushes the boundaries visually and verbally, as she described to us in her interview:

> I do a whole Paralympic thing about liking to watch wheelchair users crash, you know, because you know that it's OK. 'Cause at the end of the day nothing's gonna happen to them. You know, "What's the worst that's gonna happen? They'll never walk again?" . . . But the point to all that is about them [the public] saying "Paralympians are amazing. They're so amazing. Look at them and their limbs. Look at the man that runs on blades. Ooh!" And, it's like, you know, it's so "inspirational." I say, "No. They just make the rest of

us look lazy." And you know, they fuckin' do. I'm political and I think most of my jokes make a comment like that.

The set up for this may seem unusually crass, like a cruel form of superiority humor that takes pleasure in wheelchair users crashing. But this is where incongruity theory provides insight. Carr's use of the image of crashing wheelchairs as a shocking hook sets up the audience for a more sophisticated examination of the "Supercrip syndrome"—the extraordinary disabled hero who overcomes issues of disability by working very hard (Mitchell 1989; Silva and How 2012). Through this bit, Carr explores notions of being inspirational and engages embodiment by challenging a disability corollary of racial color-blindness. She argues that good comedy means acknowledging the reality in the room:

> You know what they're thinking. . . I think if you acknowledge what's happening, that comes across in any comedy. I mean, that's a basic thing you're taught, . . . you know, acknowledge what's happening in the room. . . . If a glass is broken in the room, comment on that. . . . It will relate to what we've all heard. . . . So basically, . . . whether it's your appearance, or whether it's their reaction, . . . go with that and acknowledge it.

From her own references to what she looks like to commenting on having to be carried onto an inaccessible stage in her wheelchair, Carr's embodiment combined with her wit can help create incongruity for audiences by conflicting with their expectations about what disability is and who should perform humor onstage. Carr does not simply acknowledge her physical reality, however. She also draws on her understanding of the audience's interpretations and thought process in relation to these realities. She explained to us in her interview that in one piece called "You're Not Laughing," she actually works the audience through some of their discomfort:

> I go, "I can feel you. You're not sure. . . . I know that you're not laughing because your granny uses a wheelchair. I know you're not saying anything because you think Stephen Hawking is amazing. I know you're not [laughing] because you know you work with people like me." It's kind of an accumulation of knowledge. What I'm getting at is knowing that people's reasons for not being with you are vast. . . . So, you can be naughty with it and go, "Don't worry. I know what you're playin' at." Or, you can be warm as well and go, "It's OK. Don't worry. Laugh at it. It's fine. . . . You're not going to hell. You are, but so am I." Or that kind of thing.

Like most of the comedians we interviewed, Carr does some work during the show to make sure the audience is with her as she leads them into uncomfortable terrain. But like Blue, just when they get comfortable, she can pull the rug out from under them.

Acknowledging the reality in the room sometimes requires more than a nudge or a wink, especially when the audience members actively resist. Most of the comedians we interviewed described attempts by others to define what is appropriate to perform onstage. Often these comedians use a combination of their bodies, movement, and words as a way to challenge and reframe these views. While speaking about disarming the audience, Davis explains audience discomfort with her embodiment and the ways that her performance was incongruent with some audience members' expectations of how she should behave:

> In the UK they are so uptight. . . . You have to disarm them. I've had people in the front row turn their chairs away from me 'cause they're so uncomfortable and they cannot get over the fact that I'm so comfortable. And I've had people come up to me after my shows going, "You shouldn't talk about your condition," and I'm like, "Oh, so me talking about how wonderful my life is makes you uncomfortable? Whose fucking problem is that?" [*laughs*] And in their minds I should not be as honest in talking about it as I do.

There can be no doubt that Davis's humor challenges perceptions of disability in some audience members. Her level of comfort with and in her own body rankles some who believe she should not talk about her "condition." But she wants to use her body, "the visual aspect," to put people in her "zone." Nina G. also spoke to how she uses embodiment to push the audience from the very beginning of her routine. She gave a specific example, too, of how she has responded to an audience member who, literally, did not want to face the reality of stuttering onstage during her performance:

> They're afraid to laugh. Once I had a woman, . . . it was at a at a at an open mike, and I started to st-stutter and she did this [*covering her face*]. So I went r-r-right up i-i-in in front of her and I went right in her face I did n-n-n-n-na-na. [*laughs*] A-and and it won them [audience] over . . . and she totally got it, and she was fine after that. . . . I called her out on it, in a way that was funny too.

Nina G.'s performance clearly acknowledges the reality in the room. This type of embodiment brings a critical realism to the stage, generating an incongruity that discomforts while also creating audience laughter. There is no sterilized attempt to hide her stuttering; absent are victim-oriented assumptions that it is embarrassing for the speaker or inappropriate for the stage; gone also are psychological explanations of stuttering as an indicator of a lack of confidence. Nina G. has the stage and, more importantly, the microphone. And her performances, such as "Stupid Shit Fluent People Say," expose raw thoughts and ideas about disability in taboo ways. Flaunting her name for the crowd with an extended "Nnnnnnnnnnn-Nina," she is no exhibitionist seeking pity or a cheap laugh; quite the opposite, in fact.

The combination of embodiment with powerful and often searing wit creates an incongruity that challenges, reframes, and often functions as a social corrective.

In Sum: Humor and Comedy as Sociocritical Tools

In this chapter, we have used the everyday experiences and stage performances of disabled comedians to explore connections between humor aesthetic and critical analysis, with specific attention to the relationships between theories of what makes something funny (types of humor) and lenses through which disability is viewed. Incongruity humor is, by far, the most common form of humor used by the comedians we interviewed, most often as a way to hold everyday practices and norms up to ideals. Disability humor based on incongruity relies on understandings of cultural and social phenomena as a standard form of evaluation and analysis. All of the comedians with whom we spoke use this kind of humor onstage as a method of unveiling and analyzing common treatment of people with disabilities (and as a way to highlight the unknown advantages of the disability experience). Many of their most critically insightful jokes are built from this kind of humor. By focusing on social structures and norms, this form of humor is most clearly aligned with the social model approach to disability.

Relief humor is also commonly used onstage and in everyday interactions. Indeed, many of the comedians we interviewed spoke of their use of relief humor from an early age as a way to navigate social situations and to make others feel comfortable. This has translated into their stage performances, particularly when they face the challenge of working audiences through the first five minutes of a show so that they are comfortable with listening to the rest of their set (which typically involves more socially critical humor about disability and other issues). Relief humor, then, can be used as a strategy for getting audience members comfortable with going into unknown, awkward, or critical territory. This type of humor also provides representation of voice and can operate as a tool of navigation and sensemaking.

While a few comedians expressed discomfort with using inferiority and superiority humor as part of their performance, others see these two types as part of a toolkit that can be employed both on and off the stage. Superiority humor tended to be used more often offstage, as a way to enact agency, particularly during interpersonal interactions in which someone was using disabling humor toward the comedian. Superiority humor can also be used in the retelling of these situations during a stage performance, with the offending party as the butt of the joke. Rather than simply putting down individual members of the audience, superiority humor is often employed by the comedians we interviewed to unveil ableist assumptions and actions of others at large. Earlier in this chapter, though, we also reviewed jokes about disability that function to devalue and stigmatize, jokes that link superiority theory humor to individual-, moral-, and medical-lens interpretations and evaluations of disability. This type of laughter not only serves the ego needs of the storyteller, but also functions to reinforce traditional norms of disability, particularly in their focus on the individual and pathological. Superiority humor is, however, also used by these performers to fight back against devaluation, discrimination, and ableist thinking.

Inferiority humor, on the other hand, is used in ways similar to relief humor—as a bridge to a comfort level that is needed for audiences to receive more socially critical humor. Indeed, some of these comedians used self-deprecation as a tool of power and autonomy to navigate, reframe, and engage in emotion management with the audience. Making oneself seem vulnerable is employed as a strategy for more transgressive activities to come in the show. This might begin, as Blue indicates, with "taking the piss out of" himself before he turns his scrutiny to the rest of society. Several of the comedians we interviewed describe ways that they acknowledge the fact that audience members are not sure whether or not to laugh, and they draw on relief and inferiority humor as a performance strategy to address this. These comedians strategize carefully and take steps to make sure the audience is with them, perhaps because they have had to do the same their entire lives while navigating everyday interactions.

In this chapter, we have shown that all four of the types of humor we explored can be employed as tools in the arsenals available to comedians who seek to use humor to push back against the disabling assumptions, beliefs, and actions of people living in an ableist world. That is, all four humor paradigms can provide an interpretive lens through which individuals can be encouraged to bear witness to the unexperienced and to reframe their previous ideas of normality. In everyday life and onstage, these performers move deftly among these types of humor to keep the ball rolling and the laughter coming. In the process, they challenge the assumption that disability is a tragedy and that disabled lives are individual problems in need of pity and remedial effort. As Oliver Double (2005) points out, observational comedy has almost overused the "have you ever noticed approach." These comedians build their observational comedy on a "you've never noticed" approach using a range of humor types that allow them to mediate the complexity of the disability experience, as Minty articulates:

> The joy of the social model if you use it in terms of comedy is that you are poking fun at everyone else for not thinking about this, for behaving a certain way like that. . . . So, there is a joy in that sense that you can just use all the things that are wrong, but you throw it back at them and you say by the way

"I am not quite happy about this." And if you do it well enough and witty enough, they laugh because they say, "Oh, yeah, how stupid are we?!"

In performing new narratives of disability through humor, the comedians we interviewed are aligning themselves not only with a tradition of comedy that unmasks "inept individuals" and "ineffectual institutions" (M. Davis 1993) but also idealist philosophical traditions that have examined the gaps between actual social life and cultural ideals (p. 218). Indeed, by doing so, they are reexamining and redefining notions of competence (and incompetence) using various types of humor as their tools. Their work is not unlike that of the sociologist:

> The humorist, then, is a humanist—sustaining a precariously balanced world-view between pairs of extreme philosophic positions that give precedence to extra human structures and processes. . . . Like the humanist constructivist schools (Marxism, Simmelianism, symbolic interactionism, and dramaturgical sociology), comedy assumes that human beings construct their organizations of the world, though henceforth experience its structure as preexisting naturally. Unlike even these constructionist schools, however, comedy focuses not on how the world is constructed but on how it can be deconstructed. (M. Davis 1993, p. 310)

The comedians we interviewed articulate the disability experience and address the goals of disability studies in ways that are more accessible and more embodied than the approaches that are typical of academic scholarship. Paradoxically, these comedians communicate issues of pain in an entertaining manner while also demonstrating that the disability experience can be filled with many pleasures—making this form of humor all the more worthy of appreciation as a sophisticated form of entertainment activism. These comedians are purposefully using comedy in ways that parallel a gathering sentiment in disability studies—specifically, that the disability experience is neither solely individual nor solely social in nature and, thus, it cannot be fully understood using a single, traditional lens, such as the medical or social model (Anderberg 2005; Shakespeare 2006; Siebers 2006). Rather, disability is viewed as a complex experience that stands at the intersection of bodily differences and a social location embued with negative cultural valuations, social disadvantages, and economic oppression. This emerging view, which is sometimes referred to as "critical realism," can be seen in the humor of the comedians we interviewed. They are using humor in ways that bring to a broader audience this nuanced and holistic view of disability in which bodily experience intersects with ableist public attitudes and the social and economic disadvantages imposed on people with disabilities in everday life. These comedians spoke candidly about their bodies in ways that foreground impairments such as stuttering, physical stature, facial features, and bone structure, rather than attempting to sterilize these elements or focus only on the sociocultural disadvantages of the disability experience. This sophisticated multidimensional treatment of disability is quite consistent with the nuanced views emerging among academics and activists.

The comedy performed by the comedians we interviewed is also consistent with the purposefully transgressive perspective of crip theory, which is emerging at the intersection of disability studies and queer theory (McRuer 2006; Kafer 2013). Crip theory argues against the binary distinction between normality and disability and challenges the very idea of normality itself. Disability is seen as a measuring stick in relation to which normality or ablebodiedness is constantly compared in the never quite successful attempt to define what it means to be normal. Through this lens, disability is conceived as an "open mesh of possibilities, gaps, overlaps, dissonances and resonances; lapses and excesses of meaning when the constituent elements of bodily, mental, or behavioral functioning aren't made (or *can't be* made) to signifiy monolithically" (McRuer 2006, pp. 156–157). The work of the comedians we interviewed provides a cognitive shift in thinking about the body. The coupling of traditional expectations about impaired bodies with wit and cleverness provides an incongruity that challenges binary thinking about ability and disability. The comedians we interviewed revel in the "open mesh of possibilities" provided by their bodily and social experiences. They use the "dissonances and resonances" of the disabilitiy experience—both physical and social—to challenge the idea that disability is a tragic state. They actively challenge audience assumptions about the normal-disabled binary and its relationship to life well lived. They are comfortable in their bodies and use them as props to push public attitudes beyond monolithic ideas of what normality signifies and what kinds of bodies should be signified as normal. Perhaps the most transgressive element of this comedy, though, can be found in the ways that it parallels public sociology, a point we explore in more detail in the final chapter of this book. Generally, discussions that draw on the social model and emerging models of disability remain quarantined to academic and policy-oriented arenas while a more medical lens on disability still dominates the widely shared cultural narrative of disability. The work of these comedians creates and amplifies new narratives of the disability experience in very public and more accessible ways.

This kind of social indictment, however, is not undertaken without risks. The comedians we interviewed for this project certainly ride a fine line of comforting and discomforting the audience. Their work is criticized by people with and without disabilities. However, their work and its critique raise a range of questions relevant for disability studies, mainstream audiences, and activism: What is funny, and who should be laughing? What makes a joke about disability funny? Is it okay for someone with a disability to joke about himself or herself, or does the humor have to turn the gun on everyone else? Should all humor be subject to political correctness, or free from censorship? What roles do shared meaning, context, and the First Amendment play in these debates? These are issues faced by the comedians we interviewed in very real ways, on and off the stage, as they do the delicate dance between entertainment and activism. We explore the strategies they use to manage these tensions in the next chapter.

6

Disability Humor in a Politically Correct World

I'm pretty opposite of PC [politically correct], man. I'll say the truth. I feel
like I say what you shouldn't say. Well, it's funny—you're laughing because
you understood that this is what it is, you know?   —*Josh Blue*

Liz Carr did not begin her career as a professional stand-up comedian until
she was thirty years old. She is quick to point out, however, "That doesn't
mean I wasn't funny before then . . . it just means that's when I started to
. . . perform publicly." Once she hit the stage, her career took off quickly,
partly, she believes, because "when you're a disabled comedian, I think
you're more memorable." Carr now appears as a regular on the BBC's
crime drama series *Silent Witness,* but has also performed stand-up as a solo
artist as well as a member of the groups Nasty Girls and Abnormally Funny
People. If it is not shocking enough that she hosted the call-in game "Vegetable, Vegetable, Vegetable" (described in the previous chapter), she is currently writing *Assisted Suicide—The Musical.* Carr clearly pushes her audiences beyond their comfort zones and works at the boundaries of what
many would consider politically correct. Carr is far from alone. A number
of comedians with disabilities use humor in ways that test notions of political correctness. Chris McCausland opened one of his performances with
Abnormally Funny People by pointing out to the audience that they were in
for "a blind guy doing observational comedy." Steve Day, a deaf comedian
in the Abnormally Funny People lineup, pulls back the curtain on the everyday follies he experiences by explaining to the audience that closed-caption
television can quickly alter a harmless interview statement from "let me
give you an analogy" to "let me give you anal joy." As winner of the 2006
Last Comic Standing reality show and a headlining solo comedian who
tours frequently, Josh Blue might be the most widely known and financially

successful disabled comedian. In spite of his popularity, though, his work is not without critics. The title of his first stand-up album alone might be enough to raise the eyebrows of the politically correct: *Good Josh, Bad Arm*. His use of his arm as a separate character onstage, scolding it ("Bad arm, bad arm!") for its uncontrollable actions associated with CP might leave some people with disabilities and their advocates cold. Like many comedians doing disability humor, though, Blue does a complicated dance, sliding between self-deprecation and witty, clever, and power-filled riffs that challenge traditional views of disability. A categorical dismissal of his work as pandering self-effacement or trading on his disability oversimplifies the way in which he uses the richness of humor as an analytical and humanizing tool.

Comedians who incorporate disability into their acts can open themselves to the same challenges as those who have addressed other sensitive topics, such as race, class, gender, and sexuality, from the comedy stage. In a very public way, these entertainers must balance artistic autonomy with the pressure of representing an entire group. As we showed in Chapter 4, this can be a daunting task for comedians such as those we interviewed for this project. They want to connect with a broader audience while communicating the story of their own lived experience. Primarily, though, they want to make people laugh. They have to spin many plates to successfully negotiate this tricky social territory. Blue, himself, would likely poke fun at the metaphorical image of him attempting to spin all of these plates with palsied hands. This juggling act poses a number of poignant questions: Who has poetic license to joke about disability? Should comedians with disabilities be required to represent or speak for all people with disabilities? How do comedians doing disability humor think about political correctness as it relates to comedy and humor?

These questions are not easy to answer. Disability studies scholars and activists take a social constructionist view of disability. Rather than equating disability with impairment, this perspective defines *disability* as the social and cultural disadvantages that are layered on top of impairment by the labor demands of Western capitalism, barriers imposed by negative public attitudes and structural constraints, and hegemonic notions of what constitutes normal human experience (Barnes 2005). Disability studies scholars often critique the everyday turns of phrases that, with or without intent, create and reinforce these disadvantages. They draw attention to obvious hate speech (use of "spastic" and "retard" as pejorative words), but also to more subtle ways in which language can demean people whose bodies do not fit neatly within current notions of what constitutes the normal. By deconstructing everyday turns of phrase, disability scholars seek to illuminate the power and potentially damaging effects of speech, actions, and the printed word (R. J. Berger 2013).

While artists, poets, writers, and performers (especially comedians) have historically been given license to say, write, and do things in the context of their creative work that would be deemed inappropriate in other settings, their work is being increasingly scrutinized for language that falls outside the realm of what is sometimes called the "politically correct." This trend creates an interesting paradox for comedians with disabilities who seek to use disability content in performance. Both the comedian and the disability scholar often use language as a tool to illuminate the taken for granted—to stare back at society. While the disability scholar is generally concerned with ways in which others use language and actions as weapons of oppression, the comedian uses language and action as tools with which to stir up an audience. The language and antics used by comedians with disabilities to do this stirring up may, however, be considered politically incorrect by members of the audience and even inappropriate by some in the disability movement. The purpose of this chapter is to explore the ways in which comedians with disabilities negotiate this sticky territory.

In this chapter, we examine the intersections of disability humor and political correctness, with particular attention to the ways that disability humor problematizes popularized notions of what it means to use politically correct humor and language. We begin with an examination of the convoluted evolution of the term *political correctness* and the various ways it has been used in and outside of academia. We then move on to explore the ways in which disability humor can inform and bring complexity to debates about political correctness. We pay particular attention to the tension between politically correct ideology and praxis within the context of disability humor, and we utilize our interview data to explore ideas about political correctness held by modern professional comedians with disabilities who must grapple with this complex challenge in their work.

Evolution of the Term *Political Correctness*

The term *politically correct* is as debated, elusive, and contested as is the term *disability*. The meaning has shifted, and still shifts, with the agenda and philosophical stance of the person who employs it as a modifier. Feldstein argues that the term *politically correct* originated in the 1940s among members of the left as a slur against others "who shared similar views but adhered to a rigid acceptance of communist dogma" (1997, p. 4). This left-on-left critique emerged amid socialists' moral condemnation of communist alliances with Joseph Stalin and Adolf Hitler; Jewish socialists, in particular, mocked those who "unthinkingly took the party line" (Feldstein 1997, p. 4). Both Richard Feldstein (1997) and Eugene Goodheart (1993) point out that the term *politically correct* then continued to be used for left-on-left mockery in academia in an ironic way that unveiled an inability to live up to one's own ideals and as a way to distance oneself from someone with similar ideas but more uncouth ways of communicating them.

Feldstein (1997, p. 6) argues that conservatives have more recently appropriated the term *politically correct* to create a mythic form of it that inflames and divides. Conservative writers and commentators—such as editor Roger Kimball (2003); political commentator and author of *Illiberal Education* (1991), Dinesh D'Souza; and philosopher Alan Bloom, who penned *The Closing of the American Mind* (1987)—use the term *politically correct* to vilify those who take a social constructionist stance. They argue that those who insist that language is not innocent and can be a powerful tool of oppression that should be used thoughtfully by people in the public trust are totalitarians seeking to legislate freedom of speech and thought in the name of multiculturalism while engaging in a moral relativism that leaves no room for objective truth. Kimball jests that political correctness amounts to:

> Self-righteous, non-smoking, ecologically sensitive, vegetarian, feminist, non-racist, multicultural, Birkenstock wearing, anti-capitalist beneficiaries of capitalism—faculty as well as students—who parade their outworn radicalism in the classroom and their social life. Mostly, it was a joke. Who could take these people seriously? It was also overwhelmingly an academic phenomenon, a species of rhetoric and behavior that flourished chiefly in and around the protected redoubts of the university. (Kimball 2003, p. 139)

While this is clearly parody or mockery, members of the conservative right find nothing funny about what they view as paternalistic moralizing by the political left. The issue of language—what and how to talk about certain issues—has become a dominant lightning rod and definitional frame for public interpretations. Conservative ire often centers on politically correct surveillance and control of language as a means to change social consciousness. And while language is only one element of political correctness, it highlights a severe philosophical difference in interpretations of reality held by its proponents and critics.

Believing that life is ordered in an objective way that can be known empirically, conservatives value traditional forms of knowledge such as nature or "wisdom" (Choi and Murphy 1992). They take a positivist stance that reality is knowable in a value-free way. Social constructionists, on the other hand, argue that our understanding of reality is shaped and controlled by social context and power relations (Choi and Murphy 1992). Indeed, unlike conservatives, social constructionists (including disability studies scholars) seek to unpack issues of power in all aspects of life; and, since they see language as essential to our construction of reality, they take keen interest in linguistics. Critics argue, however, that intense scrutiny of language can be taken too far. Geoffrey Hughes, author of *Political Correctness: A History of Semantics and Culture,* points out that attempting to avoid "judgmental terms" can create "an artificial currency of polysyllabic abstract euphemistic substitutions" (2009, p. 14). Social constructionists counter that this kind of linguistic or semantic engineering is necessary to attempt to "level the playing field" and "improve social relations" (Hughes 2009, p. 25).

While these debates rage within academe, the practice of policing words and language, along with a redefinition and appropriation of the original term *politically correct,* has leaked out to the general public (Choi and Murphy 1992; Feldstein 1997). In this chapter, we use the terms *politically correct philosophy* and *politically correct movement* when talking about the ways in which the surveillance of speech is publicly enacted as opposed to the theoretical perspective of social constructionism that, at least in part, gave rise to this surveillance. That is, in this chapter, we are talking about a formula story of what is politically correct. This public construction of political correctness, with its narrow focus on the rigid censorship of language, masks some of the more seminal aspects of social constructionist thought: an emphasis on representation of diverse voices, a focus on unraveling certitudes and dogma, contesting the sacrosanct, and a focus on power and hegemony (Choi and Murphy 1992). These elements of social constructionist philosophy certainly share common ground with the transgressive functions of disability humor that we have explored in previous chapters. Just as social constructionism argues that reality is constructed and alternative ways of knowing are possible, humor presents alternative perspectives and ways of understanding social life, especially from the perspective of those outside of the dominant group. As we showed in Chapters 2 and 3, humor has long provided a voice for the powerless. Yet in practice, the two rarely work in tandem, despite their common ground. Indeed, stand-up comedy's brash political approach has long pitted it against more subtle interpretations of humor. Early on, criticism of political stand-up comedy came from members of the conservative right, who attempted to exert their own ideas of correctness. The contemporary omen who brashly put comedy on a collision course with modern notions of political correctness and norms of decency was comedian Lenny Bruce, whose act was aimed at challenging conservative notions of decency, power, and authority. Bruce "pried open the vault containing society's taboos" (Boskin 1997, p. 78) by taking on every major social structure— organized religion, the legal system, racial boundaries, and sexuality. Long before the politically correct movement attempted to insert created or altered language into the mainstream lexicon, Bruce did his own original experimentation with new words and new meanings for old ones (Boskin 1997, p. 78).

Bruce collided with the word police, literally, meeting legal resistance throughout the 1960s for his specific choice of words. Ironically, he forced the conservative establishment into politically correct word control long before the conservative right began critiquing the politically correct movement for similar activities. His arrest on an obscenity charge in San Francisco ended in an acquittal, but this began a series of arrests and court appearances that would attempt to control his language. Other arrests followed in Los Angeles, Chicago, and New York City. After undercover officers observed his New York City show in 1964, he was indicted for violating New York Penal Code 1140: "obscene, indecent, immoral, and impure drama, play, exhibition, and entertainment." Despite testimony from a range of artists, cultural critics, and sociologist Herbert Gans, Bruce was sentenced to four months in the workhouse. Bruce died, though, before his appeal could be heard. Bruce's humor challenged "objective truths" of religion by satirizing sacred figures. Likewise, he exposed US cultural hypocrisy on issues of race and injected sexualized language into his show to demonstrate how language is a construction that depends on context.

Bruce's repertoire did not include disability. However, his attacks on the sacred objective definitions of decency and obscenity and his control of language ushered in an era of more radical, politically active comedians. This newer style of comedy engaged multiculturalism and differed greatly from the more status quo, apolitical lounge acts that preceded it. In the midst of the civil rights movement and well into the 1970s, these comedians brought a more subversive, taboo, and critical humor to the public in ways that entertained, discomfited, and pushed cultural boundaries. In an era of rapid social change and unrest, they continued the legacy of using humor to speak truth to power and to address the forbidden. Comedians such as Dick Gregory, Mort Sahl, George Carlin, Richard Pryor, and Jackie "Moms" Mabley were all doing prototype stand-up comedy that directly challenged power and authority (Krefting 2014). Similar to Bruce, they faced significant resistance from the conservative right in their efforts to speak truth to power in such public ways. Pryor's short-lived 1977 variety show faced regular censorship (Haggins 2007). Despite its success as one of the highest-ranking shows on television during its three seasons, *The Smothers Brothers Show* was eventually canceled by CBS executives who regularly censored the brothers' satirical take on controversial political topics. Carlin's bit "7 Words You Can't Say on Television" landed him in jail for disturbing the peace while performing the routine in Milwaukee. A radio broadcast from Carlin brought a Federal Communications Commission (FCC) complaint from a member of Morality in Media, which later led to a 5–4 Supreme Court decision upholding the FCC's right to regulate indecency. All the while the liberal establishment, including activists and academics, often lent their support to the work of these comedians. During

Bruce's obscenity trial, for example, sociologist Gans and Columbia University literature professor Daniel Dodson testified on the social functions and value of Bruce's work (Collins 2002). This more multicultural humor of the 1960s and 1970s, though, soon gave way to a backlash, as the social Darwinist policies of the 1980s Ronald Reagan administration found cultural parallels in entertainment and humor (Boskin 1997). The backlash included the use of brash insults aimed at particular groups and, ironically, it helped to spawn the strong public movement of political correctness in the late 1980s and early 1990s.

When the activist and revolutionary philosophies behind the brash and overtly political humor of the 1960s and 1970s met a virulent conservative backlash during the 1980s, jokes became a way to cloak aggression and inject scapegoating, and even hate, into the public psyche. Shock comics and hate humor of comedians such as Andrew Dice Clay enjoyed immense popularity, as did jokes about gays, AIDS, and people of Polish descent. This led feminist comedian Kate Clinton to quip, "Under Reagan we had the de-regulation of comedy" (Clinton, as quoted in L. Williams 1991, C1). Not coincidentally, the politically correct movement developed significant momentum during this period and, in the process, a surveillance of humor emerged in ways that sparked significant debate and discussion around what it means to make a joke. Stories of the decline of humor due to political correctness swirled in major newspapers, including the *Washington Post, New York Times,* and *Wall Street Journal,* with the latter announcing in 1997 that "humor hits a bear market" (Pullam and McGeehan 1997). Universities also began cracking down on student-generated humor deemed inappropriate, from a school-funded student newspaper at George Washington University to the antics of the Pep Band at the University of Virginia.

In the midst of this environment, the politically correct movement appeared humorless, and many of its proponents were criticized for taking themselves too seriously. Indeed, Roger Kimball and others have pointed out the "earnest humorlessness" (2003, p. 164) of politically correct champions. One reason that politically correct philosophy and practice have been lampooned is that many humorists and comics resist efforts at conformity and control, or any constructed forces of appropriateness. As Doris Lessing, no fan of the conservative right, argues (2004, p. 76), political correctness is a form of dogma, and dogma and humor are incompatible. The symbolic aspects of political correctness, particularly language, thus become easily satirized. Kimball, for example, skewered major newspapers for refusing to run housing advertisements that were thought to exclude various groups because of words used to describe the properties. Claiming that a home had a "good view" discriminated against the blind, listing a house "on a quiet street" excluded the deaf, pointing out a property as "walking distance" to the train was "unfair to the lame" (Kimball 2003, p. 160). Even liberal-leaning Carlin, who made a career of dissecting language use, critiqued political correctness in a classic bit on euphemisms, which also invokes disability:

> I don't like words that conceal reality. I don't like euphemisms. . . . And American English is loaded with euphemisms. . . . Americans have trouble facing the truth, so they invent the kind of a soft language to protect themselves from it, and it gets worse with every generation. For some reason, it just keeps getting worse. I'll give you an example of that. There's a condition in combat. Most people know about it. It's when a fighting person's nervous system has been stressed to its absolute peak and maximum. Can't take anymore input. The nervous system has either [click] snapped or is about to snap. In the First World War, that condition was called *shell shock*. Simple, honest, direct language. Two syllables, *shell shock*. Almost sounds like the guns themselves. That was seventy years ago. Then a whole generation went by and the Second World War came along and the very same combat condition was called *battle fatigue*. Four syllables now. Takes a little longer to say. Doesn't seem to hurt as much. Fatigue is a nicer word than shock. Shell shock! Battle fatigue. Then we had the war in Korea, 1950. Madison Avenue was riding high by that time, and the very same combat condition was called operational exhaustion. Hey, we're up to eight syllables now! And the humanity has been squeezed completely out of the phrase. It's totally sterile now. Operational exhaustion. Sounds like something that might happen to your car. Then of course, came the war in Vietnam, which has only been over for about sixteen or seventeen years, and thanks to the lies and deceits surrounding that war, I guess it's no surprise that the very same condition was called post-traumatic stress disorder. Still eight syllables, but we've added a hyphen! And the pain is completely buried under jargon. Post-traumatic stress disorder. I'll bet you if we'd still been calling it shell shock, some of those Vietnam veterans might have gotten the attention they needed at the time. (Carlin 2001, pp. 197–198; emphasis in original)

Using humor, Carlin unraveld the ways that the mechanical fixes of language can dehumanize, and he did this in a particular way to make the exact point that politically correct proponents argue: language is not innocent (Choi and Murphy 1992).

Others have taken a similar approach. James Garner, author of *Politically Correct Bedtime Stories,* created an entire series satirizing politically correct thought. He begins by sarcastically admitting:

> The stories were sexist, discriminatory, unfair, culturally biased, and in general, demeaning to witches, animals, goblins, and fairies everywhere. . . . We'd like to think that future generations of fairy tale fans will see this as a worthy attempt to develop meaningful literature that is totally free of bias and purged from the influences of the flawed cultural past. (Garner 1994, pp. ix–x)

In addition to the expected list of bias—sexist, racist, ethno-centrist—he apologizes for inadvertently displaying regionalist, speciesist, and "other types of bias as yet unnamed" (1994, p. x).

In a similar vein, William Safire (1991) spoofs the linguistic methods of political correctness by defining its language as "adverbially premodified adjectival lexical unity." Such critiques point to obstacles that social constructionists face in arguing for the fluidity and subjectivity of truths, as the politically correct movement spawned by this perspective enacts more mechanical and exacting linguistic methods of speaking as a way to raise the consciousness of the public.

Despite its seemingly unnatural linguistic clunkiness and its vulnerability to satire, the social justice elements of the politically correct movement can be observed through disability-related language, which highlights the individual rather than generalized categories. This form of language reconstruction has, at times, coalesced into policy. For example, Rosa's Law, which was signed by President Barack Obama in 2010, requires federal agencies to replace the terms "mental retardation" and "mentally retarded" with "intellectual disability" in federal education, health, and labor laws. (Ironically, the *American Journal of Mental Retardation* made such a change only a few years prior to Rosa's Law.) Grassroots efforts have been made to end use of the word "retarded," including the website www .r-word.org, which has almost half a million pledges to end the use of the word and whose slogan is "spread the word to end the word."

Performance comedy, certainly, saw the implications of such shifts, too. It is not a coincidence that Bobcat Goldthwait's act became stale as cultural and legal interpretations of disability, and the language to describe it, were changing. The reaction to Jerry Lewis in the 1980s and 1990s followed a similar trajectory. What's more, these evolving audience reactions went far beyond efforts of academics who mount arguments within insular scholastic circles. Protest over disability-related jokes when they are perpetrated by comedians without disabilities has increased, as comedians such as Jimmy Carr and Ricky Gervais have found out. In the 2010 documentary *Joan Rivers: A Piece of Work,* the comedian is heckled in Wisconsin by the father of a deaf son after she jokes that Helen Keller would make a great daughter since she could not speak. An audience member responded by yelling, "It's not funny if you have a deaf son." Rivers responds to the critic in the crowd by indignantly chastising him about her family history and lecturing him with the following:

> Let me tell you what comedy is about, you stupid son of a bitch! I had a deaf mother. I also fucked a guy for three years who had one leg! He lost it in France in WWII, and I think it's terrible, because he should go back and

get it because that's littering! Comedy is a way for us to deal with things! (*Stern* 2010)

Rivers later admitted that it was her father, not her mother, who was deaf (Rivers, as quoted in Turnquist 2011). Rivers's experience demonstrates how the issue gets more complicated when the individual biography of the joke teller (and presumed individual license) combines with a form of superiority humor that reinforces tired disability ideologies. This license is often assumed with significant risk, as Tea Party comedian Eric Golub found out at a 2011 rally for Sarah Palin, who is also the mother of a child with Down syndrome and a self-proclaimed proponent of disability rights. Golub stated that "[Sarah Palin] has a beautiful, adorable special needs child. For that reason alone, the left should worship Sarah Palin and adopt her as one of their own. Because the leftist haters are an entire political ideology of special needs children" (Golub, as quoted in "Tea Party Comedian Compares Liberals to Trig Palin" 2011). For his comments Golub was criticized, mostly by the left. (In an irony that illustrates the politics of political correctness, Palin did not distance herself from Golub's comments, despite previously publicly admonishing writers of *Family Guy* and the *Late Show with David Letterman* for referencing her son in jokes.)

There can be no doubt that politically correct thought has been tied to positive shifts in thinking about disability. Yet linguistic strategies of political correctness themselves have been the subject of satire and have even been lampooned by comedians doing disability humor. But this should not be too surprising, given the incompatibility between any rigid dogma and the deconstructive lens of humor. That is, just as they have been used to disrupt conservative approaches to race and gender, humor and comedy can quickly complicate and problematize aspects of political correctness:

> Political correctness is a serious matter, grounded in suffering, prejudice, and difference, and has certainly made everyone consider the plight of others, giving a new emphasis to respect. But it has also provoked a great deal of satire, irony, and humor, which have their place in a study of this kind. Some of it is unexpected: we have become used to Jews and blacks telling jokes about themselves and reclaiming ethnic slurs; but now we have jokes being told about cripples, by cripples who insist on using that designation. Consequently, the earlier tendency to see things in dichotomous terms of plain black and white is increasingly complicated. (Hughes 2009, p. x)

Since the emergence of the politically correct movement, humor scholars have more broadly addressed the topic of political correctness in important practical and theoretical ways that can inform our examination of disability humor. In 1997 nineteen humor scholars engaged in a debate about political correctness, with the interaction published in *Humor: The Interna-*

tional Journal of Humor Research. Their ideas broadly centered on the role that context and ambiguity play in humor. For example, humor scholar Elliott Orring pointed out:

> Context is one of the key elements we normally employ in our efforts to decide among the possible messages underlying texts of jokes. What we often call PC is an unwillingness to recognize or entertain the ambiguities of such expressions; to deny the benefit of the doubt to persons other than oneself. . . . PC is ultimately a form of moral bureaucracy; an attempt to legislate hard and fast rules of social interaction rather than recognize a process in which meaning and intention are constantly being negotiated. (Orring, as quoted in P. Lewis 1997, p. 469)

Humor plays off of merging scripts, double entendre, and incongruities of meaning; ironically, politically correct approaches to humor, function in objective certainty and rule-based approaches. Scholars, Orring argues, can debate what certain jokes mean or the intentions behind them, but political correctness "begins with certain knowledge" (Orring, as quoted in P. Lewis 1997, p. 492). Coupled with this certainty is an interpretation of humor through the lens of victimization, which requires a continuous "monitoring" that detracts from the "sensitivity" necessary to appreciate the ambiguity of a joke (Orring, as quoted in P. Lewis 1997, p. 462). Of course, individuals can laugh at the same joke for very different reasons. John Morreall, for example, poignantly explains in the debate that feminists laughing at a sexist joke demonstrates another realm of enjoying a joke—it can be appreciated for the way it "represents mistaken stereotypes that we know ignorant people endorse . . . what we are really laughing at is the way people think" (Morreall, as quoted in P. Lewis 1997, p. 486). He offers the critically acclaimed and highly rated show *All in the Family* as an example. In essence, this line of thinking implies that, if the same joke can be interpreted in many ways by different people, it makes no sense for the politically correct crowd to assume that its meaning is interpretively fixed.

This unique debate illustrates the wide-ranging perspectives on the ways that humor and political correctness relate to and impact each other. The discussion also spawned a number of questions that are specifically relevant to disability humor. For example, is it insightful and productive to take, as some argue political correctness does (Orring, as quoted in P. Lewis 1997, p. 462), a "victimization" approach to humor? Or, conversely, does censure of humor about certain groups actually function as a form of exclusion, thereby accentuating their "weakness" and powerlessness (Nilson, as quoted in P. Lewis 1997, p. 488)? Does making a group "off limits" to humor actually make them more invisible (Nelson, as quoted in P. Lewis 1997, p. 488)? Is humor as a form of communication categorically different from more serious and formal methods? Or, should we view all forms of communication (artistic, comedic, etc.) using the same lens and criteria, as politically correct proponents do (Ziv, as quoted in P. Lewis, p. 472)? Is being amused by a "linguistic representation" of something through the form of a joke the same thing as experiencing the serious assertion of that scenario in real life (Morreall, as quoted in P. Lewis 1997, p. 486)? These types of questions shed insight into some of the challenges that politically correct thought faces in application to disability humor.

Our interviews with comedians with disabilities suggest that disability humor can contrast sharply with politically correct thought. For example, a version of political correctness that was much more popular earlier in the movement's history—the idea that certain groups lack a voice, or that these groups are completely dominated—gives little credence to the ability of these humorists to construct their own stories in a very public way or open a window into the unexperienced. Likewise, the self-deprecation and inferiority humor that is used by the comedians we interviewed, particularly with the involvement of embodiment, is a much more complex and nuanced performativity than the exploitation and victimization apparent in past use of disability in public performances. This is not to suggest that there is nothing to be critiqued in disability humor. Rather, we suggest that it cannot be encompassed by absolutist or categorical thought. Strict politically correct assumptions that humor about disability always injures lacks an understanding of the role disability humor plays as a form of public sociology—a way of encountering disability.

Disability humor illustrates the way in which humor can complicate more dogmatic approaches to political correctness, especially because it puts representation and examination of power into praxis while simultaneously playing with and challenging some of the more formulaic aspects of politically correct thought and language. Steady Eddy (Christopher Widdows), an Australian comedian with cerebral palsy, for example, riffed with the audience on the emergence of political correctness in the United States in the 1990s: "I just got back from America. I found out something really interesting about myself: I'm no longer disabled. Apparently now I'm physically challenged. Sounds like a bloody game show, doesn't it?" (Widdows 1995). Others, such as Blue, intertwine self-deprecating humor so closely with social critique that they complicate what in past decades was a more black and white view of politically correct. Still others, such as Liz Carr, push the boundaries further, all the while embedding a critical social element in her comedy. (See the example provided in Chapter 5 in which Carr draws on Christopher Reeve's accident to make a point about the inaccessibility of buildings.)

These examples lead us to poignant questions about the complexity of disability humor and the ways in which it complicates politically correct approaches to humor: Should comedians doing disability humor shoulder the responsibility of representation or voicing an entire group? Or, should they have the autonomy to talk about their own bodies the way they want to? Is censorship of performance comedy analogous to the act of censoring or banning books and, if so, shouldn't all progressives, including proponents of political correctness, be as rankled by the former as the latter? Is it productive to simply take one joke in isolation without looking at the larger context, function, and reach of a comedian's performance? As we show from the interviews with comedians, disability humor provides an illuminating lens to examine some of the strengths and weaknesses of politically correct thought, particularly as it approaches humor and attempts to engage issues of disability. The humorist's playful imagination and analytical lens, one that adeptly engages audiences, has much insight to offer the politically correct movement, particularly on the front of reaching a broader public with issues of social justice. This is especially evident considering the paradoxical approaches of social constructionist thought with political correctness in public praxis. Social constructionists often critique conservative thought for its lack of fluidity and its absolutism (Hibberd 2005); yet the public enactment of political correctness often takes this same objective and positivist approach toward humor.

Comedic Views on Political Correctness

> I think the joy of what we do means that some of the political correctness boundaries can be relaxed, particularly because this is our own voice. And I think in that the individual voice is allowed to be heard. —*Simon Minty*

Most of the comedians we interviewed reject the kind of strict politically correct approaches to disability and humor that have leaked into the public narrative. They especially object to rigid public censorship of performance on the comedy stage, which they view as uniquely situated to speak candidly and unabashedly with the audience about life. Blue sees no other place where he can get away with saying the things he says: "Because you're on the stage it gives you that liberty, that poetic license to be raw. I mean I always use Chris Rock as an example. The things he says should not be funny." As a place of freedom, the stage can be an arena in which to directly challenge the tragedy narrative of disability. Liz Carr, who has worked in radio (BBC), television, journalism, and the comedy stage, points out a continuum of freedom and autonomy that exists within these media:

> I do a lot of radio. If I said some of the things I said onstage on radio I'd be killed. . . . If I wrote it in print, it would not get past an editor. . . . But for that ten, fifteen, twenty minutes onstage I can fuckin' say whatever I want, though I mightn't get the response I want. But I could go onstage and say anything. It's the one realm where there is no censorship, . . . and there are no rules. . . .

The audience may not like what you're gonna say and you may not get the response you want, but actually there are so few ways that there is the potential for you to say anything. You could be so topical. That's the beauty of it. By the time you get something past an editor and in the paper or even online, that moment's gone, but something might happen this afternoon that I can then talk about tonight: totally topical, totally relevant and fresh. That's that's the dynamism of comedy.

If the comedy stage provides a unique uncensored venue in which to explore disability in new ways, Carr believes that politically correct control of language can detract from this dynamism. The more practical concerns of disabled people—such as demeaning treatment, inadequate or discriminatory public policy, devaluation of disabled lives, and other real-world issues that these comedians often speak of in their routines—can get lost when there is an overemphasis on surveillance of language. The comedians we interviewed expressed concern that policing words might be taking the easy way out and might actually serve to mask the real issues of discrimination and devaluation faced by disabled people. Carr says, for example,

I do believe in the power of language, ironically, but I think you can do too much over obsessing about . . . words. . . . Why don't the press give a shit about the real issues that disabled people are facing? . . . Everyone gets on the bandwagon about "mong," but what about benefits being cut? People being put into homes? . . . Euthanasia is being talked about as a very real . . . issue over here and I think that's dangerous at the moment. . . . If you wanna get on the bandwagon, do it about something that has real importance over people's lives.

Steve Danner makes a similar argument. He expresses doubt about whether changing the word used to describe him would have a substantial impact on the way he is treated in the world. Regarding the word "midget," which is currently considered an offensive term by the organization Little People of America and many people with dwarfism, he says:

They're trying to wipe it clear of society, but to me, even if they called me a "giant" they're still laughing at me. Even if they call me a "giant" they're still treating me how I've been treated. . . . You're just trying to get rid of a word. . . . It has to be more than one word, you know? Get them to understand why to just stop calling me that. I don't really care about the "midget" word. I couldn't care less, you know? It's just a word. . . . I dropped it out of my vocabulary as much as possible, out of respect for them [Little People of America]. Me, personally, I don't care. Call me whatever you want, 'cause I'm gonna read how you're treating me rather than what you're saying.

The views of Danner and Liz Carr echo Carlin's arguments about language use, particularly that such an emphasis on language can distract and detract from concern with everyday treatment.

A number of the comedians interviewed actively resist the efforts of others to control their own language choice. Several provided specific examples. Like Danner, Maysoon Zayid speaks of choosing her battles, even as others attempt to restrict what she can say:

> So when people come up to me and say, "You can't say 'crazy' and you can't say 'lame,' because those are ableist terms and they make disability a negative thing. You can't say 'crippled,' cripple is a negative word," and I'm like, "Those are words I use to express my feelings." Because what you are doing is focusing on a word and . . . I don't fit into the box of the disabled advocate because I'm like this crazy disabled activist. . . . I am going to pick and choose my battles, and my battle is policy and education. . . . My battles are very specific.

Indeed, Zayid adds that she uses specific words to claim her disability (and reclaim that language) when in front of audiences. She indicates that she will often leave the stage saying, "By the way, I am a cripple." Blue also objects to having people try to tell him what he should not say, adding the twist of people without disabilities attempting to speak with him about the way he talks about disability:

> One time, I had a whole table leave my show and they they waited around the whole time just to like scold me and go, "I have a friend in a wheelchair and I found what you said just just horrible," and I'm like, "Well, why don't you ask your friend in the wheelchair what they think about what I'm saying? I bet they'd really like what I'm saying," and . . . it's those kinds of people who feel like they're doing their disabled friend justice by standing up to me. I'm like, ". . .You obviously haven't heard a word I said." Because as mean as I am about disability, I'm only saying it because it makes you think. Or it makes you go, "Oh, oh man he's aware of how I'm looking at him."

The comedians we interviewed, however, were not in complete agreement on the issue of using words in performance that have often been used to demean people with disabilities in everyday interactions. Simon Minty expresses concern about the confusion that might be faced by people without disabilities if people with disabilities are using terms that many consider hurtful: "I get slightly irked if someone constantly uses the world 'crippled,' maybe, and I'm saying, 'Hang on guys, you spent twenty years telling everyone off for using this damn word.' . . . And I just think it is confusing. So jump one way or the other. . . . Eighty percent of these people are now bunkered because they don't know what to do."

Danner spoke of the business side that must be considered when determining how far comedians should go in using controversial language onstage:

> Well, comedy is supposed to be that one thing where we're not supposed to be censored. . . . Comedy's like that one thing that you're not supposed to censor yourself. You're supposed to be able to say whatever's at the top of your mind, whether people like you or not, you know? You are your own person . . . but at the same time there's the business side of it. How often am I gonna get hired back? I'm always looking more at the business side of it like: "Oh that'll get me hired." If I have one or two people that are offended by what I'm saying, . . . I'm not gonna go back and retract what I said, I said it and I believe it. Or, even if I don't believe it, I believe it's funny.

Despite these very practical concerns, Danner's routines are certainly not vanilla; he pushes the envelope with his humor, but his comment above speaks to the difficulty of balancing the relative risks and rewards faced by many of the comedians we interviewed. He also says, however, that the views of the audience are diverse and that you can't please everyone:

> I think people go a little too far to try and protect everybody's feelings. . . . You have so many different people with different personalities and perspectives on life. One person may go, "You know, it's OK," another may go, "No, it's not OK." It's hard to make a hundred percent of the people happy, that's one thing I've learned being a supervisor. . . . I wanted to please everyone, you know? I wanted to be that supervisor that fixed everything and pleased everybody but you find two years later that nobody's happy. . . . You're just running around driving yourself crazy.

Danner's insight speaks to the socially constructed aspects of humor. It is shaped by personal experiences, background, and context. Audience members can home in on any or all of these. Sometimes "it" is not even disability, but some other language choice deemed politically incorrect. Blue describes an interaction he had about twelve hours prior to our interview:

> Just last night I had someone who . . . was very adamant about waiting around to talk to me and tell me that . . . I was "very talented except that . . . language!" . . . Then she said, "Red Skelton, he never said one swear word, and he was the funniest man alive." And I was just like, "Well, I'm sorry. I'm not Red Skelton, you know. . . . That's just what comes out of me and I'm not gonna curtail it just for you, you know. It's a comedy club."

Sometimes the risks of violating rules of political correctness are, however, great. As a US-born Muslim comedian of Palestinian descent, Zayid has a unique perspective on the power of language and its role in altering the consciousness of an audience. In many ways, her experience is representative of the comedians we interviewed, who strongly value autonomy to construct their own narratives. However, she also has unique experience with the forces and consequences of censorship:

I started doing stand-up comedy in Jordan and Palestine in 2002 and I'm seeing comedy on the rise in those two countries. . . . I see the immediate clamping down of the authorities on the language we use and the messages we con-
vey. . . . I show that in my standard comedy . . . which got me kicked out of
the line in the comedy shuffle . . . even though I had sold out stand-up and an
invitation for the first ever Arab language show ever done in Jordan. We got
attacked in Egypt onstage by the minister of travel and tourism in the festival,
and I had my guy who did all my posters and [sold] my tickets interrupted by
Palestinian authorities the night of the show in Palestine. But I continue to do
the comedy I want.

In this context, the stakes are high and clamping down on language carries
ramifications that are potentially far more serious than postperformance
audience complaints or reduced ticket sales. As a witty and outspoken
woman with a disability who lives in the United States, Zayid must navigate compound challenges when performing in the Middle East, making her
work all the more courageously transgressive. Her embrace of personal
control over language and narrative was shared by other comedians who
have recognized that they cannot please everyone, especially as they balance the aims of laughter with insight and activism.

Despite attempts like these to control the content of their performance,
the comedians we interviewed embrace the comedy club and stage as a
dynamic space for narrative construction and dissemination, and as a place
where the risk of using questionable language to push audiences beyond
their comfort levels comes with potential rewards. While they recognize the
power of language, they tend to focus on using language to call attention to
practical issues related to disability and daily life. Their views and
approaches are certainly not completely homogenous. Blue, Zayid, Galloway, and Liz Carr, for example, push the boundaries in more extreme
ways than some of the other comedians we interviewed. However, all of the
comedians we interviewed exploit the shock of the comedy club atmosphere in their own way to challenge more absolutist ways of thinking about
disability. Self-deprecation might breed approachability. Biting, witty
observations can surprise. Pithy insight, not pity, is built on novel linkages
made through clever incongruous humor. Our interviews suggest that these
comedians believe strict adherence to politically correct language can actually prevent them from critically exploring relevant aspects of the disability
experience and bringing these to the attention of audiences. While there is
a range of approaches to the question of political correctness among them,
including how far each is willing to go, none see the stage as a place to tip-
toe around audience sensitivity to language. Rather, they see the comedy
stage as a dynamic autonomous place in which to be fearless, exert individ-
uality, and merge wit with perspective.

Two Thumbs Up for "My Midga," Roger Ebert

During our interviews, Danner described to us his personal indifference to the word "midget." But he also respects the fact that the organization Little People of America and many people of short stature see this word as highly offensive. Like other comedians, however, he sometimes reclaims the word by creatively playing with it onstage. Riffing off the African American use of "my Nigga" as an endearing in-group term, Danner uses the term "my Midga." In researching the history of "midget" as a pejorative word, we came across a fascinating online interaction that took place in April 2005, between comedian and actor Daniel Woodburn, a little person, and the late film critic Roger Ebert. Woodburn wrote Ebert with a cordial request to stop using the word "midget" in his film reviews (see Ebert 2005 for the link). What transpired was a congenial and informative back and forth of differing perspectives that illustrates the complex way in which innocent, even preferred, words for people in marginalized groups can evolve into hate speech over time when they are used with the intent to harm. Ebert (2005) said in his first response to Woodburn that he had no idea "midget" was an offensive word and that he would no longer use the word. He asked Woodburn what his thoughts were on the word "dwarf." Ebert's response (2005) to Woodburn included a copy of an essay by Leonard Sawisch, titled "What Offends Us."

In the essay, Sawisch, a little person, wrote candidly about growing up in a generation where "midget" was equivalent to the word "nigger." He recounted a story involving his own son who was getting into fights at school when kids would ask:

> "Aren't you the kid whose parents are midgets?" Regardless of the intent of the question, Brandon was raised in the dwarf community where midget was the nigger word. . . . I had spent over a decade of my life as a disability advocate and spokesperson for the dwarf community promoting "politically correct" use of terminology. I had helped make the word midget such a powerfully negative word that it was endangering my son! And we had never actually talked about the word—he [son] just picked up the value from growing up with little people. So we sat him right down and began desensitizing the word midget. I had made a classic mistake. I had confused the word midget with the way it was used by people who intended to make me feel bad. (quoted by Woodburn in Ebert 2005)

Sawisch goes on to explain that the word was originally coined to refer to the "members of the dwarf community who were the most socially acceptable" because their limbs were proportionate. Even into the 1950s, he argues, it was "still considered more socially acceptable to be a midget than to be any other kind of dwarf." Many little people would fight over who could be called a "midget" and who could not. However, "midget" had already become a mainstream word used to refer to all little people. As is often the case, with mainstream use, came mainstream abuse, and the word became associated with derogatory attitudes and mistreatment (Sawisch 2012).

In his response to Ebert, posted on Ebert's website (2005), Woodburn passionately explains that in his own experience, "midget" has been used in such a dehumanizing way that he thinks "to fully claim the word in empowerment, the way black Americans have claimed the word 'nigger,' entails getting it away from those who abuse it or misuse it." Woodburn agrees with Ebert's point that "various discriminated-against groups use words among themselves that would be fighting words if used about them by others" (2005). (Ebert points out, for example, that in correspondence he has had with members of the disability community over the ending of the movie *Million Dollar Baby,* they have used the words "crip" and "gimp.") In his final letter, Ebert agrees to "retire the word 'midget' right here and now" (2005). Woodburn ends the interchange by saying:

> When I have felt a particular closeness with someone of color or disability we have often exchanged those derogatory terms for one another. I think that when you do have that bond and have used those terms with someone in an even, equal exchange, it is then that the words are truly owned. It is a recognition of having defeated the hate that comes with the terms. (correspondence posted in Ebert 2005)

He then signs off by saying: "So in closing I would just like to say to you Mr. Ebert—'You my Midga'" (correspondence posted in Ebert 2005).

This complex interchange illustrates both the power of bigotry to taint innocent terms and the challenges involved in using censorship as a single strategy to combat the pain of exploitation and discrimination, and the demeaning treatment that is endemic to racism, sexism, and ableism. Hate speech is hurtful precisely because it is intended to be. Any word that is used with the intent to harm becomes hate speech. No matter what word is used, the intent to harm generally comes through to its target with crystal and unequivocal clarity. The problem is that rarely is it the word itself that is to blame. Changing the word to something less painful works only if, and only for as long as, the new word is not infused with hateful intent. As long as there is hate, the new word will soon be tainted. Until harmful attitudes of racism, sexism, and ableism are truly eradicated, politically correct language is only a pause in the negotiations. No amount of word policing will be successful in the long run until we change our attitudes toward one another. In the meantime, reclaiming the words that have been used in hateful ways may be an effective weapon if used with skill and a sophisticated and nuanced talent, but it is risky business and the price can be high. It is often comedic performers who are on the front lines in taking this risk and who sometimes bear the scars of doing so.

In this chapter, we have drawn on the experiences and views of professional disabled comedians to demonstrate the many ways in which disability humor can problematize simplistic public applications of political correctness to humor and language. In doing this, we have responded to calls for this type of extended exploration made by others. Rebecca Mallett, for example, says,

> What could be deemed prejudicial comments or actions should not be necessarily interpreted as merely perpetuating such prejudice. Instead, I have advocated readings which pay attention to the social and political contexts of the texts and have drawn on existing considerations of comedy and identity to begin to unpack the disability-related comedy in *The Office* and how so many find *Little Britain* equally pleasurable and offensive. (2010, p. 12)

Mallett and others such as Tom Coogan (2013) and Tom Shakespeare (1999) have called for extended consideration of this type of humor, particularly because it is often assumed that "negativity" within jokes automatically reinforces discriminatory attitudes (Mallett 2010, p. 7). These calls also poignantly point out that disability humor often traverses the terrain of "black comedy" (Coogan 2013; Meszaros 2003). Beth Meszaros (2003), for example, says,

> Black comedy is, to put it mildly, not everyone's cup of tea. It is a genre that discovers humor in pain, suffering, and even terror. An edgy, disquieting mode, it has no truck at all with decorum or sentiment. Even to our cool, postmodern sensibility, it hovers just one short step this side of bad taste. It is discordant, subversive, impolite. Black comedy appropriates, as its own special province, subjects that are usually off-limits, subjects that it often dismantles with casual cruelty, flippancy, sometimes even brutality. The end result is unexpectedly hilarious. It provides a mechanism whereby an audience is lured into grappling with matters it has heretofore deemed unthinkable. In essence, black comedy is a literature of intense engagement that pretends to do otherwise.

Defining humor as a "literature of intense engagement" is bold, but also warranted. The disability humor performed by the comedians we interviewed addresses many goals of the disability movement. The forms of disability humor reviewed here incorporate important aspects of classic social constructionist philosophy such as increased democratic representation, pluralism, and autonomy. Our interviewees meld these elements into a counter-hegemonic sword that certainly punctures more than just traditional representations of disability. This form of humor also lances approaches that would attempt to "legislate hard and fast rules of social interaction rather than recognize a process in which meaning and intention are constantly being negotiated" (Orring, as quoted in P. Lewis 1997, p. 469).

The comedians we interviewed take enormous risks in bringing this kind of transgressive humor to mainstream audiences. Their work problematizes both strict rules of political correctness and traditional notions of disability as tragedy. They force audiences to see the messiness of the human condition that includes disability and impairment. In this way, their work aligns with emerging lenses of both critical realism and crip theory and may well contribute to new cultural narratives of disability in the future. Our final chapter contextualizes their work within the larger history of the relationship between humor and disability. In the final chapter, we also examine specific ways in which the work of these comedians allows them and others to reimagine social life. In doing so, we return to the original research questions raised in the first chapter by providing additional insight into the ways in which they "play" with theory and use humor to encounter disability (for themselves and their audiences).

7

Using Disability Humor to Reimagine Society

Most discussions of humor obscure the fact that humor is a relational term, in all its contexts. The main reason that so many discussions of humor run aground is, I think, because it is not understood that an opposing term is always lurking nearby, controlling our perception of what is humorous.
—*Susan Sontag 1987, pp. 99–100*

In the mid-1990s an aspiring comedian named Greg began showing up at open mike night at McCurdy's Comedy Theatre in Sarasota, Florida. He brought a box of props with him. This was a different kind of comedian than the longtime club owner Les McCurdy was used to—Greg has a developmental disability. McCurdy says, "He got up there for his first time on stage and he got hooked, and he has never stopped coming back. I started to wonder if there were more Gregs" (McCurdy 2013). For the past nine years, McCurdy has conducted workshops with individuals who have a range of intellectual disabilities, some of whom are nonverbal. McCurdy wanted to do something "to open the door for more people" (2013) to do stand-up, so he began offering workshops that culminated in each student performing a three- to seven-minute joke set to 250 people. Unlike the professional comedians we interviewed for this book, McCurdy's students do not draw on disability issues for material. Their jokes range from one-liners to funny stories. Like the comedians we interviewed, though, they welcome the experience of having others laugh at their jokes rather than their disabilities. The audience—parents, family, and friends—shift between nervousness, discomfort, and pride. According to friends and family, the performers get more than just a mic and the stage. They gain skills in concentration, articulation, and confidence. McCurdy, who understands that many of the comedy students have spent their lives avoiding being laughed at, sees the process of preparing for the stage as beneficial:

Teachers, caregivers and parents have told me the therapeutic benefits have been wonderful and in some cases almost miraculous, but the most important thing to me is the tremendous joy each student experienced in the moment when the laughter is created, and it did not matter if they were laughing at them or with them. All that mattered was laughter. And I am grateful for the opportunity. (McCurdy 2013)

It is easy for a comedy club owner to say that laughter is all that matters within the safe space he provides. This is less evident, though, in the everyday lived experience of disability, where disabling humor persists as a form of cruelty and tool of oppression. The discomfort of friends and family members in the audience may stem in part from knowledge of this persistence. McCurdy is also pushing against a formula story in which disability is still equated with personal tragedy and that calls into question the legitimacy of any combination of disability and humor—even in the hands of disabled comedians.

The words of Susan Sontag with which we began this chapter bring us back to where we started in Chapter 1. Perceptions of disability as taboo and tragic might render humor and disability an odd coupling. But as we showed in Chapter 3, they have functioned in tandem for centuries, albeit in different ways across the years. In its most recent form, disability humor is a unique aesthetic that functions as a mediator of social experience, a method of social analysis, and a strategy of social activism. Disability humor tends to poke a sharp stick in the eye of more sterile approaches to humor and disability, which often run aground with polarized and oppositional thinking that limits definitions of both. Throughout this book, we have explored disability humor by drawing on history, theories of humor, disability studies perspectives, attitudes about political correctness, and, most importantly, the works and views of professional comedians with disabilities. Taking these as a whole, what broader conclusion can be drawn about this unique form of humor?

In this final chapter, we bring these elements together and return to the major questions posed in Chapter 1. How does humor function as a tool to investigate and analyze the disability experience, and how is disability humor used to mediate the disability experience to audiences? As we attempted to address these questions, we have made three primary contributions to understandings of disability humor. First, we have created a historical examination of the relationship between disability and humor over extended periods of time. Second, we have drawn together theories from disability studies and humor studies, illuminating common analytical lenses. Finally, and perhaps most importantly, we have sought to engage in emancipatory research that brings comedic voices to scholarly discourse through interviews with comedians about their aims, their understanding of what they are doing with their comedy, and their thoughts on issues such as the tension between political correctness and activist humor. We have threaded all of these together in discussion of the ways that humor enables us to encounter disability on multiple levels. This chapter ends with suggestions for future research in this area. Since our focus has been on the work, ideas, and insights of comedians themselves, we briefly turn to the audience to discuss methodological difficulties and potential avenues for exploring their reception of disability humor. We include some preliminary findings on online audience reception from the larger project on which this book is based. We explore other avenues of research as well, including the use of humor by individuals with disabilities in everyday interactions.

Historical Threads: Folly, Disability, and Critique

As the historical record demonstrates, disability humor as we know it can be traced back to long-standing connections between folly and disability. At times, the two have been entangled, working together as an aesthetic (both physical and verbal), a form of analysis (both individual and social), and a symbolic tool to challenge the sacred and powerful. Indeed, figures such as Erasmus, through his "ironic praise," saw "abnormality" as a central element of folly. Disability humor, though, has not had a linear progressive path. The rise of the medical model lens on disability helped to decouple folly from disability. Further, in an era in which disability is viewed through more progressive lenses, attempts to solve the problem of hate speech and disabling actions (including humor) by strict enforcement of politically correct speech can shut down important discussions and narratives about disability. It is important not to overromanticize views or treatment of disability in the distant past. It is also important to point out that, long before the twentieth century, disability had a significant role in folly and folly had a value. Even at a time when disability was absent from the public performance of comedy, figures such as Marshall P. Wilder used the comedy stage as a space for social critique.

The comedians we interviewed for this project continue a legacy of folly linked to disability and critique. Of course, they perform in a culture and context that, in many ways, is vastly more open to disability; all have attended college and have had opportunities they would not have had just a few decades ago. In some ways, though, these comedians are also constrained by ideologies that did not exist in previous times. They struggle with a culture that sees disability and humor as oppositional. They face the paradoxical challenges of traditional views of disability as personal tragedy and politically correct views about what one can say about disability and how one can say it—both of which have implications for their humor. But their work is very much in the vein of folly as it existed centuries ago—

they create, to use William Willeford's words, an "aberration of sense and understanding" (1969, p. 29). From Erasmus to Wilder to Liz Carr, there is a tradition of jester types as a "great disturber of designs" (Prentki 2011, p. 9). If, as Ben Shepard argues, classical carnival folly provided an arena for "participants to design interactions of their own" (2005, pp. 456–457), this tradition threads directly into the work of the contemporary comedians we interviewed as well as the overall evolution of disability humor. It is the carnivalesque activism of disability humor that connects it in interesting ways to the emerging perspective of crip theory.

Comedians Playing with Theory?

Chapter 5 provides detailed parallels drawn between humor theories and models of disability, which helps us understand how humor functions as a critical lens and as a method of constructing new narratives of disability. Murray Davis (1993) argues that comedians and sociologists are alike in that they (1) focus on contemporary life; (2) deconstruct and debunk social expectations, organizations, and behavior; (3) reorder and reverse the audience's perspective; (4) compare social ideas to the way things are; (5) play off expected outcomes; (6) compare and contrast groups; (7) challenge hypocrisy; (8) examine "presentation of self" in everyday life; and (9) demonstrate the ambiguity and fluidity of social life. Comedians, Davis points out, disorder the orderly world of human constructions and social expectations. Stephanie Koziski makes a similar case, comparing comedians to anthropologists: "What many standup comedians and anthropologists do is, as anthropologist Victor Turner describes, 'cut out a piece of society for the inspection of his audience and set up a frame within which image and symbols of what has been sectioned off can be scrutinized, assessed, and perhaps remodeled'" (Turner, as quoted in Koziski 1984, p. 60). Koziski goes on to argue that the anthropologist and the comedian possess a challenging "habit of mind" (1984, p. 63) that is prone to explore structures of society and illuminate cultural knowledge underlying the outlook of certain groups. Both collect, analyze, and compare how "various groups structure their reality" (Koziski 1984, p. 60), and then bring all of this to the public for examination and discussion. The lecture environment, Koziski argues, is not unlike the stage of the comedian. In essence, comedians and anthropologists "share a way of seeing" that requires the ability to "stand outside themselves and to empathize with people who are different in order to more fully understand their actions and beliefs" (1984, p. 73). But this, she cautions, does not make them the same. The comedian's basic aim is to entertain, not to "elucidate culture theory" (1984, p. 61). According to Koziski, the comedian uses no scientific objectivity, which is why comedic observations are "broadly refracted and highly distilled" images (1984, p. 63). The anthropologist, conversely, uses scientific objectivity and does not aim to entertain.

Our research demonstrates that while comedians find, frame, and edit "reality into an artistic construction—the comedy routine" (Koziski 1984, p. 63), some comedians who perform disability humor do, indeed, have specific analytic aims that go beyond laughter and entertainment. Several of our interviewees described this goal as educational; others talked about it as perspective shifting. We showed in Chapter 4 that these comedians are not, as Josh Blue points out, telling the audience "how it is" by laying out a hard and fixed reality. Instead, they often use humor to create ambivalence in the audience—situations of oppositional possibilities: they comfort through laughter, but they discomfort (and even shock) by addressing the taboo onstage. Several comedians spoke about taking audience members to a different place, breaking through a wall, and bringing new perspectives that, in fact, build onto the larger theoretical perspectives we have discussed. Some, for example, specifically push against the medical model and support the social model in their work. Some made unsolicited references to these models when discussing their humor routines with us. Their work intentionally unpacks cultural concepts that are important in disability studies such as: the inspirational Supercrip, embodiment, boundary work, linguistics, and representation. Most importantly, their work poses a direct and powerful challenge to the persistently prevailing notion that disability is always and only a personal tragedy. And certainly, as we have shown in Chapters 4 and 5, the fact that their work parallels broader cultural theories is no mere accident. While not all of them, as Simon Minty puts it, have had a "sit down where we said, 'how do we educate people?'" they all strategically employ humor to provide insight into disability that goes beyond a micro-level understanding. By creating ambivalence, they challenge broader theories of how the world works. In this sense, contrary to Koziski's (1984) claim, we argue that they are doing theory work (or play).

Behind the Mic: The Comedians' Perspective

One of the most rewarding aspects of this project was the opportunity to speak directly with comedians about their work and hear their interpretations of what they hope to accomplish through their comedy. This took us in the direction of emancipatory research, as we aimed to bring comedic voices to scholarly discourse. Michael Oliver argues that this type of research is not about empowering people; rather, once they have decided to empower themselves, it involves asking what research can do to facilitate this process (1992, p. 111). Oliver also specifies ways in which this type of research can contribute to combatting the oppression of people with disabilities. These include: "1) [a] description of experience and of collective experience in the face of academics who abstract and distort the experience of disabled people; and 2) a redefinition of the problem of disability" (Oliver 1997, p. 20). In this vein, we have aimed to provide an account of the experiences of comedians doing disability humor, both as individuals and as a larger group, as they fulfill a unique role and function. We also aimed to highlight the strategies, techniques, and autonomy they use to construct new narratives of disability. Their insight into such issues as political correctness and representation, taken from interviews and performances, sheds important light on the broader and evolving definitions of humor and disability. In particular, their experiences and observations help us to deconstruct the assumed polarity between the two.

It remains rare for an individual with a disability to have regular access to a captive audience of people without disabilities outside of academe or activism, which makes the insights of these comedians all the more poignant. Representation was a prominent theme that emerged from our interviews. Specifically, representation of their own individual disability experience is a central aim of everyone we interviewed. While some embraced the role of representing an entire group, others made sure to point out that they were telling their own story, and that they did not want the responsibility of having to represent a larger group. Some articulated an added pressure to get it right when performing for groups who share their disability. The ability to represent their own experience, though, is interpreted as an immense form of freedom and power—they see the stage as a unique venue in which to represent disability in ways not possible elsewhere. While there are different approaches to the issue of representation, all of the comedians with whom we spoke believe that within their everyday lives there are novel experiences that have the potential to shift audience perspectives. Minty says (in Chapter 6) that there is joy in being able to throw the ableist actions and assumptions of others back at them by using these negative social experiences as material for comedic performance. He also feels that, if done with enough wit and skill, performance of this material can leave able-bodied members of the audience thinking: "Oh, yeah, how stupid are we?!"

Through our interviews, we also learned a great deal about the comedians' ideas on how humor works, its functions, and its techniques. Inferiority humor, for example, is used in counterintuitive ways that mix self-deprecation with cleverness and power. Superiority humor is used not just to bring down individuals, but to unveil ableist thinking and to depict the disabled body in a more dynamic light. Incongruity humor is employed deftly to unveil common treatment of people with disabilities as well as to highlight the advantages of the disability experience. And while many speak to their own individual daily experiences, most do aim to connect their humor to larger universal experiences of human life. Terry Galloway, for example, speaks to communication breakdown while Alan Shain has written an entire performance piece around his anxious anticipation when waiting for a date. These comedians not only speak to issues relevant to a broader audience, they reflect astute insight into how far they can go with an audience and describe specific strategies for guiding the audience into unknown and awkward territory without losing them in the process. This might begin, as Blue indicates, with "taking the piss out of" himself before he turns his scrutiny to everyone else. Several comedians acknowledged the fact that audience members are not sure whether or not to laugh, and they have developed specific techniques to address this problem, which they incorporate into their performances. These comedians work to make sure the audience is with them, perhaps because they have had to do the same their entire lives while navigating everyday interactions. Carr says that disabled comedians "don't need any advice on what it takes to be a great comedian because you've broken through all the other shit that people have to break through to even listen to you."

While their humor styles are heterogeneous, the comedians we interviewed tend to reject censorship of their performances. Most indicated greater concern for practical aspects of everyday treatment than for politically correct language. They see the fight against unjust actions and demeaning attitudes as more important than avoiding particular words. And while some indicated that growing up with a disability meant making sure others around them were comfortable, onstage they do not attempt to please everyone. Indeed, some indicated that this is an impossibility. A primary reason that their approaches to humor create problems for more rule-based approaches of political correctness is that they use humor to craft an engaging story and depict a true, novel, and humanistic experience. This breathes life into narratives of disability in ways that more sterile, politically correct approaches cannot. It is, as Beth Meszaros eloquently articulates, a "literature of intense engagement" (2003) that transcends the victimology and euphemistic language that often puts politically correct philosophy at odds with the rich insights that can be provided by critical humor.

While the focus of this book was on the comedians themselves, we have gained some preliminary insight into audience response from these interviews. Overwhelmingly, the comedians reported positive reception of their humor, and their continued success as professional comedians attests to this. More importantly, though, they explained that many audience members tell them in postperformance interactions that they have gained insight from their comedy. These comments often come from audience members without disabilities, many of whom say to the comedians things like "I totally do that!" Positive responses also come from individuals with disabilities, who express feelings of solidarity, sentiments of shared experiences, or gratitude for a positive representation of disability to a public audience. Nina G.'s example of the widespread adoption of her empowering joke about being a "S.I.L.F." by other women who stutter provides a powerful example of the kind of solidarity that can come from the public performance of disability humor.

Some of the comedians we interviewed feel that they can get away with things that non-disabled comedians cannot. They tend to feel that the license to joke about their own experience of disability comes from a position of understanding and truth telling. They also believe, however, that although an insider position is one way to establish one's credentials to use disability humor, skilled and empathetic nondisabled people can also sometimes get it right and make it clear that the intent of their humor is not to demean or disable. They articulated a preference for more sophisticated humor about the disability experience (from both disabled and nondisabled humorists), rather than cheap laughs based on an easy joke at someone's expense. Their own skillful use of self-deprecation and embodiment to help prepare an audience to hear more critical material, for example, poses a challenge to the assumption that self-deprecating disability humor is always victimizing and exploitive rather than empowering. Yet the stage does not exist completely outside of broader cultural norms that exert their force, as evidenced by the stories of audience members not being prepared for this type of humor. Despite the unique function of the comedy stage as a place of sociocultural freedom, the comedians we interviewed do experience resistance during and after performances. Most comedians, in general, face tough crowds and heckling at some point and may even interpret this as evidence of success. Comedians who perform disability humor, however, also encounter unique obstacles not likely to be faced by other comedians, and they have developed skillful ways of navigating these situations.

Encountering Disability Through Humor

As we discussed in Chapter 2, humor has most often been described in the literature as a coping strategy in times of stress: as a defense against being sucked under by tragedy (Herth 1993; Vaid 1999; Vilaythong et al. 2003). Indeed, in both popular culture and the literature on coping, the value of humor is framed in opposition to negative words such as "struggle" and "suffer." Framing the relationship between disability and humor in this way is based on the assumption that disability is a tragedy that humor helps one endure. Yet if we move beyond these more traditional interpretations of coping and disability, we find significant insight into the functions of humor and the disability experience. The insights of the comedians we interviewed, together with analysis of their humor, help to illustrate the coping functions of humor at multiple levels: as a tool for processing and navigating the indignities of living in an ableist world; as a tool of social analysis; and as a way to embody or engage in social activism. As we began to understand this process, and the multiple levels it involves, we came to redefine our notions of the word "coping" as a more interdisciplinary and complex concept than generally described. Indeed, we found it more helpful to expand our own understanding of coping through one of its synonyms—"encounter." The use of this word is more than semantics or a politically correct attempt to leave behind the baggage associated with coping. Through the concept of encounter, we have a more holistic way to explore humor functioning at the individual, socioanalytical, and activist levels.

Humor in Everyday Life: Processing the Individual Experience of Disability

On the individual level, the comedians we interviewed provide specific insight into the role that relief humor can play, not only for the audience, but also for the individual comedians themselves. In Chapter 4 and in the biographical sketches included in the Appendix, we showed that humor has had a vital role in the everyday lives of these comedians from early childhood on. They describe themselves as natural humorists and were raised in families in which a humorous approach to life was encouraged. As adults, they are willing to use humor to set well-intentioned others at ease to engage in positive social interaction, but have no patience with those who use disabling humor with intent to harm or bully. They have no difficulty recognizing hate speech that is wrapped in humorous packaging. Using nuanced skills honed over a lifetime of experience, they make in-the-moment distinctions between humorous attempts that disable and humor that has the potential to forge human connections. The power differential between jokester and target, the intent of the person telling the joke, the tone with which it is delivered, the sophistication of the humor, and the degree to which it accurately portrays something about the disability experience are all factors in the acceptability of humorous treatment of disability in everyday interactions. Even when the intent is good, our interviewees' patience can be tried by jokes that are repetitive, simplistic, or rely on clichéd understandings of the disability experience. They use their own humor in daily encounters with others to manage their emotions and those of well-meaning people they encounter. When the intent is not so positive, but there is hope that a lesson might be learned, they use humor to educate. This kind of education is sometimes gentle and sometimes more severe—depending on their own level of frustration and the seriousness of the infraction. In using humor in their everyday lives, they consciously attempt to counter the tragedy narrative of disability with a humorous narrative to help others grasp the complexity of the human experience—one that includes disability and impairment.

They also take this humorous narrative of disability and humanity to the stage. In their stage performances, they use humor as a way to control the situation, redefine themselves, and deal with the frustrations of living in an ableist world—in essence, to process and reframe the daily experience with disability. Nina G. turns the microaggressions of others into poignant and biting stage material. Steve Danner recalls how he has taken what would otherwise be a negative experience—buying kid-sized shoes—and used humor to process and reinterpret the situation so that he feels in control. Moreover, he specifically says that performing stand-up comedy helped him with this processing. In her explanation of this function of humor, Galloway specifically uses the words "empowering" and "dignity" when discussing her humor workshop called "Actual Lives." These lived experiences starkly contrast with coping synonyms such as "struggle" or "overcome."

Our interviewees described the comedy stage as a liberating place to wrestle with the frustrations of the disability experience. Their use of humor, then, is not one-dimensional coping in the sense of self-pity, or simply laughing to keep from crying, nor is it merely a form of deflection. We use the term *encounter* to describe the way in which these comedians use humor as an active, empowering, and autonomous tool. Encountering creates a "space for participants to design interactions of their own invention and creation" (Shepard 2005, pp. 456–457). It "enables" agency while stamping out feelings of being helpless (Emerson 1997). All of the comedians with whom we spoke reference their use of humor in this manner.

Encountering Disability in Social Context

Yet using humor and comedy to encounter disability goes beyond simply interpreting the individual experience. It can provide a new frame for navigating the social environment, one that takes into account the complexities of interpreting, analyzing, and navigating situations. More than coping, dealing with, or enduring, folly provides comedians and the audience with a way to engage a critical perspective on the disability experience writ large—a way to analyze and understand the broader disability experience in its social context. Thus, encountering disability through humor can shift the perspective from the individual to a sociological level. Recall Rollo May's claim (in Chapter 2) that humor is "an expression of our own uniquely human capacity to experience ourselves as subjects who are not swallowed up in the objective situation. It is the healthy way of feeling a 'distance' between oneself and the problem, a way of standing off and looking at one's problems with perspective" (1953, p. 54). Paradoxically, humor allows comedians and their audiences to distance themselves from situations so they may encounter them in a more deliberate and strategic way. The use of incongruous analysis, and its ensuing explorations of responses, structures, and norms, affords both the humorist and the audience an ability to locate themselves in a larger social context. Such distancing has several effects, according to Herbert Lefcourt, particularly allowing individuals to "actively engage" within stressful situations but with a lesser "emotional reaction" to those situations (1996, p. 59).

In the examples discussed in the previous chapters, the comedians use humor as a lens that transforms the frame of disability from individual problems to social issues. The internal structure of the jokes told by the comedians we interviewed is built on a cognitive shift that forces the audience to contrast the lived experience of the comedian with norms, ideals, and assumptions about disability. In the jokes discussed, these incongruities unveil hidden structures and interactions as well as limitations imposed by social structures on individuals with disabilities. In this way, developing the structure of the joke necessitates a functioning sociological imagination that can tap into these norms, structures, and assumptions to then contest, invert, and implode them.

Also imploded are constraints around the concept of disability itself. Humor can facilitate freedom from these conceptual restraints, allowing alternative ways to encounter disability. The critical consciousness connected to this type of folly, then, has specific implications for reframing—liberating the mind as it interprets and constructs disability—by dissolving fixed definitions of disability and norms, if but temporarily. To use Mikhail Bakhtin's words, it frees human thought and fosters "imagination for new potentialities" (1984, p. 49) for interpreting disability. According to Bakhtin, it "purifies" from dogmatic thinking about disability and liberates from "fear and intimidation, from the single meaning" (1984, p. 123). That is, certain types of humor can unravel disability so that it no longer has a unified singular meaning. As previously stated, disability humor that draws on incongruity reframes traditional ways of interpreting disability (the medical model) into a more sociological interpretation (the social model) while questioning ideals and categories (crip theory). Inferiority humor creates new potential ways of understanding the disability experience by connecting it with the broader human experience and portraying the diversity of disability through embodiment. As we showed with relief theory, certain types of humor offer a range of new freedoms. It is an outlet for subverting social constraints, as Blue demonstrates through discussing his response when people mistake cerebral palsy for drunkenness. Likewise, it is an avenue for bringing discussions of the body into public dialogue, as Carr demonstrates in various ways. It is also an arena in which to confront fear, as Nina G. illustrates when she describes her response to an audience member's discomfort with her stuttering. Whatever individual fears might exist in relation to disability, laughter and humor can create an arena in which there is more freedom to unravel those fears. As Bakhtin points out, "Laughter demolishes fear and piety before an object, before a world, making it an object of familiar contact and thus clearing the ground for an absolutely free investigation of it. Laughter is a vital factor in laying down that prerequisite for fearlessness" (1981, p. 23). For example, some of the comedians we interviewed indulge this free investigation and fearlessness by examining issues of disability and sexuality in their stand-up routines. In this unique context, then, their humor offers an alternative way to portray and consider new paradigms for understanding and interpreting—encountering—disability. The doorway to this freedom is the aesthetics of humor behind the stage action. Without the structural lens of humor, there is no performance, no laughter, and no possibility of temporarily transcending norms or fears. In essence, specific types of humor can be used to facilitate these encounters onstage and offstage.

Public Comedy as a Means of Encountering Disability

We have explored how the comedians we interviewed offer insight into the potential of humor to provide the individual with a means of processing everyday disability experiences as well as how humor can move analytical encounters with disability to a more sociological level. But this takes us only so far in understanding how humor mediates and spreads new narratives. The public comedy arena—particularly the stage—has few parallels. As we asked in Chapter 1, where else will a diverse crowd of people without disabilities pay money to hear someone talk about disability and consider it entertainment? And where else is disability explored in public discussion in ways that create laughter, rather than fear or pity? From a social action perspective, how might the public performance of disability humor help audiences encounter disability?

Let's consider first what humor scholars have to say about these potentialities: the performance of live stand-up comedy provides audience members with what Victor Turner calls "plural reflexivity," or the ways that a "group or community seeks to portray, understand, and then act on itself" (Turner, as quoted in Mintz 1985, p. 73). Comedy scholar Lawrence Mintz, the first to apply the idea of plural reflexivity to studying humor in culture, argues that the comedic interaction provides the group with a unique "comunitas weighing structure," where it can affirm, invert, or reject values; explore new paradigms; and modify norms and values (1985, p. 73). Humor, especially through comedic performance, can provide both analytic tools and an arena in which individuals can "disrupt popular accounts or depictions," disorder shared meaning, and provide counternarratives that redefine disability (Reid, Stoughton, and Smith 2006, p. 637). Alternative images presented through humor can provide important descriptive information for an audience (Reid, Stoughton, and Smith 2006). If the audience members have no personal experience with disability, their efforts to decode and understand it, and be amused by it, can be a process through which new information is conveyed (Zhao 1988).

We have presented several examples of how comedians engage in inferiority humor to expose and identify their own flaws and imperfections in some way. When comedians do this, Mintz (1985) argues, they are often exempted from ordinary expectations and able to move into a more ambivalent role. Historically, this type of public comedy allowed audiences to ridicule and feel superior to the comedian (superiority theory). Ironically, though, to the extent that we identify with the comedian, he or she can become a comic spokesperson (Mintz 1985). Mintz believes that this public ritual of stand-up comedy—the comedian as shaman—leads us to celebrate a community of shared culture, of homogeneous understanding and expectation (1985, p. 74). However, our interviews and analysis focus on just the opposite: encounters with the new through disruption of homogeneous understanding (of disability). Through a unique combination of wit, vulnerability, and entertainment, these comedians seem to foster a form of legitimacy and social capital that simultaneously allows audiences to identify with and learn from them. Often combining all of the types of humor we discussed—inferiority, superiority, incongruity, and relief—these comedians function in the true tradition of the jester. They make themselves familiar enough to engage the audience and strange enough to lead them into new territory. Indeed, in a society where novelty and differentiation matter significantly, perhaps it is this paradox that is so engaging. Many audience members can likely relate to Shain's experience of waiting for a date, Danner's search for the right clothing, or Nina G's experience of being the target of microaggressions in everyday encounters. But these comedians bring the uniqueness of their own disability experience to the story—thereby grabbing audience attention. As Tanyalee Davis points out,

> You know [*laughs*] I have a really interesting life. I have a fun life. . . . I'm in a very male-dominated business. . . . Generic white guys, you know, they can talk about the same boring shit over and over. You can have six male comics talking about the same crap over and over again. . . . I get up there and talk about me for forty-five minutes. . . . I've got people's attention and they're so engaged, and that's the true test of a . . . of a good comedian. . . . You don't have to make people laugh for forty-five minutes to an hour, but you have to keep them engaged and wanting more.

Ironically, the process of making the disability experience accessible for audiences—facilitating audience encounter with disability in an engaging and entertaining way—also bears recognition here, particularly because this very public form of humor parallels more formal types of public sociology. Navigating this world of play, most of the comedians we interviewed are nonacademic actors who are engaging models of social life and acting on them by creating and circulating new narratives of disability to a broad audience. While many of these comedians have been schooled in various models of disability, even those who haven't do have an experiential understanding of these models and the cultural narratives based on them. In their comedy, though, they are circulating counternarratives of disability in much more accessible ways than many of us in the world of academe. Rather than discussing hegemonic discourses, for example, Nina G. posts a clip on YouTube titled "Shit Fluent People Say to People Who Stutter." Whether it be online or in person, the language and narrative techniques used in their comedy are familiar enough to audiences to keep them engaged and novel enough to provide a new perspective.

These comedians also use the stage to cut through politically correct filters that might otherwise prevent a (re)coupling of folly and disability and its potentialities. We have covered a number of examples where comedians use humor to trump dogmatic approaches to disability—conservative and liberal. We have also examined how these comedians put into praxis core tenets of political correctness (representation and voice), without sterilizing their experiences, a common pitfall of politically correct approaches to humor. In other words, deftly using hyperbole, shock, and inversion to reach the audience, these comedians move audiences from one-dimensional assumptions about disability as the tragedy of impairment to more real, raw, and reinterpretive narratives. What's more, proponents of politically correct philosophy cannot argue with the fact that these comedians bring to a broader audience an encounter with the structures, norms, and values that shape the disability experience. Yet they also retain personal control over their own narrative and, thus, how they are represented.

While this project has not incorporated a full-fledged audience reception component, there are good reasons to believe that this humor does, indeed, provoke thought and poignant response from audiences. Certainly, the professional success of these comedians—live shows, DVDs, Internet clips accessed, podcasts, and radio interviews—along with their own assessments of how their audiences respond suggest that audiences are encountering disability in novel ways. Preliminary research supports this assessment. For example, early analyses of audience reception of Blue's humor—online posts in response to videos of his performances on the web—show a range of different reactions that suggest that something more than just entertainment is taking place. Melissa Welch, Shawn Bingham, and Sara Green (2016) suggest that most of these responses can be coded into several categories: many posts affirmed Blue's talent without mentioning disability. This is done by either quoting jokes back in the comment section, or by comparing Blue favorably to other mainstream comics without disabilities. A second category includes comments that affirmed Blue's talent and specifically mentioned his disability in the process. Others commented on Blue as an "inspirational/motivational" figure, with little focus on the humor itself (Welch, Bingham, and Green 2016). A number of comments related to the posters' personal experiences with disability. These posters not only commented on their shared experience with Blue, but also sometimes said that he taught them something about how to handle certain experiences such as interactions with other people or managing personal feelings. A smaller group could be classified as "hecklers," posters who believed that Josh Blue won *Last Comic Standing* because his disability got him "sympathy votes." Finally, some posts engaged in "education and debate," which often included discussion that moved away from Blue to various disability topics. These posts were apparently made for the purpose of educating other posters about disability, and they often came from people with disabilities or family members of people with disabilities. These online comments illustrate the varied functions of humor as well as Blue's role as more than an entertainer. Blue is clearly succeeding as a professional comic but his humor has other potential functions, including serving as a catalyst for public discussion and debate about the disability experience.[1]

What's Next: Suggestions for Future Research

Much of our inquiry for this project has focused on the experiences and insights of comedians doing disability humor. Our preliminary work on audience reception is drawn from Internet posts. We know little directly from audience members about what they are thinking during performances, or about the impact, if any, on their views of disability postperformance. There is some evidence that individuals view deprecating humor about disability more positively when they have information that the creator of that humor has a disability (Ellithorpe, Esralew, and Holbert 2014); however, this research on who has license to joke about disability was conducted on cartoons that use disability as a major theme, not on audience responses to stand-up comedy, which is more fluid and multidimensional. Given the increasing numbers of performers with disabilities over the past decade, we need to know more about how their live audiences respond. Audience reception interviews could reveal a range of interesting insights into the functions and outcomes of this type of humor; for example, whether the comedians' aims are actually being met, and audience perceptions of political correctness as it pertains to the various types of humor. Comparing the reactions of disabled and non-disabled audience members would also be useful. However, audience reception in the comedy clubs remains an elusive form of inquiry. Comedy clubs continue to earn most of their income through the sale of alcohol. Audience members are not likely to follow an evening of entertainment, drinking, and laughter with a formal social science interview. All of the comedians we interviewed have performed on college campuses. This could provide a fruitful, though not necessarily generalizable, alternative environment for research on audience reception. While their performances might be similar to what they do in more public club settings, the audience and context are much different.

Many of the comedians we interviewed indicated a lack of physical accessibility in comedy clubs, which impacts both the comedian and the audience. A number of clubs we have attended are in basements; in spaces retrofitted for a comedy club design; or, due to the need for low overhead, in older facilities. At the same time, many more people are accessing humor through the Internet. This is now the dominant outlet for stand-up comedy of all kinds. It has the advantage of allowing quick circulation of jokes, links to video clips, and audience responses. This context, with less of an emphasis on physical embodiment, is certainly relevant to discussions of disability and humor: How does the Internet impact the spread of disability narratives through humor? Since Internet comedy clips are often shorter in length, how does seeing a comedy segment (or bit) in isolation from a larger show impact reception?

There are also larger questions about the future of disabling and disability humor. Companies such as the BBC are now engaging disability humor through podcasts that require minimal financial investments. Are these avenues likely to be the future for disability humor? (By comparison, two of the more recent television comedies that prominently featured characters with disabilities were cancelled in the fall of 2014—*Growing Up Fisher* and *The Michael J. Fox Show*.) If certain media forms seem more prone to traditional disabling humor (e.g., morning radio shows), what role will new media (e.g., Twitter) play in circulating newer and older narratives? Has disabling humor after the Americans with Disabilities Act become more subtle and sophisticated in its presentation in the media? With some audience members still unable to see humor and disability as compatible, can disability humor emerge as a truly robust method for disability activism and education? This evolution certainly bears further inquiry.

There is also the more unique phenomenon of professional comedians and comedy writers teaching individuals with disabilities to perform stand-up comedy. Released in 2013, the Showtime documentary *Comedy Warriors: Healing Through Humor* chronicles a program in which professional comedians work with veterans to developed stand-up comedy routines that explore and interpret war, injury, and postmilitary life. Five veterans who have experienced severe burns, post-traumatic stress disorder, or amputation worked with performers and comedy writers such as Lewis Black, Zach Galifianakis, B. J. Novak, and Bob Saget over the course of two weeks, culminating in live shows at the Improv and Laugh Factory in Los Angeles. Much of the performance is relief humor for the comedians and the audience. One comic stands in front of the audience in awkward silence before saying anything and then simply states, "You should see the other guy" (*Comedy Warriors* 2013). The film has won at least seven festival awards, including the 2013 Audience Award for Best Documentary at the Naples International Film Festival, and several of the comedians are now performing around the nation.

Comedy Warriors (2013) and *Special O'Laughics* (2008) chronicle the range of ways in which humor can function, but also portray efforts to coach individuals in the use of humor to exploit perceived weaknesses and deploy them as strengths. These types of workshops raise a wide range of questions about the individual comedian, the audience, and the forms of activism. What type of humor is being taught? What stories about disability are being told, and what are the implications for the storytellers and the audience? How are the comedians and the coaches navigating the tricky territory of inferiority humor?

Beyond our focus here on the professional disabled comedian, what about the use of humor in everyday interactions by individuals with disabilities who are not comedians? There has been some research in this area (Stebbins 1996), but important questions remain. For example, how do individuals with disabilities differentiate between humor that is stigmatizing or disabling and humor that is not? Do they use different types of humor in their everyday lives (superiority, inferiority, etc.)? And how might they use humor to counter stigmatizing reactions of others, to relate to others, or to process particular situations? Clearly, there are multiple ways in which humor and disability intersect far beyond the comedy stage, which provide a number of avenues through which to explore the complex relationship between disability and humor.

The Final Act

When the radical comics of the late 1950s and 1960s began to emerge along with the new comedy scene, "black comedy" was infamously referred to as "sick humor" ("The Sickniks" 1959, p. 42), the result of putting things together that presumably had nothing to do with humor. Some equated black humor with "psychological sickness or maladjustment" (Kercher 2006, p. 95). Robert Ruark called it a "state of inverted mental sickness" (1963, p. 38). Others saw it not as an illness but as a reaction against a stodgy culture and a form of "intuitive wisdom" (Kercher 2006, 96). In his 1960 *LP I Am Not a Nut, Elect Me!* Lenny Bruce replied to the label by stating: "The kind of sickness I wish *Time* had written about, is that school teachers in Oklahoma get a top annual salary of $4000, while Sammy Davis Jr. gets $10,000 for a week in Vegas" (1960). Certainly, there are many parallels to the humor we have covered here, which makes daring leaps by pairing humor with the disability experience in insightful ways. It might be called disability humor, crip humor, or politically incorrect humor. It has been called a "literature of intense engagement" (Meszaros 2003) and likened to public sociology. However it is labeled, in true jester fashion disability humor is a raucous inversion of the assumption that people with disabilities live sick or pitiful lives. By pointing out the social ills that disable individuals with impairments, this kind of humor makes the slur "sick humor" all the more ironic.

In the 1960s-era strip mall comedy club that we wrote about at the beginning of this chapter and in Chapter 1, surrounded by pictures of Chris Rock, Louis C.K., Tommy Chong, and Paula Poundstone, and with an audience of mostly blue-haired retirees, Blue employs disability humor as a touchstone that illuminates the flaws in social ideals of equality, challenges our comfortable assumptions about disability, and problematizes the success of efforts to construct a more egalitarian approach to disability. Indeed, a range of comedians with disabilities are deftly employing this type of humor to unveil, unravel, and bend fixed notions of the body. Disability is not only "deep in comedy's DNA" (Logan 2011), it continues to play a part in the evolution of stand-up comedy. Likewise, comedy is providing new ways to encounter disability. In the words of Carr: "You're there on the stage and you have the power. You've got the stage. . . . Sideswipe them with the comedy and you get in there and you break down some of those barriers." As the social model of disability slowly makes its way from the halls of academe and the world of disability activism into the cultural narrative of disability that is widely shared by the public, disabled comedians around the world are pushing the cultural narrative of disability even further into the emerging territory of critical realism and crip theory. By doing the dangerous dance of embodying disability onstage in humorous fashion, they are performing crooked comedy for audiences around the world and bringing carnival consciousness to new audiences in unique ways. In the process, they exemplify for the public the complex and often ridiculous messiness of the human condition and the joyous freedom to be found in breaking free from the constraints imposed by narrow definitions of what it means to live a good life. In the words of Galloway, they are saying to the world: "Behold the glory! This is me."

Note

1. It is important to keep in mind that, because these clips are much more accessible than a live comedy club performance, reactions could vary from audience members who invest money and time to attend a live performance. In addition, live audiences have access to much more stage material, allowing Josh Blue to build rapport with the audience and allowing the audience greater access to content and context.

Appendix
Biographical Sketches of the Comedians Interviewed

Josh Blue (www.joshblue.com) is a comedian with cerebral palsy who was born in Cameroon, West Africa, and grew up in Saint Paul, Minnesota. As the son of a college professor, he had the opportunity to travel fairly extensively during his childhood—including trips to Senegal, where he spent an entire year when he was fifteen years old. During his extended stay, Blue learned both French and Wolof (the native language of Senegal). He credits his travels with helping him to put his identity as a person with cerebral palsy into perspective. In his interview, Blue says, "What has really helped me is the time in Africa and seeing other parts of the world and realizing how other people live their lives and you know just struggle to have shoes on or whatever. . . . I do have shoes. Yes, I have cerebral palsy, but I got shoes you know? It just kinda makes you go . . . 'OK, this . . . ain't that big a deal.'"

Blue sees himself as a natural observer of human and social behavior and thinks that his disability may be at least partly responsible for enhancing this skill: "I feel like I see things . . . like I have a broader picture of just what's in front of me. . . . I don't know whether it has to do with my disability or just the brain I was given . . . but if you don't have any hindrances . . . you might not even see the thing you're gonna trip over." He values this observational skill as a gift that gives him a constant flow of material for his comedy. He also sees his humor as a natural talent. He's grateful for this ability to make people laugh, but he wasn't content to rely entirely on his untrained natural talent. Blue honed his skills more formally in what he describes as a creative, self-tailored, postsecondary education program that focused on creative writing and stand-up comedy.

Blue uses his life experiences as a father, person with cerebral palsy, and Paralympic soccer player as fuel for his often wickedly brutal stand-up performance. While he's had his share of experiences as the target of disabling humor, he also began using humor as a weapon against disabling cruelty at an early age. In his professional routines, he pulls no punches. He skillfully pokes fun at himself to put people at ease and as a way to soften them up before challenging their negative attitudes and incorrect assumptions about disability. Blue is a highly successful comedian who consistently draws audiences willing to pay to be pushed past their comfort zones. He is the 2006 winner of NBC's *Last Comic Standing*. Building on successful tours on the college campus circuit, Blue now tours widely—performing at comedy clubs and festivals such as HBO's Aspen Comedy Festival, Comedy Central's South Beach Comedy Festival, and the Comedy Festival of Las Vegas. His television appearances include: Comedy Central's *Mind of Mencia; The Ellen DeGeneres Show;* Ron White's *Salute to the Troops; Live with Regis and Kelly; The Late, Late Show with Craig Ferguson;* and a television special, *Comedy Central Presents: Josh Blue.* He also has a significant Internet presence with millions of views on his videos. He has been interviewed widely by the press.

In addition to comedy, Blue has recently become a popular disability speaker. He finds this work more challenging than stand-up comedy, which remains his professional passion. In both types of work, his goal is simple but profound. He seeks to encourage others to see disabled people as "viable humans."

Liz Carr (www.lizcarr.co.uk) is an actress and comedian who was born in the United Kingdom and spent her early childhood near Liverpool. She became a wheelchair user at the age of eleven after an extended illness that she acquired when she was seven years old—during a two-year period in which her family lived in the United States. In her interview, she says, "I broke my spine at that point because of the . . . steroids. This was the seventies. We didn't know about the dangers of drugs like that and I hate . . . that most people find the things that you need to be on to help you, can do more damage." Carr's family moved back to the UK to be near relatives after her illness and she completed her primary, secondary, and postsecondary education there—studying law at Nottingham University.

Carr's parents valued education "hugely" and made sure that she and her brother "had great educations." Carr says, "I think there was a feeling 'Oh blast, you know, she can't do stuff physically, but let's therefore make sure she gets a good education and that will set her up for life.'" She went to mainstream schools and, until she went away to the university, "didn't have a sense of identity as a disabled person." Carr "started to get political in university." In her twenties, she became a disability activist, "working within the disabled people's movement in the UK" and "working with young disabled people, working with the independent living movement."

After college, she became even more involved in disability activism and "did a lot of disability comedy and a lot of campaigning." Her activist orientation continues to the present. "I'm still involved with direct action. . . . I've been over to the United States and have been part of . . . ADAPT [Americans Disabled for Attendant Programs Today, previously known as Americans Disabled for Accessible Transportation] actions . . . as well as . . . becoming . . . very involved in identity politics."

Once Carr hit the stage, her career took off quickly. She feels this is partly because "when you're a disabled comedian, I think you're more memorable." Over the past decade, she has performed widely and extensively as a solo performer and with the comedy groups Nasty Girls and Abnormally Funny People (with Tanyalee Davis and Simon Minty, who were also interviewed for this project). Carr has also made substantial contributions to the BBC radio disability podcast *Ouch!* She describes her feelings about being a stand-up comedian who both has a disability and uses disability content in performance as follows:

> I think I love . . . being in the moment. I think there's nothing more wonderful than making people laugh, and I think that's the driving force. However, . . . I couldn't just go on stage and talk about fluffy things. I just wouldn't find it worthwhile. . . . I tend to talk a lot of current affairs, the state of the country, what's happening in the world. . . . I guess I talk about disability because it's who I am and it's a big part of my life. . . . I'm a lesbian as well and I talk about that.

In 2010, Carr cut back on her grueling schedule of stage performances and took a job in the television industry. Of this decision, she says:

> I was getting married that year and I wanted a different life. . . . I was tired of driving around the country and getting home at three, four in the morning . . . and I was having some panic attacks. . . . A lot of the stages I performed on, I would have to be lifted onto . . . and I would start to develop this anxiety on stage. . . . You just kind of go "this isn't worth [it]. I need to think about what's important."

Carr has now returned to the stage at a more measured pace. "I still do comedy, but I do less and I'm much more selective. . . . I'd say it's two or three nights a month now. . . . Ironically, I think . . . I'm a better comedian now." In 2013, Carr joined the cast of the long running BBC crime series *Silent Witness*.

Steve Danner (https://www.facebook.com/pages/Official-Steve -Danner-Fan-Page/129627290381210) lives in the Napa Valley area of California. Danner now identifies himself as a member of the community of little people, but he grew up without much contact with other members of that community. "I always knew I was kind of a little person but . . . never really knew how I fit in." He did, however, grow up in a family in which disability was part of the mix. In his interview, he says, "My parents were foster parents . . . and . . . a couple kids . . . were . . . developmentally delayed. . . . I actually live with one foster brother now. . . . We both moved out of the parents' house and then a couple years later, I said, "Hey, you need a roommate? I need a roommate."

In terms of his own childhood experience growing up with a bodily difference, Danner "didn't really have a whole lot of negativity. . . . Kids, of course, are always cruel and I quickly developed friends who kind of protected [me] from the negativity. Not that I needed protection, but it always helped." As an adult, he is quite understanding of people's curiosity about his difference and uses "humor a lot in . . . interactions with people."

Danner "always kind of wanted to be an entertainer" and studied broadcasting for a while in college, but "didn't have the right help then." Ironically, his break came in 2010 when, as a member of the audience at a comedy club, he was heckled from the stage by a stand-up comedian who "looked at me and he goes 'Are you a MIDGET?'" Undaunted by the use of a word considered highly derogatory in the community of little people, Danner heckled right back—so successfully, in fact, that the stage performer sought him out afterward, asking, "Are you a comedian?" Danner said that he wasn't, "and the performer goes, 'You're a pretty funny guy.'" They hung out after the show for a while and Danner began to think "You know, I could try this . . . and a month later, I entered an open mic and I felt awesome about it and I just went full speed from there."

In the past few years, in addition to becoming a professional comedian, Danner has also become more involved in the community of little people. "There's an organization, Little People of America [LPA], which I didn't start attending until I was thirty—maybe twenty-nine. . . . There's like 3,200 little people there. . . . I've met some very nice people at LPA." Ironically, however, even in this social space, Danner feels stigmatized by some members of the community because of bodily difference:

> I don't even know what kind of dwarf I am . . . I had . . . a guy pointing at me. He says . . . "Hey, we're playing guess your diagnosis. . . . What are you?" I was just like, "Hi, I'm Steve." You know, it's just kind of like they pick me apart that quick 'cause I don't really look like any of the other dwarfs. . . . So, I'm learning a lot more about myself. . . . I'm gonna figure out some kind of diagnosis—what kind of dwarfism I have.

In classic comedic style, Danner uses this experience and others in which he's asked what kind of little person he is as fuel for his stage performance.

In his interview, Danner talks about a joke in which he says to his audience: "I have people asking me all the time. They say: 'What makes you a little person?' . . . I'll just stop. . . . I'll look at the ground and I'll say: 'Well, I wear kids' shoes. Does that help?'"

In addition to solo performances, Danner is a member of the Comedians with Disabilities Act comedy group with Nina G. (who was also interviewed for this project), Michael O'Connell (a wheelchair user), and Eric Mee (who is blind). This group has been highly successful—performing at a variety of well-known comedy venues such as San Francisco's Punch Line and the Laugh Factory in Hollywood.

Tanyalee Davis (tanyaleedavis.com) was born in northern Canada and grew up in Winnipeg, where her parents moved "because it was a big city and they knew I had health issues, but they couldn't figure out what the hell was wrong with me so I needed to . . . move to the big city of Winnipeg for diagnosis." Unlike Danner, Davis now knows "what kind of dwarf" she is—having eventually received a diagnosis of diastrophic dysplasia. As an adult who is three foot six, Davis is very comfortable with her bodily difference today. As a child, however, she was teased and bullied, and she used humor to try to circumvent the negative attitudes of others. Like other performers we interviewed, Davis has been able to draw on these negative childhood experiences as a source of material for her stand-up comedy. In her interview, she says, "I think my opening line . . . the first time I went on stage [was]: 'Hey, did you guys know that there is a midget here? Uh, no?' I walked in and they were like: 'Hey, look at the midget.' And I was like: 'Where?' It did get a good laugh because I disarmed people and they didn't see that coming."

Davis knew she "wanted to be a performer from a young age." During her school years, she "was always in school plays and stuff like that" and fell in love with stage performance. After high school, her mother wanted her to "go to university and get a real job," but she was determined to be a performer. Eventually, she gave in and said, "Okay, fine, I'll go to university and . . . study theater." Studying theater, however, did not hold the same appeal for her as performing on stage. Before long, she began to think, "Why can't I just perform?"

> So, I started doing Community Theater . . . children's theater and I got the lead in the first production. I was Perry the Penguin. It's damn cute and . . . there was another adult in the production. He played the villain and apparently he had a thing for penguins. . . . So [we] kinda started dating and then he said to me one night: "Do you want to come down to see me at an open mic at a comedy club?" I had never been to [a] comedy club; never watched stand-up; didn't really know what I was in for. So, I went out there and

watched him die on his ass and . . . I knew exactly what he was doing wrong.
. . . His timing was off. His material was shit. . . . I just kind of knew. So, I
got really excited telling him how crappy he was. He was like: "Oh, really?
Here's a comedy book. Write some material. . . ." About three weeks later,
January 23rd, 1990, was my first time on stage and I kicked ass.

Davis uses humor in a variety of ways for a variety of professional
and personal purposes. She uses humor to fit in and put others at ease with
her bodily difference when she senses that this kindness on her part is warranted by good intentions on the part of others. She also uses humor to
resist the common disability as tragedy narrative for receptive audiences.
Like our other interviewees, however, she has a "rolodex" of interactions
in which she has been the target of stigmatizing attitudes and behaviors,
and she uses these as fodder for the more critical aspects of her comedic
performance.

In addition to performing in comedy clubs in her native Canada, Davis
(now a US citizen) tours internationally and has received numerous awards
for her comedy. She has performed in the United States (including a six-
month engagement in a Las Vegas venue "just off the strip"); at international comedy festivals (including the Edinburgh Fringe Festival, where her
one-woman show received four-star reviews); and in Canadian, UK, and
US television programs and films. She performs both as a solo headliner
and with the comedy group Abnormally Funny People. Her website says,
"Tanyalee has made a small yet significant dent in the entertainment scene.
. . . What she lacks in height, she makes up in tenacity." She is "known as
'the little lady with a lot of BIG LAUGHS.'"

Nina G. (ninagcomedian.com) describes herself as a single woman of
"white, Italian American descent" who was raised in the San Francisco Bay
area of California; attended the University of California, Berkeley; and holds
a doctoral degree. In elementary school, Nina G. was diagnosed with learning
disabilities and also began to stutter. As a child, she struggled with an educational system that underestimated her ability and kids who teased and bullied
her—taking the hit to self-esteem that these disabling attitudes can cause. She
still encounters stigmatizing behavior in her interactions with others:

> What I hate most is when I go out with my friends at night or something and
> I'm . . . all dressed up and I think that I'm going out and dancing and it's a
> time to relax, and someone makes fun of me and it's . . . not what I was ex-
> pecting. . . . Like: "remember you are d-different fr-fr-from everyone else."
> . . . When you're out at night you don't really want to be called out on that.

Nina G. feels, however, that her disability experiences have pushed her to
carve out a creative life path for herself as a "disability activist" and a
"comedian/disability educator." In her interview, she says,

> I think my learning disability has affected me more than my stuttering in terms o-o-of my ch-choices in my career. . . . I wasn't going to be able to work as a cashier because my math skills suck . . . and my processing isn't very good for those kinds of situations. So, I had to go on and get more education . . . if I wanted a-a-a job . . . or . . . the things that that that I want to do in my life. . . . My stuttering is what I talk about in my comedy.

Nina G. eventually went on to graduate school to pursue her career goal of being a disability educator. She uses her personal experience as a woman with learning disabilities who stutters as source material for this work. In her stand-up performances, Nina G. also talks about the way she and others who stutter are treated. She pushes back against the disabling attitudes of others and seeks to educate the audience in mass. "Because I am [a] . . . stand-up comic, I don't have to educate every single person every single time. . . . It's kind of addressing [it] in bulk."

Like most of the comedians we interviewed, Nina G. has been attracted to comedy since she was a young child. "As a four-year-old, I remember being fascinated by Steve Martin because that's when he was really p-p-popular . . . and I've just always been a fan of his c-c-comedy." As an adult professional comedian, her interests have turned to comedians who use humor as a weapon against discrimination and the stigmatizing attitudes of others:

> When I was a kid I really liked G-G-Gilda Radner and Lily Tomlin umm I went through different phases. . . . I think now as a comedian . . . I am more influenced by people who take o-on social issues. So for me, Lenny Bruce has always been someone I really idolized and someone who I look toward now—as well as some of the other African American comedians like Paul M-M-Mooney who is very angry and talks about a lot of issues around discrimination and racism. . . . I really respect people [like] Geri Jewell who-who would really o-open things up, but I don't think comedy and disability have gotten to the place that Chris Rock brings racism a-a-and comedy, which is where I guess I want to eventually go, but I'm no Chr-Chris Rock.

In addition to stand-up performance, Nina G. is a disability educator who presents at conferences and workshops and in schools, businesses, non-profit organizations, and the Centers for Independent Living. She has recently authored a children's book entitled *Once upon an Accommodation: A Book About Learning Disabilities.*

Terry Galloway (theterrygalloway.com) describes herself as a "deaf, queer writer and performer." She uses the term *little d deaf* to distinguish herself from members of the Deaf community who are fluent in American Sign Language (ASL) and capitalize the word to emphasize their preferred status as a cultural and linguistic minority group. She tours nationally and internationally and is based in Tallahassee, Florida. Like most of the comedians we interviewed, Galloway has lifelong experience with both disability and humor. She credits the "queerness of disability" as a source of creativity that has had a positive impact on her career as a professional comedic performer. Galloway's hearing impairment was discovered during early childhood when she "started having hallucinations" associated with congenital health issues thought to be associated with medication her mother was given during pregnancy. Her parents "had never dealt with disability. . . . So . . . they really had no idea what to do." Galloway says, "When I was a kid, I was not sent to deaf school. I was mainstreamed" and, thus, was not taught ASL as a child. She says she was "never close with the deaf community . . . because I'm so deficient in my sign." Although she didn't grow up with a Deaf cultural identity, she did identify with other disabled children.

> I was sent to a camp called Alliance Camp for Crippled Children. . . . You had kids . . . with cerebral palsy, with MS, kids who were quadriplegic, . . . kids with vision impairment, hearing impairment. . . . So my experience with disability isn't with other Deaf children. It's with kids who were disabled. . . . I identify with the disabled . . . that was my first and most profound identification.

Galloway's disability identity, which remains important to her, is currently being challenged. At the time of her interview, she had recently received a cochlear implant, which she says "has been a miraculous occurrence." She is well aware, however, that the improvements to her hearing that have resulted from the implant pose a challenge to her identity as a disabled person and performer. She still has a hearing impairment without the device, but not when it is in place and working properly.

This challenge to Galloway's disability identity has ramifications for her professional life as well as her personal identity. Both disability and humor have played important parts in the creative professional path that Galloway has created for herself. She uses humor to narrate the disability experience for others through her stage performances: "I think it's a way of redefining myself, of taking a hold of my own personal narrative. . . . I take my narrative and I talk about it in ways I want to talk about it and I use humor to do that. . . . I become a figure more of fun . . . than a figure to be pitied . . . or to be mocked or scorned or anything like that. So, humor is the way that I do that." Galloway also helps others to use humor to renarrate their disability experience in ways that not only empower the storyteller but also challenge the perception that disability is always and only tragic. In Austin, Galloway cofounded Actual Lives Austin—an award-winning activist theater group for adults with disabilities. She is currently cofounder and artistic director of the Tallahassee-based Mickee

Faust Club—a nonprofit theater group for the "queer, disabled and minority community."

Galloway is the recipient of numerous awards, fellowships, and grants for her work including: multiple awards from the Corporation for Public Broadcasting and National Public Radio. In 2000, Galloway and Donna Marie Nudd received the Leslie Irene Coger Award for lifetime achievement in performance from the National Communication Association. In addition to performing at festivals, on college campuses, and in other venues around the world, she has been a visiting artist at California Institute for the Arts, University of Texas at Austin, and Florida State University. She has published articles, monographs, poems, and performance texts. Her memoir, *Mean Little Deaf Queer,* was published by Beacon Press in 2009 and received the Golden Crown Award for Non-fiction.

Kim Kilpatrick (www.ottawastorytellers.ca/kim-kilpatrick/) is a Canadian storyteller who lives in Ottawa and has "been blind since birth" due to a "condition called retinopathy of prematurity." Kilpatrick was "lucky enough to grow up in a family . . . that wasn't overprotective." In her interview, she says,

> They decided that I just would do whatever everyone did. . . . It was kind of 'Oh, well, we have a blind daughter . . . that's the way it is and we're going to do whatever we do. . . . My family was quite . . . active. . . . So, I did a lot of sports . . . recreationally, but then I did some competitive swimming and I did . . . national Paralympic stuff when I was younger. . . . I just feel normal. I feel [*laughs*] you know [*laughs*] like I live an interesting life and . . . it feels good and well rounded . . . mostly.

While Kilpatrick is happy with her life and comfortable with her blindness, she often encounters experiences in public places that set her apart: "You're always on display. . . . You can't be anonymous. [*laughs*] . . . You know, first I had a cane, then I had a guide dog and they're really magnets . . . of people. . . . You're different. . . . You do things differently. . . . So, you're never invisible, never sort of faded into the crowd."

In addition to everyday life, humor plays an important role in Kilpatrick's professional storytelling performances. In fact, she uses the negative experiences she encounters in interactions with others as source material for her performances:

> You just have to say: "Well, you know what, that'll be good storytelling fodder" . . . and you make it into your art. . . . There's so many things that become good stories. . . . Instead of "Oh, Jesus, people . . . get on my nerves" . . . you're . . . kind of: "Oh, look at you, now you're going to be in the story." . . . It really makes you feel much less upset with it in a way. . . . You still ed-

> ucate . . . but . . . you're already in that creation—like: "Thank you for giving me [*laughs*] . . . some material."

Kilpatrick's career as a disability educator and storyteller evolved gradually over time:

> I studied music and . . . worked for . . . ten years or so as a music therapist—mostly with people with dementia and palliative care. . . . Then I . . . needed a break and I started . . . helping people with disabilities get volunteer jobs. . . . Then I . . . started storytelling . . . because I really loved it. . . . After a while, I started mostly doing that. . . . It just kind of evolved.

Kilpatrick believes that her visual impairment encouraged a love of orally transmitted stories that set her up for a career as a storyteller: "I've always enjoyed reading . . . braille but also listening . . . [to] audiobooks and people reading to me. . . . I think language and hearing language became very important. So, I think storytelling was a . . . natural place to go." She views storytelling and humor as powerful tools for disability education and the promotion of disability awareness: "I did a lot of disability awareness . . . presentations and I still do. . . . I've noticed . . . when I do storytelling in school, that they get it more . . . than . . . if you just said: 'I'm totally blind and this is how I use braille.' If you tell a story, they think about it and they ask you questions . . . which are deeper. . . . It's powerful!" Kilpatrick is a member of the Ottawa StoryTellers (along with Alan Shain who was also interviewed for this project). She performs across Canada in schools and other settings including festivals, clubs, pubs, and other private venues.

Simon Minty (www.sminty.net) is a London-based businessman who cofounded, produces, and performs with Abnormally Funny People—one of the comedy groups with which several of our interviewees have performed. As a person of short stature with some mobility limitations, he is well aware of the public reactions received by people who are different and the discrimination they often face in the community. He uses both serious and humorous approaches to combat discrimination and encourages broad participation by people with disabilities of all types. Minty has undergraduate degrees in sociology and philosophy and a postgraduate diploma in disability management at work. He has worked as a financial services officer and disability trainer and is an associate to the Employer's Forum on Disability and the Broadcasters and Creative Industries Disability Network. He has produced numerous disability-related training videos and published widely. Minty is currently a disability consultant and entrepreneur. His consulting company works with major firms and organizations in the United Kingdom, the United States, and around the world on issues related to disability equity and mainstreaming. The underlying aim of that work is to help "organisations understand why disability inclusion is important and show them how to remove any barriers to achieving it, ensuring this is tailored to their current position and resources" (www.sminty.net). Minty also seeks to improve media portrayals of people with bodily differences.

In addition to his serious engagement in the disability awareness business, Minty sees comedic performances by individuals with disabilities as a way for them to share their talents with wide audiences. In doing so, Abnormally Funny People may also help bring new narratives of the disability experience to these audiences, but this is a secondary goal. In his interview, he describes the formation of Abnormally Funny People:

> I think initially our idea was to be funny. That was the bottom line really, is to come out and do really funny stuff. Whether people touched upon disability was after that. They had to be funny. . . . We had a guy who was blind who hardly talked about his disability and then we had others who that is all they did was talk about it . . . but there was never a sit-down where we said, "How do we educate people?"

While the primary intent of the Abnormally Funny People shows was clearly to entertain, Minty recognizes that its very existence challenges stereotypes and stretches boundaries because of the relatively small number of disabled comedians performing professionally. He believes that people with disabilities are sometimes afraid to offend others by being funny, but that the very act of doing so stretches boundaries because it stands in direct challenge to the idea that disability is tragic. This can make audiences uncomfortable. At the same time, though, it opens eyes. Minty feels that, once the audience comes to grips with the idea that they are being entertained by a group of disabled comedians, they relax and start to laugh.

Since it was founded, Abnormally Funny People has performed in clubs and festivals throughout the UK including London's Soho Theatre and the prestigious Edinburgh Fringe Festival. In 2014, Minty also launched a comedy podcast featuring comedians with disabilities. Like Abnormally Funny People, this podcast seeks to address the serious goal of increasing disability awareness while avoiding the pitfall of being pigeonholed as being "lectury."

Alan Shain (www.alanshain.com) is a stand-up comedian, actor, dancer, storyteller, and disability advocate who is based in Ottawa, Canada. Shain believes that people with disabilities are on the verge of developing a "culture of disability" and taking pride in themselves as disabled people. He feels that this is taking place most prominently in the arts, where visual and performing artists and writers are beginning to redefine culturally accepted notions of what it means to be beautiful, independent, and strong. He thinks that humor is a good way to dispel the stereotype that disability is a tragedy and that disabled people are helpless and passive victims. His production company is named Smashing Stereotypes Productions. In his performance, Shain uses humor, drama, and other forms of expression to challenge the notion that people with disabilities are one-dimensional. His work explores love, sex, dating, masculinity, relationships, and other aspects of social and family life that are often erroneously assumed to be irrelevant to the disability experience.

Shain studied acting at Trevor John Studios in Ottawa and with the Ottawa Little Theatre. He has undergraduate degrees in political science and sociology and a master's degree in social work, for which he wrote his thesis on theater and disability. Shain sees himself as an artist first, but says that his writing, performance, and comedy are clearly rooted in the struggle against ableism and are thus an alternative form of activism. His writing and performance as a stand-up comedian draw on his lived experience as a person who has speech and mobility impairments due to cerebral palsy. In his act, he rebuffs prevailing public attitudes toward disability.

Shain got his start as a stand-up comedian at Yuk Yuk's Komedy Kabaret. He is also a member of the Ottawa StoryTellers and has appeared regularly at storytelling festivals. He also performs at comedy festivals, clubs, pubs, and other venues—including university campuses and schools. His original play *Still Waiting for That Special Bus* has toured widely to considerable acclaim. Shain has also performed comedy, dance, and theater, both solo and with others, in various locations in Australia, Canada, the United Kingdom, and the United States. He was the only Canadian artist invited to participate in the Paralympic Arts Festival in Sydney in 2000. He has performed on national television in Canada as well as in major artistic venues such as the John F. Kennedy Center for the Performing Arts. His work has received grant funding and has been favorably reviewed by both the disability and the general press (print, television, and radio).

Maysoon Zayid (www.maysoon.com) is a Palestinian American writer, actress, and stand-up comedian who was born in Cliffside Park, New Jersey—a small town in the northeastern United States, where she thinks that she and her extended family may have been the only Arab Americans in town. While she was aware as a child that anti-Arab racism and anti-Muslim religious prejudice existed, she did not find it evident in her experience growing up in Cliffside Park. Zayid's father was proud of their Palestinian background and made sure she felt connected to her religious and cultural heritage. She was widely accepted by her friends and family, and she believes that her mainstream school experience gave her both educational and social advantages. "I had the same girlfriends since I was five. They were my bridesmaids. . . . So I didn't suffer the way other children did."

Like several of the other comedians who participated in this project, Zayid believes that her disability may have contributed in some ways to her choice of career. "I feel like it [disability] definitely had a hand in the career that I chose. . . . My parents were more flexible with me, as immigrant parents, than most parents because they just wanted me to do something. They didn't really care what it was." She feels that they were open to her choice of a career in the arts and performance in part because of her disability. Her parents and friends were supportive of her performance endeavors as a young child:

> I became a dancer at the age of five. Which is where my . . . career in art began. I've been on stage since I was five. . . . We did the dance as a form of physical therapy because we didn't have insurance and my parents couldn't afford physical therapy. So I went to a local hometown dancing school. . . . I just functioned completely oblivious of my disability until I got to college.

Things changed rather dramatically when she went away to college and later entered the adult world of work, where she had to face low expectations and barriers to full participation. Like other performers we interviewed, Zayid used humor to navigate and push back against the disadvantages imposed by an ableist world. "I have done . . . that . . . since I was like five years old. . . . People say some stuff to me and I would just you know immediately respond back and it's how I deal with the disability now." Like many of our other interviewees, she also values comedic performance as a cathartic experience: "Comedy is a great way to get over whatever is bothering you. . . . I always say I have a great job because like no matter how down I get, when I jump up on stage, I'm making people laugh." Zayid incorporates her experiences as a person with a disability and her experiences as an American of Palestinian decent into her comedy routines that lie at the intersection of disability experience and political critique—specifically calling attention to media misrepresentations of current affairs in the Middle East.

Despite the considerable number of significant obstacles Zayid has had to face due to the discrimination associated with her intersecting minority group statuses, she has created a successful career in performance. She has appeared on a wide variety of television programs, tours widely in the United States and the Middle East, and performs in top comedy clubs in New York City. She also seeks to share her success with other Arab American performing artists, playwrights, and filmmakers through her work as the cofounder and co–executive producer (with fellow comedian Dean Obeidallah) of the New York Arab American Comedy Festival. She shares her commitment to the value of the arts in the lives of children with disabilities by spending several months each year in the Palestinian Territories, where she runs an arts program for disabled and orphaned children living in refugee camps.

References

Abnormally Funny People. 2006. London: Media Trust Productions.

Abel, Millicent. "Humor, Stress and Coping Strategies." *Humor: International Journal of Humor Research* 15, no. 4 (2002): 365–381.

Adelson, Betty. "Dwarfs: The Changing Lives of Archetypal 'Curiosities'—And Echoes of the Past." *Disability Studies Quarterly* 25, no. 3 (2005). http://dsq -sds.org/article/view/576/753 (accessed December 12, 2015).

Albrecht, Gary. *The Disability Business: Rehabilitation in America*. Thousand Oaks, CA: Sage, 1992.

———. "Disability Humor: What's in a Joke?" *Body and Society* 5, no. 4 (1999): 67–74.

Amarasingam, Amarnath. "Laughter the Best Medicine: Muslim Comedians and Social Criticism in Post-9/11 America." *Journal of Muslim Minority Affairs* 30, no. 4 (2010): 463–477.

Anderberg, Peter. "Making Both Ends Meet." *Disability Studies Quarterly* 25, no. 3 (2005). http://dsq-sds.org/article/view/585/672 (accessed June 1, 2012).

Apte, Mahadev. "Disciplinary Boundaries in Humorology: An Anthropologist's Ruminations." *Humor: International Journal of Humor Research* 1, no. 1 (1988): 5–25.

Aristotle. "Poetics." In *The Complete Works of Aristotle,* edited by Jonathan Barnes, 2316–2340. Princeton, NJ: Princeton Universityu Press, 1984.

———. *The Politics*. Translated by T. A. Sinclair. London: Penguin, 1992.

———. *Nicomachean Ethics, Revised Edition. E*dited by Roger Crisp. Cambridge: Cambridge University Press, 2000.

Bakhtin, Mikhail. *The Dialogic Imagination: Four Essays*. Austin: University of Texas Press, 1981.

———. *Rabelais and His World*. Bloomington: Indiana University Press, 1984.

Barnes, Collin, and Geof Mercer, eds. *The Social Model of Disability: Europe and the Majority World*. Leeds, UK: Disability Press, 2005.

Bartholomy, Jonathan. "The Importance of Disability Humor in the United States and How Disabled Comedians Have Changed the Way We Think About Disability and Comedy from 1978 to 2006." Paper presented at the Society for Disability Studies conference, Denver, Colorado, June 2012.

Bauer, Patricia. "What's So Funny About Disability? Well . . ." *New York Times,* December 11, 2005.

Baum, R. Bruce. "Humor and Disability." *The Bridge* 8, no. 4 (1998): 3–5.

Beckett, Angharad. *Citizenship and Vulnerability: Disability and Issues of Social and Political Engagement.* Hampshire, UK: Palgrave Macmillan, 2006.

Bell, Michael, and Michael Gardiner. "Bakhtin and the Human Sciences: A Brief Introduction." In *Bakhtin and the Human Sciences,* edited by Michael Bell and Michael Gardiner, 1–12. London: Sage, 1998.

Bemiller, Michelle, and Rachel Schneider. "It's Not Just a Joke." *Sociological Spectrum* 30, no. 4 (2010): 459–479.

Berger, Peter. *Invitation to Sociology: A Humanistic Perspective.* Garden City, NY: Doubleday, 1963.

Berger, Ronald J. *Introducing Disability Studies.* Boulder, CO: Lynne Rienner, 2013.

———. "What's So Funny About Disability?" April 9, 2016. https://wiseguys2015.com/2016/04/09/whats-so-funny-about-disability/ (accessed June 2, 2016).

Berger, Ronald J., Jon A. Feucht, and Jennifer Flad. *Disability, Augmentative Communication and the American Dream: A Qualitative Inquiry.* Lanham, MD: Lexington Books, 2013.

Bergson, Henry. *Laughter: An Essay on the Meaning of the Comic.* New York: Macmillan, 1911.

Berk, Ronald. "Does Humor in Course Tests Reduce Anxiety and Improve Performance?" *College Teaching* 48, no. 4 (2000): 151–158.

Billington, Sandra. *A Social History of the Fool.* New York: St. Martin's Press, 1984.

Bingham, Shawn. "Seeing Beyond the Verge of Sight: Art as Social Inquiry." In *The Art of Social Critique: Painting Mirrors of Social Life,* edited by Shawn Bingham, 1–20. Lanham, MD: Lexington Books, 2012.

Bingham, Shawn, and Sara Green. "Aesthetic as Analysis: Synthesizing Theories of Humor and Disability Through Stand-up Comedy." *Humanity & Society.* http://has.sagepub.com/cgi/reprint/01605976156211594v1.pdf? (accessed December 18, 2015).

Bingham, Shawn, and Alex Hernandez. "'Laughing Matters': The Comedian as Social Observer, Teacher, and Conduit of the Sociological Perspective." *Teaching Sociology* 37, no. 4 (2009): 335–352.

Bishop, Kathryn. "Whoopi Goldberg: From Sidekick to Star." *Cincinnati Inquirer.* August 29, 1986, 74.

Blaikie, Norman. *Approaches to Social Enquiry.* Cambridge, UK: Polity Press, 1993.

Bloom, Alan. *The Closing of the American Mind.* New York: Simon & Schuster, 1987.

Blue, Josh. *7 More Days in the Tank.* Denver, CO: Bad Arm Productions, 2006a.

———. "Josh Blue at Last Comic Standing." 2006b. Season 4, Episode 5. www.youtube.com/watch?v=qMSrpZi_6WM (accessed June 12, 2011).

———. *Q&A.* Posted May 29, 2008. www.youtube.com/watch?v=tck4WU4b9mg (accessed July 1, 2012).

———. http://www.joshblue.com/bio.html. 2014.

Bogdan, Robert. *Freak Show: Presenting Human Oddities for Amusement and Profit.* Chicago: University of Chicago Press, 1988.

Bonaiuto, Marino, Elio Castellana, and Antonio Pierro. "Arguing and Laughing: The Use of Humor to Negotiate in Group Discussions." *Humor: International Journal of Humor Research* 16, no. 2 (2003): 183–224.

Boskin, Joseph. *Rebellious Laughter: People's Humor in American Culture.* Syracuse, NY: Syracuse University Press, 1997.

Bragg, Lois. "From the Mute God to the Lesser God: Disability in Medieval Celtic and Old Norse Literature." *Disability and Society* 12, no. 2 (1997): 165–177.

Brett. Paul. *The King's Speech.* 2010. Beverly Hills, CA: UK Film Council.

Brewer, Paul, Dannagal Young, and Michelle Morreale. "The Impact of Real News About 'Fake News': Intertextual Processes and Political Satire." *International Journal of Public Opinion Research* 25, no. 3 (2013): 323–343.

Brody, Roberta. "Buoys in the Gap: Satire, Sarcasm, and Irony as Sense-making Strategies." Paper presented at the annual meeting of the International Communication Association, San Francisco, California, May 1999.

Brooks, Nancy, Diana Guthrie, and Curtis Gaylord. "Therapeutic Humor in the Family: An Exploratory Study." *Humor: International Journal of Humor Research* 12, no. 2 (1999): 151–160.

Bruce, Lenny. "The Tribunal." *I Am Not a Nut, Elect Me!* (LP). Fantasy. 7007. 1960.

———. "To Is a Preposition, Come Is a Verb," *What I Got Arrested For.* Fantasy Records, 1971.

Cahill, Spencer, and Robin Eggleston. "Managing Emotions in Public: The Case of Wheelchair Users." *Social Psychology Quarterly* 57, no. 4 (1994): 300–312.

Cann, Arnie, Kitty Holt, and Lawrence Calhoun. "The Roles of Humor and Sense of Humor in Responses to Stressors." *Humor: International Journal of Humor Research* 12, no. 2 (1999): 177–193.

Carey, Allison. *On the Margins of Citizenship: Intellectual Disability and Civil Rights in Twentieth-Century America.* Philadelphia: Temple University Press, 2009.

Carlin, George. *Napalm and Silly Putty.* New York: Hyperion, 2001.

Carlyle, Thomas. *The Works of Thomas Carlyle.* New York: Peter Fenelon Collier, 1897.

Carr, Jimmy. *Making People Laugh.* London: Bwark Productions, 2010.

Carr, Liz. "Liz @ Knock2Bag." March 2, 2010. www.youtube.com/watch?v=nHIc KDV7Trw (accessed February 2, 2012).

Carroll, James L. "Changes in Humor Appreciation of College Students." *Psychological Reports* 65, no. 3 (1989): 863–866.

Case, Dick. 2011. "Helen Keller Once Appeared in Syracuse at an Old Vaudeville House on South Salina Street." *Post Standard* (Syracuse), March 22, 2011.

Casper, Kevin. "I Didn't Do it, Man, I Only Said It: The Asignifying Force of *The Lenny Bruce Performance Film.*" *Rhetoric Society Quarterly* 44, no. 4 (2014): 343–362.

Castellani, Robert. *From Snake Pits to Cash Cows: Politics and Public Institutions in New York.* Albany: State University of New York Press, 2005.

Chakravarti, Paromita. "Natural Fools and the Historiography of Renaissance Folly." *Renaissance Studies* 25, no. 2 (2011): 208–227.

Choi, Jung, and John Murphy. *The Politics and Philosophy of Political Correctness.* Westport, CT: Praeger, 1992.

Collins, Ronald. *The Trials of Lenny Bruce: The Fall and Rise of an American Icon.* Naperville, IL: Sourcebooks MediaFusion, 2002.

Coogan, Tom. "Usually I Love *The Onion,* but This Time You've Gone Too Far." *Journal of Literary and Cultural Disability Studies* 7, no. 1 (2013): 1–17.

Crewe, Nancy, and Irving Kenneth Zola, eds. *Independent Living for Physically Disabled People.* San Francisco: Jossey-Bass, 1983.

Crowther, Bosley. "Jerry Lewis, New Comedian, a Bright Spot in Silly Film, 'My Friend Irma.'" *New York Times,* September 29, 1949.

Crutchfield, Susan. "'Play[ing] Her Part Correctly': Helen Keller as Vaudevillian Freak." *Disability Studies Quarterly* 25, no. 3 (2005). http://dsq-sds.org /article/view/577 (accessed August 14, 2012).

Daily Mail Reporter. "Fury as Ricky Gervais Ridicules Down's Syndrome Children with 'Two Mongs Don't Make a Right' Twitter." *MailOnline,* October 20, 2011. www.dailymail.co.uk/news/article-2050854/Ricky-Gervais-Twitter-joke -ridiculing-Downs-syndrome-children-sparks-fury.html (accessed September 12, 2013).

Darling, Rosalyn Benjamin. *Disability and Identity: Negotiating Self in a Changing Society.* Boulder, CO: Lynne Rienner, 2013.

Davies, Telory. "Freedom and Prosthetic Actuality in Joseph Chaikin's *Body Pieces.*" *Disability Studies Quarterly* 25, no. 3 (2005). http://dsq-sds.org/article /view/578/755 (accessed August 1, 2015).

Davis, Murray. *What's So Funny? The Comic Conception of Culture and Society.* Chicago: University of Chicago Press, 1993.

Davis, Tanyalee. "Performance at Winnipeg Comedy Festival." 2006. www. youtube.com/watch?v=br2g2OD630U (accessed March 11, 2012).

Decker, Elaine. "Making Sense with the Sense of Humor: An Examination of the Joke as a Hermeneutic Unit and Its Potential Place in Education." PhD dissertation, University of British Columbia, 2004.

Dedman, Meg. "Little People of America Celebrates Its 50th Anniversary." 2007. http://www.lpaonline.org/assets/documents/Little%20People%20of%20 America%20Celebrates%20Its%2050th%20Anniversary.pdf (accessed February 12, 2014).

DeJong, Gerben. "Defining and Implementing the Independent Living Concept." In *Independent Living for Physically Disabled People,* edited by Nancy Crewe and Irving Kenneth Zola, 4–27. San Francisco: Jossey-Bass, 1983. (Orig. pub. 1979.)

Derks, Peter, and Jack Berkowitz. "Some Determinants of Attitudes Toward a Joker." *Humor: International Journal of Humor Research* 2, no. 4 (1989): 385–396.

Dimeglio, John. *Vaudeville, U.S.A.* Bowling Green, OH: Bowling Green State University Press, 1973.

Double, Oliver. *Getting the Joke: The Inner Workings of Stand-up Comedy.* London: Methuen, 2005.

Douglas, Mary. "The Social Control of Cognition: Some Factors in Joke Perception." *Man* 3, no. 3 (1968): 361–376.

———. *Implicit Meanings: Selected Essays in Anthropology.* London: Routledge & Kegan Paul, 1975.

D'Souza, Dinesh. *Illiberal Education: The Politics of Race and Sex on Campus.* New York: Free Press, 1991.

Dudley-Marling, Curt. "The Social Construction of Learning Disabilities." *Journal of Learning Disabilities* 37, no. 6 (2004): 482–490.

du Pre, Athena. *Humor and the Healing Arts: A Multimethod Analysis of Humor Use in Health Care.* Mahuwah, NJ: Lawrence Erlbaum Publishers, 1997.

Dutton, Dennis. *The Art Instinct.* New York: Bloomsbury Press, 2009.

Ebert, Roger. "Dwarfs, Little People, and the M-Word." *Roger Ebert's Journal.* 2005. http://www.rogerebert.com/rogers-journal/dwarfs-little-people-and-the -m-word (accessed November 1 2012).

Edwards, Martha. "Constructions of Physical Disability in the Ancient World: The Community Concept." In *The Body and Physical Difference: Discourses of Disability,* edited by David T. Mitchell and Sharon L. Snyder, 35–50. Ann Arbor: University of Michigan Press, 1997.

Ellithorpe, Morgan, Sarah Esralew, and R. Lance Holbert. "Putting the 'Self' in Self-deprecation: When Deprecating Humor About Minorities Is Acceptable." *Humor: International Journal of Humor Research* 27, no. 3 (2014): 401–422.

Emerson, Caryl. *The First Hundred Years of Mikhail Bakhtin.* Princeton, NJ: Princeton University Press, 1997.

Erasmus, Desiderius. *Praise of Folly.* Translated by Betty Radice. Harmondsworth, UK: Penguin, 1973.

Feldstein, Richard. *Political Correctness: A Response from the Cultural Left.* Minneapolis: University of Minnesota Press, 1997.

Fine, Gary Alan, and Christine Wood. "Accounting for Jokes: Jocular Performance in a Critical Age. *Western Folklore* 69, nos. 3–4 (2010): 299–321.

Fisher, Pamela, and Dan Goodley. "The Linear Medical Model of Disability: Mothers of Disabled Babies Resist with Counter-narratives." *Sociology of Health and Illness* 29, no. 1 (2007): 66–81.

Fleischer, Doris, and Frieda Zames. *The Disability Rights Movement: From Charity to Confrontation.* Philadelphia: Temple University Press, 2000.

Foot, Hugh. 1991. "The Psychology of Humor and Laughter." In *Psychology and Social Issues,* edited by Raymond Cochrane and Douglas Carroll, 1–14. London: Falmer Press, 1991.

Foucault, Michel. *Madness and Civilization: A History of Insanity in an Age of Reason.* New York: Vintage Books, 1964.

———. *History of Madness.* New York: Routledge, 2006.

Francis, Linda. "Laughter, the Best Mediation: Humor as Emotion Management in Interaction." *Symbolic Interactionism* 17, no. 2 (1994): 147–163.

Freud, Sigmund. "Humor." *International Journal of Psychoanalysis* 9, no. 1 (1928): 1–6.

———. *Jokes and Their Relation to the Unconscious.* New York: Norton, 1960.

Garland, Robert. *Eye of the Beholder: Deformity and Disability in the Graeco-Roman World.* Ithaca, NY: Cornell University Press, 1995.

Garland-Thomson, Rosemarie. *Extraordinary Bodies: Figuring Physical Disability in American Culture and Literature.* New York: Columbia University Press, 1997.

Garner, James. *Politically Correct Bedtime Stories.* New York: Macmillan, 1994.

Gentili, Vanna. "Madmen and Fools Are a Staple Commodity: On Madness as a System in Elizabethan and Jacobean Plays." *Cahiers Elizabethains: Late Medieval and Renaissance Studies* 34 (1988): 11–24.

Gilbert, Douglas. *American Vaudeville: Its Life and Times.* New York: Dover, 1963.

Goffman, Erving. *Stigma: Notes on the Management of Spoiled Identity.* London: Penguin, 1963.

Goodheart, Eugene. "PC or Not PC." *Partisan Review* 15, no. 4 (1993): 550–556.

Gracer, Bonnie. "What the Rabbis Heard: Deafness in the Mishnah." *Disability Studies Quarterly* 23, no. 2 (2003): 192–205.

Graham, Elizabeth, Michael Papa, and Gordon Brooks. "Functions of Humor in Conversation: Conceptualization and Measurement." *Western Journal of Communication* 56, no. 2 (1992): 163–181.

Green, Sara. "Components of Perceived Stigma and Perceptions of Well-being

Among University Students with and Without Disability Experience." *Health Sociology Review* 16, nos. 3–4 (2007): 328–360.

———. "Staying True to Their Stories: Interviews with Parents of Children with Disabilities." In *Disability and Qualitative Inquiry: Methods for Rethinking an Ableist World,* edited by Ronald Berger and Laura Lorenz, 57–74. Surrey, UK: Ashgate, 2015.

Green, Sara, and Shawn Bingham. "I Could Have So Easily Been Excluded": Exploring Narratives of Inclusion and Exclusion in the Lives of Professional Performers with Disabilities. In *Working with Families for Inclusive Education: International Perspectives on Inclusive Education*, vol. 9, edited by Kate Scorgie, Richard Sobsey. Bingley, UK: Emerald Group Publishing Limited, forthcoming.

Green, Sara, Rosalyn Benjamin Darling, and Loren Wilbers. "Has the Parent Experience Changed over Time? A Meta-analysis of Qualitative Studies of Parents of Children with Disabilities from 1960–2012." In *Research in Social Science and Disability,* vol. 7, edited by Barbara Altman and Sharon Barnartt, 97–168. Bingley, UK: Emerald Group, 2013.

Griffin, Dustin. *Satire: A Critical Reintroduction.* Lexington: University Press of Kentucky, 1994.

Haggins, Bambi. *The Laughing Mad: The Black Comic Persona in Post-Soul America.* New Brunswick, NJ: Rutgers, 2007.

Haller, Beth. "Guest Editor's Introduction: Disability Humor." *Disability Studies Quarterly* 23, nos. 3–4 (2003). http://dsq-sds.org/article/view/430/607 (accessed March 12, 2015).

———. *Representing Disability in an Abelist World: Essays on Mass Media.* Louisville, KY: Advocado Press, 2010.

Haller, Beth, and Amy Becker. "Stepping Backwards with Disability Humor? The Case of NY Gov. David Paterson's Representation on 'Saturday Night Live.'" *Disability Studies Quarterly* 34, no. 1 (2014). http://dsq- sds.org/article/view /3459/3527 (accessed March 11, 2015).

Haller, Beth, and Sue Ralph. "John Callahan's Pelswick Cartoon and a New Phase of Disability Humor." *Disability Studies Quarterly* 23, nos. 3–4 (2003). http://dsq-sds.org/article/view/431/608 (accessed November 1, 2011).

Hampes, William. "Relation Between Humor and Generativity." *Psychological Reports* 73, no. 1 (1993): 131–136.

Heath, Robin, and Lee Blonder. "Conversational Humor Among Stroke Survivors." *Humor: International Journal of Humor Research* 16, no. 1 (2003): 91–106.

Herth, Kaye. "Hope in Older Adults in Community and Institutional Settings." *Issues in Mental Health Nursing* 14, no. 2 (1993): 139–156.

Hibberd, Fiona. *Unfolding Social Constructionism.* New York: Springer, 2005.

Hirshey, Gerri. "Comedy of Hate." *Gentlemen's Quarterly,* August 1989.

Hobbes, Thomas. "Human Nature." Reprinted in *The English Works of Thomas Hobbes of Malmesbury,* vol. 4, edited by William Molesworth, 1–76. London: Bohn, 1840 [1651].

Hobbs, Pamela. "Lawyers' Use of Humor as Persuasion." *Humor: International Journal of Humor Research* 20, no. 2 (2007): 123–156.

Holden, Stephen. "The Serious Business of Comedy Clubs." *New York Times,* June 12, 1992.

Hughes, Geoffrey. *Political Correctness: A History of Semantics and Culture.* Oxford, UK: Wiley-Blackwell, 2009.

Irving, Allan, and Tom Young. "Paradigm for Pluralism: Mikhail Bakhtin and Social Work Practice." *Social Work* 47, no. 1 (2002): 19–29.

Janik, Vicki, and Emmanuel S. Nelson. *Fools and Jesters in Literature, Art, and History*. Westport, CT: Greenwood Press, 1998.

Jarzab, Alicia. "Attack It with Humor and Make It as Wonderful as You Can." *Exceptional Parent* 34, no. 4 (2004): 38–40.

Jewell, Geri. "I Love Liberty." October 2, 2010 [1982]. www.youtube.com/watch?v =ktNqtasZCLI (accessed January 12, 2012).

Juni, Samuel, and Bernard Katz. "Self-effacing Wit as a Response to Oppression: Dynamics in Ethnic Humor." *Journal of General Psychology* 128, no. 2 (2001): 119–142.

Kafer, Alison. *Feminist Queer Crip*. Bloomington: Indiana University Press, 2013.

Kaiser, William. *Praisers of Folly*. London: Victor Gollancz, 1964.

Kennedy, Dan. "What Is Dwarfism?" *The Etymology of Dwarfism*, 2005. www.pbs.org/pov/bigenough/what-is-dwarfism/.

Kercher, Stephen. *Revel with a Cause: Liberal Satire in Postwar America*. Chicago: University of Chicago Press, 2006.

Kimball, Roger. "Political Correctness or, The Perils of Benevolence." *National Interest* 74 (2003): 158–165.

Kohl, Herbert. "The Politically Correct Bypass: Multiculturalism and the Public Schools." *Social Policy* 22, no. 1 (1991): 33–40.

Koziski, Stephanie. "The Stand-up Comedian as Anthropologist: Intentional Culture Critic." *Journal of Popular Culture* 18, no. 2 (1984): 57–76.

Krefting, Rebecca. *All Joking Aside: American Humor and Its Discontents*. Baltimore, Maryland: Johns Hopkins University Press, 2014.

Krutnik, Frank. "Jerry Lewis: Deformation of the Comic." *Film Quarterly* 48, no. 1 (1994): 12–26.

Kuppers, Petra. *Disability Culture and Community Performance: Bodies on the Edge*. New York: Routledge, 2003.

———. *Disability Culture and Community Performance: Find a Strange and Twisted Shape*. New York: Palgrave Macmillan, 2011.

Lebesco, Kathleen. "There's Something About Disabled People: The Contradictions of Freakery in the Films of the Farrelly Brothers." *Disability Studies Quarterly* 24, no. 4 (2004).

Lefcourt, Herbert. "Perspective-taking Humor and Authoritarianism as Predictors of Anthropocentrism." *Humor: International Journal of Humor Research* 9, no. 1 (1996): 57–71.

Legman, Gershon. *Rationale of the Dirty Joke: An Analysis of Sexual Humor*. New York: Simon & Schuster, 2006.

Lenfant, Dominique. "Monsters in Greek Ethnography and Society in the 5th and 4th Centuries BCE." In *From Myth to Reason? Studies in the Development of Greek Thought*, edited by Richard Buxton, 197–214. Oxford, UK: Clarendon Press, 1999.

Lessing, Doris. *Time Bites*. New York: HarperCollins, 2004.

Lewis, Ann. *Children's Understanding of Disability*. New York: Routledge, 1995.

Lewis, Paul. "The Fall of Standup Comedy." *Chicago Tribune,* March 8, 1993.

———, ed. "Debate: Humor and Political Correctness." *Humor: International Journal of Humor Research* 10, no. 4 (1997): 453–513.

Logan, Brian. "All the King's Fools: Disability Is Deep in Comedy's DNA." *The Guardian,* February 23, 2011.

Long, Debra, and Arthur Graesser. "Wit and Humor in Discourse Processing." *Discourse Processes* 11, no. 1 (1988): 35–60.

Loseke, Donileen. "The Study of Identity as Cultural, Institutional, Organizational, and Personal Narratives: Theoretical and Empirical Integrations." *Sociological Quarterly* 48 (2007): 661–688.

Lowry, Edward. *Vaudeville Humor: The Collected Jokes, Routines and Skits of Ed Lowry.* Carbondale: Southern Illinois University Press, 2006.

Mackelprang, Romel, and Richard Salsgiver. *Disability: A Diversity Model Approach in Human Services Practices,* 2nd ed. Chicago: Lyceum Books, 2009.

Mallett, Rebecca. "Claiming Comedic Immunity: Or, What Do You Get When You Cross Contemporary British Comedy with Disability?" *Review of Disability Studies: An International Journal* 6, no. 3 (2010): 5–14.

Martin, Rod, Nicholas Kuiper, L. Joan Olinger, and Kathryn Dance. "Humor, Coping with Stress, Self-concept, and Psychological Well-Being." *Humor: International Journal of Humor Research* 6, no. 1 (1993): 89–104.

Marx, Groucho. *Groucho and Me.* New York: Dell, 1959.

May, Rollo. *Man's Search for Himself.* New York: Random House, 1953.

McCurdy, Les. "Special O'Laughics: Les McCurdy at TEDxSarasota." *TEDTalk,* January 13, 2013. www.youtube.com/watch?v=25SdpolRP6s (accessed November 12, 2013).

McDonagh, Patrick. *Idiocy: A Cultural History.* Liverpool, UK: Liverpool University Press, 2008.

McRuer, Robert. *Crip Theory: Cultural Signs of Queerness and Disability.* New York: New York University Press, 2006.

———. "Compulsory Able-bodiedness and Queer/disabled Existence." In *The Disability Studies Reader,* 4th ed., edited by Lennard J. Davis, 369–381. New York: Routledge, 2013.

Meszaros, Beth. "Enlightened by Our Afflictions: Portrayals of Disability in the Comic Theatre of Beth Henley and Martin McDonagh." *Disability Studies Quarterly* 23, nos. 3–4 (2003). http://dsq-sds.org/article/view/433/610 (accessed July 7, 2013).

Metzler, Irina. "Disability in the Middle Ages: Impairment at the Intersection of Historical Inquiry and Disability Studies." *History Compass* 9, no. 1 (2011): 45–60.

Meyer, John. "Humor as a Double-edged Sword: Four Functions of Humor in Communication." *Communication Theory* 10, no. 3 (2000): 310–331.

Mills, Charles Wright. *The Sociological Imagination.* London: Oxford University Press, 1959.

Mintz, Lawrence. "Stand Up Comedy as Social and Cultural Meditation." *American Quarterly* 37, no. 1 (1985): 71–80.

Mishler, Elliot G. "Models of Narrative Analysis: A Typology." *Journal of Narrative and Life History* 5, no. 2 (1995): 87–123.

Mitchell, Laura. "Beyond the Supercrip Syndrome." *The Quill* 77, no. 10 (1989): 18–23.

Moran, Carmen. "Beyond Content: Does Using Humor Help Coping?" *Disability Studies Quarterly* 23, nos. 3–4 (2003). http://dsq-sds.org/article/view/434/611 (accessed August 1, 2012).

Morreall, John. *Taking Laughter Seriously.* New York: SUNY Press, 1983.

Nilsen, Don. "The Psychological Functions of Humor." *Humor Scholarship: A Research Bibliography.* Westport, CT: Greenwood, 1993.

Nock, Albert Jay. "The King's Jester: Modern Style." *Harper's Magazine,* March 1928.

Norden, Martin. *Cinema of Isolation: The History of Physical Disability in the Movies*. Rutgers, NJ: Rutgers University Press, 1994.

Norrick, Neal. *Conversational Joking: Humor in Everyday Talk*. Bloomington: Indiana University Press, 1993.

O'Connor, Tom. "Disability and David Lynch's 'Disabled' Body of Work." *Disability Studies Quarterly* 22, no. 1 (2002): 5–21.

Oliver, Michael. *Social Work with Disabled People*. Basingstoke, UK: Macmillan, 1983.

———. "Changing the Social Relations of Research Production." *Disability, Handicap, and Society* 7, no. 2 (1992): 101–115.

———. "Emancipatory Research: Realistic Goal or Impossible Dream?" In *Doing Disability Research*, edited by Colin Barnes and Geof Mercer, 15–31. Leeds, UK: Disability Press, 1997.

Otto, Beatrice. *Fools Are Everywhere: The Court Jester Around the World*. Chicago: University of Chicago Press, 2001.

Paris Review Interviews IV. New York: Picador, 2009.

Pernick, Martin. "Defining the Defective: Eugenics, Aesthetics, and Mass Culture in Early-twentieth-century America." In *The Body and Physical Difference: Discourses of Disability*, edited by David T. Mitchell and Sharon L. Snyder, 89–110. Ann Arbor: University of Michigan Press, 1997.

Pity the blind, No. 2. Directed by A. E. Weed, 1904, American Mutoscope and Biography.

Plato. *The Republic*, 2nd edition, translated by D. Lee. Baltimore: Penguin, 1974.

Prentki, Tim. *The Fool in European Theatre: Stages of Folly*. London: Palgrave Macmillan, 2011.

Priestley, Mark. *Disability: A Life Course Approach*. Cambridge, UK: Polity, 2003.

Pullam, Susan, and Patrick McGeehan. "Did You Hear the One About . . . Forget It: Wall Street Humor Hits a Bear Market." *Wall Street Journal*, June 18, 1997.

Reid, Kim, Edy Stoughton, and Robin Smith. "The Humorous Construction of Disability: Stand-up Comedians in the United States." *Disability and Society* 21, no. 6 (2006): 629–643.

Reid-Hresko, John, and Kim Reid. "Deconstructing Disability: Three Episodes of South Park." *Disability Studies Quarterly* 25, no. 4 (2005). http://dsq-sds.org/article/view/628/805 (accessed August 8, 2012).

Rieger, Alicja. "Make It Just as Normal as Possible with Humor." *Mental Retardation* 42, no. 6 (2004): 427–444.

———. "'It Was a Joke for Him and a Life for Me': A Discourse on Disability Related Humor Among Families of Children with Disabilities." *Disability Studies Quarterly* 23, nos. 3–4 (2005). http://dsq-sds.org/article/view/605/782 (accessed February 2, 2012).

Rieger, Alicja, and Diane Ryndak. "Explorations of Humor and Other Types of Fun Among Families of Children with Disabilities." *Research and Practice for Persons with Severe Disabilities* 29, no. 3 (2004): 194–209.

Robillard, Albert. "Wild Phenomena and Disability Jokes." *Body and Society* 5, no. 4 (1999): 61–65.

Rodrigues, Suzana, and David Collinson. "'Having Fun?' Humour as Resistance in Brazil." *Organization Studies* 16, no. 5 (1995): 739–768.

Romero, Eric, and Kevin Cruthirds. "The Use of Humor in the Workplace." *Academy of Management Perspectives* 20, no. 2 (2006): 58–69.

Rose, Lynn. "Discarding the Disabled: Infanticide in Ancient Greece." Fall Public

Lecture Series. Institute for Antiquity and Christianity, Claremont Graduate University, Claremont, CA, October 4, 2007.

Rosenbaum, Stephen A. "Hammerin' Hank: The Right to Be Raunchy or FM Freak Show?" *Disability Studies Quarterly* 23, nos. 3–4 (2003). http://www.dsq-sds.org/article/view /432/609 (accessed January 22, 2012).

Rosqvist, Hanna. "The Politics of Joking: Narratives of Humour and Joking Among Adults with Asperger's Syndrome." *Disability and Society* 27, no. 2 (2012): 235–247.

Roy, Carole. "The Irreverent Raging Grannies: Humor as Protest." *Canadian Women Studies* 25, nos. 3–4 (2006): 141–148.

Ruark, Robert. "Let's Nix the Sickniks." *Saturday Evening Post.* June 29–July 6. 1963, 38–39.

Ruch, W., and F. J. Hehl. "A Two-Mode Model of Humor Appreciation: Its Relation to Aesthetic Appreciation and Simplicity-Complexity of Personality." In *The Sense of Humor: Explorations of a Personality Characterisitic*, edited by W. Ruch, 109–142. Berlin: Mouton de Gruyter, 1998

Safire, William. "On Language; Linguistically Correct." *New York Times,* May 5, 1991.

Sandahl, Carrie, and Philip Auslander, eds. *Bodies in Commotion: Disability and Performance.* Ann Arbor: University of Michigan Press, 2005.

Sanders, Barry. *Sudden Glory: Laughter as Subversive History.* Boston: Beacon, 1995.

Sawisch, Leonard. "Essay." 2012. www.shortdwarf.com/tag/leonard-sawisch/ (accessed June 19, 2013).

Schopenhauer, Arthur. *The World as Will and Idea.* London: Kegan Paul, 1964.

Schweik, Susan. "Marshall P. Wilder and Disability Performance History." *Disability Studies Quarterly* 30, nos. 3–4 (2010). http://dsq-sds.org/article/view/1271 /1294 (accessed October 20, 2014).

Scotch, Richard. *From Good Will to Civil Rights: Transforming Federal Disability Policy,* 2nd ed. Philadelphia: Temple University Press, 2001.

Shain, Alan. "Stand-up (Actually, Sit-down) Comedy." Smashing Stereotypes Productions. www.magma.ca/~rickcurrie/shain/standup.htm (accessed October 4, 2012).

Shakespeare, Tom. "Rules of Engagement: Doing Disability Research." *Disability and Society* 11, no. 1 (1996): 115–121.

———. "Joking a Part?" *Body and Society* 5, no. 4 (1999): 47–52.

———. *Disability Rights and Wrongs.* Oxford, UK: Routledge, 2006.

———. *Disability Rights and Wrongs Revisited,* 2nd ed. London: Routledge, 2014.

Shepard, Ben. "The Use of Joyfulness as a Community Organizing Strategy." *Peace and Change* 30, no. 4 (2005): 435–468.

Shultz, Kara, and Darla Germeroth. "Should We Laugh or Should We Cry? John Callahan's Humor as a Tool to Change Societal Attitudes Toward Disability." *Howard Journal of Communications* 9, no. 3 (1998): 229–244.

"The Sickniks." *Time,* July 13, 1959, 42.

Siebers, Tobin. "Disability in Theory: From Social Constructionism to the New Realism of the Body." In *The Disability Studies Reader,* edited by Lennard J. Davis, 173–184. New York: Routledge, 2006.

———. *Disability Theory.* Ann Arbor: University of Michigan Press, 2008.

Silva, Carla, and P. David Howe. "The (In)validity of Supercrip Representation of Paralympian Athletes." *Journal of Sport and Social Issues* 36, no. 2 (2012): 174–194.

Slide, Anthony. *The Encyclopedia of Vaudeville*. Westport, CT: Greenwood Press, 1994.

Smedley, Edward, Hugh James Rose, and Henry John Rose. *Encyclopaedia Metropolitana, Or, Universal Dictionary of Knowledge: Comprising the Twofold Advantage of a Philosophical and an Alphabetical Arrangement, with Appropriate Engravings*, vol. 21. London: J. J. Griffin, 1845.

Smit, Christopher. "'Please Call Now, Before It's Too Late': Spectacle Discourse in Jerry Lewis Muscular Dystrophy Telethon." *Journal of Popular Culture* 36, no. 4 (2003): 687–703.

Snyder, Charles. *The Psychology of Hope: You Can Get There from Here*. New York: Free Press, 1994.

Sobchack, Tom. "Bakhtin's 'Carnivalesque' in 1950s British Comedy." *Journal of Popular Film and Television* 23, no. 4 (1996): 179–185.

Solomon, Robert. "Are the Three Stooges Funny? Soitainly! (or When Is It OK to Laugh?)." In *Ethics and Values in the Information Age,* edited by Graybosch Rudinow, 604–610. Cambridge, MA: Wadsworth Press, 2002.

Sontag, Susan. "In Conclusion." *East West Films Journal* 2, no. 1 (1987): 99–105.

Sorensen, Majken. "Humor as a Serious Strategy of Nonviolent Resistance to Oppression." *Peace and Change* 33, no. 2 (2008): 167–190.

Southworth, John. *Fools and Jesters in the English Court*. Phoenix Mill, UK: Sutton, 1998.

Spencer, Herbert. "The Physiology of Laughter." *Macmillan's Magazine,* 1860.

Stainton, Tim. "Reason's Other: The Emergence of the Disabled Subject in the Northern Renaissance." *Disability and Society* 19, no. 4 (2004): 224–243.

Stebbins, Robert. "Defusing Awkward Situations: Comic Relief as Interactive Strategy for People with Disabilities." *Journal of Leisurability* 23, no. 4 (1996): 3–7.

Stern, Ricki. *Joan Rivers: A Piece of Work*. New York: IFC Films, 2010.

Strick, Madelijn, Rick van Baaren, Rob Holland, and Ad van Knippenberg. "Humor in Advertisements Enhances Product Liking by Mere Association." *Psychology of Popular Media Culture* 1, no. 8 (2011): 16–31.

Stronbach, Ian, and Julie Allan. "Joking with Disability: What's the Difference Between the Comic and the Tragic in Disability Discourses?" *Body and Society* 5, no. 4 (1999): 31–45.

Taber, Katherine, Maurice Redden, and Robin Hurley. "Functional Anatomy of Humor: Positive Affect and Chronic Mental Illness." *Journal of Neuropsychiatry and Clinical Neurosciences* 19, no. 4 (2007): 358–362.

Taub, Diane, Penelope McLorg, and Patricia L. Fanflik. "Stigma Management Strategies Among Women with Physical Disabilities: Contrasting Approaches of Downplaying or Claiming a Disability Status." *Deviant Behavior* 25, no. 2 (2004): 169–190.

Tavernier-Courbin, Jaqueline. "Humor Is a Serious Matter." *Thalia: Studies in Literary Humor* 8, no. 2 (1985): 13–20.

"Tea Party Comedian Compares Liberals to Trig Palin." *Huffington Post,* September 6, 2011. www.huffingtonpost.com/2011/09/06/tea-party-comedian-compares -liberals-to-trig-palin_n_950570.html (accessed November 1, 2013).

Thomas, James. "Standing Up Racism: Richard Pryor and the Development of a Contentious Racial Politics." In *The Art of Social Critique: Painting Mirrors of Social Life,* edited by Shawn Bingham, 315–340. Lanham, MD: Lexington Books, 2012.

Titchkovsky, Tanya. *Disability, Self, and Society.* Toronto, ON: University of Toronto Press, 2003.

Turnquist, Kristi. "Joan Rivers Brings Her Tart-tongued Stand-up Routine to the Oregon Symphony." *The Oregonian: Oregon Live,* January 7, 2011. www .oregonlive.com/movies/index.ssf/2011/01/joan_rivers_brings_her_tart-to.html (accessed June 4, 2013).

Union of the Physically Impaired Against Segregation (UPIAS). *Fundamental Principles of Disability.* London: UPIAS, 1976.

"U.Va.'s 'Scramble' Band Scrambling to Survive." *Washington Post,* June 20, 1991.

Vaid, Jyotsna. "The Evolution of Humor: Do Those Who Laugh Last?" In *Evolution of the Psyche: Human Evolution, Behavior and Intelligence,* edited by David Rosen and Michael Luebbert, 123–138. Westport, CT: Praeger, 1999.

Vilaythong, Alexander, Randolph Arnau, David Rosen, and Nathan Mascaro. "Humor and Hope: Can Humor Increase Hope?" *Humor: International Journal of Humor Research* 16, no. 1 (2003): 79–89.

Walker, Peter. "Frankie Boyle Meets His Match in Mother of Down's Syndrome Child." *The Guardian,* April 8, 2010.

Weaver, Simon. "Developing a Rhetorical Analysis of Racist Humour: Examining Anti-black Jokes on the Internet." *Social Semiotics* 20, no. 5 (2010): 537–555.

Welch, Melissa, Shawn Bingham, and Sara Green. "No Laughing Matter? Examining the Reception of Disability Humor." Paper presented at the annual meeting of the Society for the Study of Social Problems, Seattle, Washington, 2016.

Welsford, Enid. *The Fool: His Social and Literary History.* London: Faber & Faber, 1968.

West, Patrick. "Frankie Boyle's Down's Syndrome 'Joke' Was Despicable—But We Still Need Him." *The Telegraph,* April 9, 2010.

White, Elwyn. *Essays of E.B. White.* New York: Harper & Row, 1977.

———. *Essays of E.B. White.* New York: McGraw-Hill, 2000.

White, Julia. "'Krazy Kripples': Using *South Park* to Talk About Disability." In *Building Pedagogical Curb Cuts: Incorporating Disability in the University Classroom and Curriculum,* edited by Liat Ben-Moshe, Rebecca C. Cory, Mia Feldbaum, and Ken Sagendorf, 67–76. Syracuse, NY: Graduate School, Syracuse University, 2005.

Wickberg, Daniel. *The Senses of Humor: Self and Laughter in Modern America.* Ithaca, NY: Cornell University Press, 1998.

Widdows, Christopher (a.k.a. Steady Eddy). "Australian Comedians in Concert." 1995. www.youtube.com/watch?v=UbGOjmNAsb8 (accessed April 9, 2012).

Wilder, Marshall. *Sunny Side of the Street.* New York: Funk & Wagnalls, 1905.

Wiles, David. *Shakespeare's Clown: Actor and Text in the Elizabethan Playhouse.* Cambridge, UK: Cambridge University Press, 1987.

Willeford, William. *Fool and His Scepter: A Study of Clowns and Jesters and Their Audience.* Evanston, IL: Northwestern University Press, 1969.

Williams, Brad. November 12, 2008. https://www.youtube.com/watch?v=xj1u G6ibmEo (accessed July 24, 2013).

Williams, Lena. "It's Not Funny and I'm Sorry: Tacky Jokes of the Past, R.I.P." *New York Times,* January 2, 1991.

Wolfe, Kathi. "For the Disabled, There's Nothing Funny About Mary." *Atlanta Journal Constitution.* August 16, 1998.

Zhang, Yong, and George Zinkhan. "Humor in Television Advertising: The Effects of Repetition and Social Setting." In *Advances in Consumer Research,* vol. 18, edited by Rebecca H. Holman and Michael R. Solomon, 813–818. Provo, UT: Association for Consumer Research, 1991.

Zhao, Yan. "The Information-Conveying Aspect of Jokes." *Humor: International Journal of Humor Research* 1, no. 3 (1988): 279–298.

Zijderveld, Anton. *Reality in a Looking Glass: Rationality Through an Analysis of Traditional Folly.* London: Routledge & Kegan Paul, 1982.

Zola, Irving Kenneth. "Bringing Our Bodies and Ourselves Back In: Reflections on a Past, Present, and Future 'Medical Sociology.'" *Journal of Health and Social Behavior* 32, no. 1 (1991): 1–16.

Index

Ableism, 67
Abnormally Funny People comedic group, 21, 80, 121
Activism, and performance, 146; balance of, 80, 85, 119; break fifth wall with, 81; creative process of, 91; disability comedy incompatibility with, 80; disabled comedians as, 9; themes of, 80
Actual Lives, 152
Affirmative activism, 68, 70
All in the Family, 131
All the King's Fools, 32
Allen, Woody, 13
Americans with Disabilities Act, 60, 158
Apte, Mahadev, 26–27
Architectural Barriers Act 1968, 57
Aristotle, 33, 34
Armin, Robert, 45
The Arsenio Hall Show, 31
Assisted Suicide: The Musical, 121
Audience, 84, 118; breaking fifth wall with, 81; of Carr, L., 82; comfortable with disability tension for, 83; disability acknowledged up front for, 82; disability comedy of, 6, 81, 82; disability education of, 86; disability unique perspective for, 81; diverse views of, 136; engaging models for, 156; inferiority humor for, 116; mediate disability experience for, 144; methodological difficulties of, 145; new perspective mechanism for,

87; performer and audience bridging gap between, 104; reception of, 158; relief humor for, 115; "room realities" for, 113; uncomfortable territory for, 81
Auslander, Philip, 3
Autonomy, on stage, 133–134

Bakhtin, Mikhail, 15, 22, 42, 153, 154
Barty, Billy, 51
Berger, Peter, 15–16
Bergson, Henri, 96, 109, 110
Best, Steve, 93
Bishop, Kathryn, 60
Black, Lewis, 159
Black comedy: brutality of, 140; intuitive wisdom of, 160; as "sick humor," 159
Bloom, Alan, 124
Blue, Josh, 1, 25, 61, 121; affirming talent of, 157; biographical sketch of, 163–164; childhood of, 163; disability self-awareness of, 135; educate audience of, 86; established comedy of, 82; *Good Josh, Bad Arm by*, 122; humor natural talent of, 163; incongruity theory and humor use by, 111; inferiority humor use of, 106, 107; life experience of, 163; as motivational exemplar, 90; natural talent of, 70–71; observational skill of, 163; political incorrect language of, 136; *7 More Days in the Tank by*,

About the Book

Exploring a paradox, Shawn Bingham and Sara Green show how humor has been used both to challenge traditional views of disability and to reinforce negative stereotypes and social inequalities.

Seriously Funny ranges from ancient Greek dramas to medieval court jesters to contemporary comedy, from stage performances to the experiences of daily life. Rich with insights into issues of identity and social stratification, it offers an eye-opening perspective on attitudes toward disability across the ages.

Shawn Chandler Bingham is assistant professor of sociology and assistant dean of academic affairs in the Honors College at the University of South Florida. **Sara E. Green** is associate professor of sociology at the University of South Florida.